Two Harwoods in the House

A Vermont Memoir

by Madeline B. Harwood

with Karen D. Lorentz

Copyright © 2001
by Madeline B. Harwood
and Karen D. Lorentz

Also by Karen D. Lorentz

Killington, A Story of Mountains and Men, Mountain Publishing, Inc., 1990

Vermont Voices, An Anthology (Editor), League of Vermont Writers, 1991

A Vermont Parent's Prevention Resource, A Guide to Raising Healthy, Drug-Free Children, PreventionWorks, 1995

Okemo, All Come Home, Mountain Publishing, Inc., 1996

Good Vermonters, The Pierces of North Shrewsbury, Mountain Publishing, 2000

ISBN:0-9625369-8-9

Printed at Daamen Printing, West Rutland, Vermont

This book is dedicated to:

My children
who meant everything to Doc and me,

Our friends and neighbors
with whom we shared so much,

Doc's patients
whom he was proud to serve,

and

Many wonderful
legislators and politicians
of both persuasions
with whom I worked.

Madeline B. Harwood

For all those who enjoy reading
about Quintessential Vermonters.

Karen D. Lorentz

Acknowledgments

When I look back on my life, it strikes me how much times have changed. That is perhaps the biggest reason for tackling this book. In 1993 I began to reflect on the many years I have enjoyed and decided I wanted to leave a written record to share those times with my family and friends.

So I began to write — in large part thanks to those of you who over the years laughed at Doc's and my adventures (all of them true) and said, "Madeline, you should write a book."

I had much help along the way, beginning with (the late) Pete Copp who was generous with his suggestions and support in getting me started. Ellen Perry Berkely read my early manuscript and shared her editing expertise and comments. My friend Mary Lou Burditt encouraged me to see this project through and introduced me to Karen Lorentz.

Karen helped me rewrite the manuscript, encouraging me to fill in the gaps. She gave shape to the narrative, added the last chapter, type-set the book, and saw the project through the printing and publication process. Without her help and patience, this book would not exist.

Proofreaders Phebe Ann Lewis, Mary Bort, Anita Albinson, Peggy Armitage, and John Lorentz made many useful suggestions and helpful corrections. It was kind of you to share your thoughts and to give so generously of your time.

A special debt of gratitude goes to Barbara Snelling for taking time from her busy schedule and campaigning to read the manuscript and pen the Foreword.

Thank you to all for your help in making my dream to publish a reality.

I hope the reader will enjoy this sharing of our lives and see how special it is to be connected to so many wonderful people.

I would enjoy hearing from anyone who would care to write to me.

Madeline B. Harwood
Manchester Center, VT 05255

Contents

Acknowledgments .... *iv*

Foreword .... *vi*

Introduction .... *viii*

Chapter One   In the Beginning 1

Chapter Two   Nursing School 17

Chapter Three   Love & Marriage 23

Chapter Four   Starting a Family Practice 33

Chapter Five   Our Year in Whitingham 41

Chapter Six   On the Move with the Army 49

Chapter Seven   The War Years 57

Chapter Eight   Manchester at Last 69

Chapter Nine   The Ups & Downs of Family Life 81

Chapter Ten   From Patients to Politics 103

Chapter Eleven   Senator Harwood Goes to Montpelier 123

Chapter Twelve   Exciting Times, A Run for the U.S. House 139

Chapter Thirteen A Meaningful Journey & New Challenges 159

Chapter Fourteen Two Harwoods in the House 177

Chapter Fifteen   A Reflection 195

Postscript   *The Community Remembers* *211*

Appendices *237*

Foreword

by Barbara W. Snelling

This is an autobiography with two levels of communication. It appears to be simply a narrative of an ordinary couple's life, but in truth, it is the story of an extraordinary husband and wife, each with exceptional contributions to their community, state, and nation.

Those of us who have known Madeline only in the second half of her life would have a hard time recognizing the vulnerable and somewhat naive young woman that her charming narrative portrays. She provides glimpses of her daily life, using selected anecdotes that illuminate her feelings and her self-awareness as she grows more sophisticated and more self-confident. Her character strength is with her from her earliest days, nurtured by her mother and father.

Her mother's motto, well remembered and acted on by Madeline, was "All that you do, do with your might; things done in halves are never done right." Her mother would be proud of the life Madeline has led.

Madeline's legacy from five generations of strong and dedicated Vermonters shines with love of family and love of country. This is a sturdy, hard working family with high principles of integrity, loyalty, faith, and love.

Madeline's ancestry is matched by Doc's five generations of Vermont Harwoods. In reading the story, one has the feeling that these families are the making of the best of Yankee stock.

But despite Madeline's strengths, she harbored many early self-doubts, and dutifully submitted to her husband's guidance regardless of her own instincts. In her later years as a mature adult, she gradually gained self-confidence. Her training as a nurse enabled her to take charge in crisis situations. She learned to recognize her power and her ability to function on her own, to make decisions and to cope with the intrigue and gamesmanship of the legislature and to become a leader both in her community and in the political world. She, with her subtle but quick sense of humor, relished those occasions when she won out over people in positions of power.

I had heard many positive comments about Madeline from my husband before I really knew her well, despite our whirlwind visits to her home. She had helped us in my husband's campaigns for statewide office, always hospitable, thoughtful, and knowledgeable and totally indefatigable. Her home was a much needed respite from the intense tempo of campaigns, and her advice was always sound.

When the Republican Party's Snelling Award was established after my husband's death, it was my most sincere pleasure to make the award to Madeline for her years of loyalty and dedication to Republican ideals. The award was created to recognize leadership and contributions to the state's well being. No one was more deserving of the first annual award than Madeline.

But despite many accolades and honors, never did her newfound self-confidence or political success separate Madeline from Doc and an all-encompassing love. Their relationship — through tough times and good times — is an exemplary model for the young couples of today's world where break-ups occur over minor disputes.

Madeline describes Doc's dedication to his patients, always putting them first. She corrects Doc's excessive modesty in his accounts of his experiences at UVM by telling of his achievements as an athlete. She also tells of his intense devotion to their four children and their devastation as parents in the loss of a son to cancer. She comments on Doc's excessive selflessness and modesty, but she also recounts his many automobile accidents. Her stern reprimand of his driving habits finally caused him to reform.

This is an honest story of a beautiful marriage and two successful careers. If one does not know and love the Harwoods when starting the first chapter, one will surely love and respect them both before the book is closed.

Barbara Snelling is a state senator from Chittenden County, former Lt. Governor of the State of Vermont, and the wife of the late Governor Richard A. Snelling, to whom she was married for many years when he died in 1991.

Introduction

During her 86 years as a Vermonter, Madeline Harwood experienced growing up on a small rural farm, education in a one-room schoolhouse, and training to become a registered nurse. She married, becoming a doctor's wife and assistant, and raised four children. She lived through the Depression, World War II, the Cold War, the fall of the Berlin Wall, and other twentieth-century world events. She also did something very unusual for women born in 1914, she entered the field of politics.

When Madeline was growing up in the first half of the twentieth century, women's lives centered around the home and domestic duties and the world treated them much differently than today. Rural Vermont children seldom obtained educations beyond the eighth grade as farm families needed the free labor they provided, and few could afford to board a child in a larger town with a high school.

But Vermonters were an ambitious lot, and some parents made sure that their children received the secondary schooling that they themselves had so often been denied. Further education or training beyond high school was possible, but it necessitated having the means. Males were more likely to be encouraged to attend college, and scholarships and jobs made that possible for hard working young men like Clifford and Clarence Harwood. But when a young woman found a way to afford further education, there were only a few choices available to her: teacher, secretary, or nurse. Many a Vermont woman simply got married and raised a family.

Madeline was fortunate to have parents who insisted on high school educations for all their children; they also encouraged her to pursue nursing. Nurse's training was different then, too. The hospital, while staffed with many female nurses, was still a male dominated environment where young women adhered to "doctor's orders" without questioning them or taking part in decision making.

Madeline cared a great deal about becoming a good nurse and being useful to others. In fact, she tried hard to adhere to the rules and living in a man's world. When she broke the rules, as she did on several occasions, it was not out of protest or being a rebel. The women's movement was still thirty years off, and Madeline was not into blazing a new trail in the 1930s. It was her honesty and wanting to be helpful that got her into trouble at this stage.

Marriage to Clifford Harwood in 1936 occurred in an era when women were not yet treated as equals. Men were in charge, largely because they had been brought up that way by their fathers who "ruled" the household, farm, or business with little or no input from wives or women in general. After all, it hadn't been too long since women had gotten the right to vote (1920).

Madeline relied on Clifford and his judgment at first. But Clifford was not the type to protect his woman. As a dedicated doctor, he could be demanding of both himself and his wife. In expecting more from Madeline rather than less, Clifford became a catalyst for change. His own high standards, expectations, and example provided a strong role model for her. Her independence and spirit were given an opportunity to blossom and a slow but meaningful change took place. Over time, she became a strong and outspoken woman who not only felt deeply about things that mattered to her but began to act upon those feelings.

Clifford's innate drive and commitment to his medical practice and to politics enabled him to understand her desire to get involved. Politically aware and active himself, he found it natural to support her efforts. He was both a conventional husband who wanted his wife at home nights, and an intelligent man who was far ahead of his time in his regard for a woman's capabilities and potential.

Their conventional marriage and dedication to community and patients meshed in a way that profoundly influenced Madeline. Being a hard worker and knowledgeable about politics through her volunteer work, she lacked only one ingredient to go down a new road, a belief that she really could do the job. That came when National Republican Platform Committee Chairman Melvin Laird requested her to serve on the Drafting Committe in 1964. It was one of those defining moments when she could dig deep and come up not only with the courage to tackle the task at hand but also the conviction to go on to pursue a new career in public service.

As they say, the rest is history. Madeline already had the quiet ambition stirring within her and the encouragement of Clifford and a whole life of experiences, including the trauma of World War II, on which to base her beliefs and fuel her desire to become a state senator. She never ran for office out of a sense of glory or power, but rather from a willingness to do the hard work that is required of legislators. Nor did she think of herself as a pioneering woman politician. But in truth, she did pave the way for many who followed in her footsteps.

The story that follows is Madeline's. The anecdotes, adventures, misadventures, and humor are part of who she is. As a co-writer, I have helped her to organize the information and prompted her to explain more so we might better understand her experience.

Today, women (and many men) are learning that it is possible to have several careers and that the fifties are often the age of discovery of a new, fulfilling direction. What is today's newest trend is something Madeline accomplished thirty-six years ago, when she transitioned from mother and nurse to a second "lifetime" as an outspoken public servant.

Although she was to be a conservative Republican, this book is not so much about her politics as it is about a strong determination to do what she felt was right. It is a story that shows us the inner workings of a real person who strived to make a difference by serving in Vermont's Citizen Legislature.

As proofreader Phebe Ann Lewis remarked, Madeline's story is a piece of Americana. It is the story of a woman who went from earning $10 a month during nurse's training to sitting at the right hand of a President. And as Barbara Snelling observed, even if you never met the Harwoods personally, by the end of Madeline's narrative you will feel that you know them.

If you come to share Barbara's respect and love for Doc and Madeline, then my purpose in assisting Madeline with her words will have been fulfilled. I believe there are many wonderful Vermonters who have made a difference in their communities and state. To help bring two of them to your attention has been a special privilege.

I share in Madeline's hope that you will enjoy her story and welcome any feedback the reader might care to give.

Karen Lorentz
October 1, 2000

Chapter One

In the Beginning . . .

I was born Madeline Leitha Bailey on July 7, 1914, acquiring the Bailey name whose spelling had been changed previously from Bayley. I was a fifth-generation descendant of General Jacob Bayley, a patriot who served his country on the battlefield, his state in its first provisional government, and his town as a founding father. General Bayley was descended from a line of Bayleys who came to this country from England and first settled in Massachusetts.

General Bayley was an important figure in early Vermont history, but because he was an independent thinker who mixed it up with some of our early Vermont "heroes," he hasn't been as favorably remembered as some like Ethan Allen, a mythic hero who also turned out to be somewhat controversial. Thanks to the work of historians, however, this is what we know of our ancestor and the more "exciting" times in our family's history.

The Bayley Family & History

Jacob's great-great grandfather, John Bayley, was a weaver in Chiooenham, England. Accompanied by his son John and daughter Joanna, he sailed for America on June 4, 1635, on the Angel Gabriel (a sturdy 240-ton, well-armed vessel built in 1617 for Sir Walter Raleigh's fleet and originally called the Jason). The convoy with which they traveled was attacked by pirates and one ship was captured. The Angel Gabriel returned fire, escaped, and sailed on for New England.

On August 14, the crew dropped anchor off the coast of Maine at Pemaquid Island to resupply the community there before continuing to their destination. They were surprised by a fierce hurricane at dawn of the next day. By afternoon the ship with its livestock and supplies had been lost to the sea along with five crew and passengers who had stayed on board. The seventeen or so who had gone ashore the previous day, including the three Bayleys, survived.

The Bayleys eventually made their way to Massachusetts where they settled in Newbury. John lived two years at Newbury and then became the first settler of Salisbury (MA), where he died in November 1651. His wife Eleanor died in England, never having ventured across the ocean to join her husband. Neither dared an ocean passage after his perilous journey, so John never saw his wife again.

Both Joanna and son John married and settled in Newbury. John's son Isaac had a son Joshua, who had nine children, including Jacob Bayley born in 1726. Like his farmer father before him, Jacob had only a basic education and became a farmer. At the age of nineteen, Jacob married Prudence (Stickney) Noyes, a sixth generation descendant of Nicholas Noyes of England and Ipswich, Massachusetts. They moved to a section of Haverhill (MA), which soon became Hampstead, New Hampshire when the state lines were redrawn.

Jacob was active in town affairs and in the militia. He served as a lieutenant and then a captain in the French and Indian War, seeing action on Lake George and during the siege of Fort William Henry (New York). He escaped from the massacre that followed the fort's surrender on August 7, 1757, by running barefoot twelve miles to Fort Edward. In 1759, he was in charge of a detachment which marched through the Mohawk Valley to Oswego. He was appointed Lieutenant Colonel in Goff's regiment and succeeded him as Colonel. He was present at the siege and surrender of Montreal and was connected with Amherst's expedition.

It was on their way back to Hampstead that Bayley and three other officers, who served with him in Goff's regiment, stayed several days at an area of Vermont known as the "lower Coos." Liking the land which bordered the Connecticut River, they looked into settling there, and thus Bayley came to Newbury, Vermont in the summer of 1762. The foursome sought a charter for both Newbury and Haverhill (a town on the eastern side of the river which is now in NH) from Governor Benning Wentworth, Royal Governor of New Hampshire (1741-1776). Wentworth chartered 138 towns, about 3-million acres or half the area of Vermont from 1749-1764. Back then part of Vermont was known as the New Hampshire Grants and part was in the Province of New York.

On May 18, 1763, Jacob Bayley and the others were granted the charter for the town of Newbury, where he was not only one of the first settlers but also a founding member and lifelong Deacon of the Newbury church. This church, which was formally organized in 1764, was the second church organized in Vermont. In 1773, Bayley obtained a charter for Newbury from the Governor of New York, which charter superseded the first and accounts for Newbury becoming a part of the Province of New York. (Both New York and New Hampshire had claimed the territory that was to become Vermont as will be explained shortly.)

Active in town and political affairs, Bayley served in many positions, including: Justice of the Peace and Quorum for the whole of the New Hampshire Grants by New York Assembly in 1766; representative to the New York Congress, 1775; delegate to the Continental Congress, April 8, 1777; and member of the Convention to draft the Constitution of the Republic and State of Vermont at Windsor, July 1777. He was solicited to serve on the Council of Safety at the behest of Thomas Chittenden who called him "the strongest man east of the mountains."

The Council of Safety was a board of twelve men who were charged with administering the affairs of the state until a government under a constitution could be organized. As the only source of authority in Vermont from August 1777 to March 1778, the Council was invested with legislative, executive, and judicial powers. It prescribed the conduct of war, raised troops, appointed officers, and transacted civil and military business with other states and with Congress. It also prepared business for the first General Assembly at which time the Council relinquished its duties as a provisional government. (At that time, Thomas Chittenden, who had headed the Council, became the first governor of Vermont. He served 1778-89, 1790-97.)

In April 1776, Bayley began to build a road to Canada at the request of George Washington, who had agreed with Bayley's suggestion that a route for commerce and communication to St. Johns would be beneficial. The road effort was discontinued when the War for Independence went badly in Quebec and it was feared the British would use it to invade Newbury and the colonies. Washington had sent Bayley 250 pounds sterling to get started on the road, but Bayley was never reimbursed for the additional 732 pounds of personal funds which he paid the 110 men on the project. [In April 1779, Washington ordered Colonel Moses Hazen to complete the road. They reached "Hazen's Notch" in the mountains of Westfield but never St. Johns 40 miles away. After the war, the 50-mile Bayley-Hazen Road greatly aided in the settlement of the northern Vermont towns through which it passed.]

During the Revolutionary War, Bayley became a Brigadier General in 1776 and a Commissary General under appointment from Washington in 1777. Joshua Coffin in his *History of Newbury, Massachusetts* wrote:

> These positions involved great responsibilities, and subjected him to danger, difficulties and sacrifices of an extraordinary character, and many anecdotes might be related of his exploits, hair breadth escapes, encounters with the enemy, Indians, and Tories, his constant vigilance to the scouts sent from Canada to take him, for whom a reward of 500 guineas had been offered dead or alive. By means of spies he acquired important intelligence of the movements of the enemy in Canada, and rendered great services with his purse, person and pen at and before the surrender of Burgoyne, where he was engaged with two or three of his sons. He made a treaty of friendship with the St. Francis Indians, and by his kindness to them won their attachment. Many of the tribe were of great service to the colonies during the Revolutionary War. He sacrificed a large estate in the service of his country, for which he never received any compensation, and was equally distinguished for his talents, his patriotism, and his piety,

Frederic P. Wells in his *History of Newbury, Vermont* adds that in addition to his military leadership and taking command of the Northern army (troops from eastern Vermont and western New Hampshire) and otherwise contributing to the war effort in New England, General Bayley expended $60,000 for the patriotic cause. His petition for compensation was never granted, and he spent the rest of his life working off that debt and died a poor man.

Despite his many contributions, Bayley remained an "unsung hero." This "oversight" was probably due to the fact that he opposed Ethan and Ira Allen and Thomas Chittenden in their initial efforts at statehood. Not trusting the Allen brothers, who were infamous for their land dealings and schemes, Bayley was in a quandary as to the future of his town and state and tried to do what he considered best for Newbury and those towns more closely allied with it in the Connecticut River Valley.

It was during the height of the War of Independence (1775-1783) that yet another battle was raging within Vermont. The struggle concerned conflicting claims as to the rightful owner of these lands; this situation arose in 1740 when King George and his Council altered the boundaries between the Massachusetts Bay and New Hampshire colonies, giving New Hampshire additional land lying west of the Connecticut River and to within twenty miles of the Hudson River. Previously, Charles II had granted all lands west of the Connecticut River to his brother, James Duke of York, thus giving the Province of New York legal claim to Vermont. (New Hampshire was given most of the lands east of the Connecticut River above the Massachusetts boundary.)

This action set the stage for the inevitable land-title disputes that arose with settlement of Vermont towns when New York realized in 1763 that Wentworth was overstepping his bounds and granting charters to land that was not his (and accounts for Bayley seeking a New York charter in 1773). It was this problem of unclear land titles that delayed settlement of much of Vermont and led to the skirmish between the Yorkers and the Green Mountain Boys as well as a "declaration of independence for Vermont" in 1777. As a leader of the Green Mountain Boys who had fought the Yorkers for Vermont's independence, Ethan Allen joined Thomas Chittenden and others in the Bennington Party to push for statehood for Vermont and admission to the Federal Union.

However, sixteen towns on the east side of the Connecticut River wished to join the new state of Vermont (as organized by the Windsor Convention of March 1778) and were received into the First Union in June. The Bennington Party opposed this move (mostly for political reasons having to do with a balance of power residing in the western section of the state) and presented protests from both New Hampshire and the Continental Congress. They managed to pass resolutions that caused uneasiness among delegates from towns on both sides of the river, many of whom subsequently seceded from the Assembly of Vermont.

There were no less than four possibilities for authority over Vermont now. The Bennington Party favored a new state of towns between Lake Champlain and the Connecticut River. The New Hampshire Party wanted to re-annex the Grants to that state, and New York wanted to exercise its right to its claim. Some thought that the state would end up being divided along the ridge of the Green Mountains between New Hampshire and New York. A fourth "College" Party suggested that the many Connecticut River Valley towns, of which Newbury was one, be kept together under one jurisdiction as part of New Hampshire or New York, or failing that, be formed into their own new independent state.

The matter was complicated by politics and geography, and the contentious matter festered for six years with Bayley opposing the Allens and representing interests on the eastern side of the Green Mountains but particularly the many river towns with which Newbury identified. But slowly, the Vermont river towns recognized the new entity of Vermont and the last two holdouts, Norwich and Newbury, joined them in 1784.

With this about face, Bayley now went along with the recommendation of the Continental Congress that a State of Vermont should have boundaries extending to the Connecticut River but not east of it. In 1786, with Bayley's and the Town of Newbury's support, Vermont pursued formal admission to the Federal Union. New York, however, still objected to giving up its claim and thus delayed statehood until it was satisfied with a payment of $30,000. At that time, the Republic of Vermont became the fourteenth state on March 4, 1791.

General Bayley went unrecognized for his heroic deeds and a century later the historian Lucius E. Chittenden called him "one of the neglected patriots of the Revolution."[1] Bayley was recognized by the people

---

[1] *Lucius, who was Thomas Chittenden's great grandson, became a lawyer and held the office of Register of the Treasury during Abraham Lincoln's first term as president. He was also a prolific writer who authored a number of historical articles and addresses on the Civil War, Lincoln, and many diverse Vermont subjects.*

of Newbury, however, where he became known as the "Father of New-bury" for his services to the town and its church.[2]

While my own adventures with guns and politics seem tame in comparison to this ancestor who was part of the action and faced real danger many times over, I sometimes wonder if there wasn't some family gene that survived or maybe it was just a streak of Yankee independence that eventually propelled me into politics. Whatever it was, I think it caused me to have an interesting life in the state legislature, during which time I also enjoyed a few "skirmishes" along the way.

Bayley to Bailey

General Bayley had ten children; a son Joshua, from whose family line I am descended, was born at Hampstead, New Hampshire. Joshua also fought in the Revolutionary War, attaining the rank of Major and Colonel in the militia. Around 1785, he built a house at Newbury Village (VT), where he served as a town representative 1791-1794, 1802-1803, and 1804-1809. Joshua was my great-great grandfather. He married Anna Fowler and they had twelve children.

Their son Jacob married Betsey Peach and they lived in the Jefferson Hill section of Newbury. They had six children, one of whom George Washington Bayley, my grandfather, was born in 1826 and also lived at Jefferson Hill. He and his wife Ann C. Felch had six children, five of whom survived. The oldest boy Herbert went West in 1898, but my father George Allen Bailey continued to live at Jefferson Hill all his life.

My father was born on December 28, 1872. He became a farmer like his father and his forebears before him. My mother Maude A. Smith was born on April 30, 1886, in Barton, Vermont. Her mother Elvina was a cook in the lumber camps so they moved around quite frequently.

---

[2]*In May 1993, the General was remembered by the Vermont Legislature in a Joint Resolution (J.R.H.13) "honoring the initiatives, services, and memory of Vermont Revolutionary War patriot, General Jacob Bayley, of Newbury. . . . as one of the state's founders and champions of liberty . . ." The resolution was sent to the Town Selectmen and to a local branch of the D.A.R., and Governor Howard Dean issued a Certificate of Special Recognition.*

Her father Aaron Smith was born in England and met his wife in Vermont.

When my parents married in September 1908, they stayed on at Jefferson Hill in the northwest corner of Newbury, not too far from South Ryegate. At that time, Newbury was a farming community with a population of 2,125. Wells described Newbury as having "about 36,450 acres that comprised a great variety of soil-rich tracts of meadow, fertile upland, high hills and

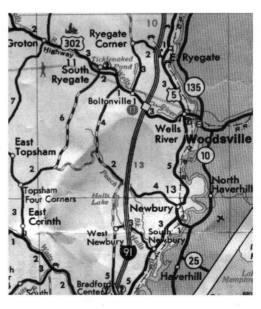

deep valleys, with some square miles of land whose broken and ledgy surface forbids cultivation." There were many villages within the town, including Newbury, Newbury Center, West Newbury, and Wells River. The Connecticut River formed the town's eastern boundary, separating the town and state from New Hampshire to the east.

Growing Up on a Farm

My two older brothers John and Lewis were born in 1909 and 1911 respectively. My two younger sisters Charlotte Mae and Evelyn arrived in 1916 and 1921. Clayton was born in February 1924 but suffered convulsions and died in June. Gerald arrived in September of 1928, when three of us were in high school.

I remember growing up on a 25-head dairy farm as a time when responsibilities and chores were shared. I helped my mother with cooking, cleaning, and caring for my younger siblings. Mother made our clothes, did the washing, mopping, ironing, cooking, and gardening among other household and farm duties. Charlotte and I washed the breakfast dishes and swept the kitchen floor before leaving for school in the morning. Evenings, we washed the supper dishes before doing our homework.

Mother's motto was, "All that you do, do with your might; things done in halves are never done right." That taught me to try to do my best in my early years.

My brothers did farm chores. As a farmer, Dad worked long hours from 5 a.m. to 7 p.m. — often later in summer. There was milking to be done by hand twice a day, horses to be fed, stables to be cleaned, wood to be cut, trees to be tapped in spring, hay fields and meadows to mow in summer. My mother was in charge of planting the gardens, but father helped with that, too. In winter, when the cows did not give as much milk (some cows would be bred in winter), and therefore milking chores were less time consuming, he would tend to their feed and cut down trees and split wood for the next year's fuel supply. In spring, he made maple syrup. These were time-honored duties that supplemented a farmer's income from milk production. All required long hours in the barn, woods, and sugarbush.

Dad was a "jack of all trades." It was necessary to be able to do whatever needed doing because there was little money to spare. In the early 1900s, rural Vermonters were still largely subsistence farmers, and there was not a lot of cash to be made. Dad took milk to the creamery in nearby South Ryegate and received his milk check every two weeks. At times my mother made butter and sold it. We had a DeLavalle Separator and the cream was used to make butter and some of the skimmed milk went to the pigs and other animals.

We had two work horses: Chub, an old black horse, and Nancy, a spirited red horse. We had many hens and chickens which provided eggs as well as poultry for the table. There were a few pigs, which were butchered for the table, and when the cows got old and not so productive, they would be slaughtered to provide beef. Mother would can the meat by cooking it first and then preserving it in jars. She preserved eggs in "water glass" (a preservative of silica and water in which they would keep for up to two years) and salt pork in brine in crocks in the cellar. She also made mincemeat, using the meat from the neck of cows, and canned peaches and berries. We had an apple orchard and stored apples in the cellar to provide some fresh fruit during the winter.

Although we were poor by today's standards and didn't have money for conveniences like refrigerators and radios, we always had enough to eat. I remember our childhood as being happy and don't recall ever feeling deprived. We enjoyed childhood games — ball, checkers, marbles, and other kids' games. We also had an old phonograph and listened to music and stories on records. Ours was a large and loving family.

But like most families, we had our share of teasing, occasional fights, and practical jokes. Lewis once found a woodchuck's entry and exit holes and told Charlotte to pull her skirt tight and sit on one of the holes. He then built a fire in the other hole to smoke out the wood-chuck. Our entertainment was of the "homemade" variety.

Our growing-up years were a lively time. Maybe because we played with our brothers, my sisters and I grew up more rough 'n tumble. We were tomboys, playing catch, baseball, or hide and seek with the boys. We were not overprotected or made to stay inside. There was a certain competitiveness among us as children. When colored grain (feed) sacks arrived at the house, my sisters and I used to fight over who was going to have her dress made out of a particular bag.

My sister Charlotte told the following story in 1986. (Doc and I were the guests at a fundraiser and had agreed to be the subjects of a "Roast.") Her memory, as written for the occasion went like this:

> It isn't that I know Madeline better than anyone here, but I've known her the longest. Without revealing our ages, it was almost seventy years ago that I first looked up to her.
>
> We had a nice home with indoor plumbing, central heat, and all. It was forced steam heat that came through cast iron radiators of various heights, depending on the area and space available.
>
> Madeline was happy, I'm sure, to have a younger sister. She liked to help mother take care of me. One time she was helping me in the bath-room. I must have been too heavy for her to lift for as she attempted to put me on the toilet, I landed on the very edge of the seat, with the rest of me on the hot radiator, which was next to and level with the toilet. Mother, who was always close by, came to my rescue.
>
> Madeline has always been a thinker and an ambitious achiever. When I was a bit older, she thought I should know how to protect myself from the Indians. She borrowed our brothers' bow and arrow, and we went outside for a lesson. She demonstrated very carefully where and how to place the arrow on the string, saying you had to "pull back hard," then let go. As she did this and released the arrow, it went flying back over her left shoulder and right through a window behind us.

It didn't take long to decide what to do next. She said we would have to tell Dad!

She took me by the hand and led me to where Dad was working, telling me every step of the way, to tell him I had broken the window.

Everything went as planned and fighting back the tears, I confessed. At that moment a familiar voice from behind said, "Madeline broke that window, not Charlotte."

Mother, having observed the whole thing, had quietly followed us.

I was so thankful Mother came to my rescue once again. I really wasn't looking forward to a spanking in an already sensitive area from a prior encounter with a hot radiator!

Madeline has been handicapped from birth, you know. She was born left handed. Could this be the reason she held the bow with the string away from her instead of towards her?

One of the things we enjoyed was going barefoot. Dad didn't mind because he didn't have to buy us so many shoes, but he always made us wait until he heard the first Bob-O-Link of spring before he allowed us to walk to school barefoot. Then, at the end of the day, we had to scrub our feet in a bucket to clean them before we could go to bed.

The Bailey Family circa mid-1940s: Gerald, Evelyn, Charlotte, Madeline, Lewis, John, Maude, and George.

We went to church most Sundays with our mother, who drove the horse hooked up to an old surrey. Father didn't usually accompany us to church because he had so many farm chores to tend to.

As children we were taught to be very quiet and to not move or say anything during the service, unless we were supposed to speak or sing. That could be very difficult for us when the children who sat in the pew behind us reached under our seats and tied our shoe laces together. I still remember my laces being tied to my sister's and not being able to say a thing about it! We endured such teasing and practical jokes on many a Sunday.

Our home was situated at the end of a long road in the Jefferson Hill area. I was told it was named for President Thomas Jefferson. Our house had a living room, dining room, kitchen, pantry, bedroom, and a bath-room on the first floor and three bedrooms and an attic on the second. We had hot and cold running water. The water heater was located in a closet, so when we made bread we would put it in the warm closet to rise. There was a pump in the basement which we had to move back and forth by hand to create the pressure to boost the water to the floor above.

We had central heat with a wood-fired furnace in the cellar and ra-diators in the rooms, but I remember that the kitchen served as our living room and dining room during the cold winter months due to the extra warmth that the wood-fired Glenwood cooking range provided. We did our school lessons by the light of kerosene lamps. I disliked the chore of washing lamp chimneys and trimming the wicks and joined others in rejoicing when electricity came to our area in the 1920s.

Dad suffered from asthma attacks, mostly in the winter. (There weren't any allergy tests available at that time. Later, when I learned more in nurse's training, I thought that he was probably allergic to the dry hay, horse hair, or even the cat that he carried to the barn each night on his shoulder.) He never had a vacation because there were always chores to do. He lived to be eighty and died in 1952.

My mother was seventy-four when she died in 1960. I think that they had a hard life (especially during the Depression), but it was also a good life and they enjoyed living to see all of us married and settled with families of our own.

When we went to grammar school, grades one through eight were housed in a one-room building. School started at 9 a.m. and we were dismissed at 4 p.m. We had two recesses and a half hour for lunch at noon. I recall about nineteen students with one teacher — no teacher's assistant in those days.

In addition to learning to read and write and do math, we studied the Bible. Religion was allowed then, and we found the teachings on how to live (be kind to one another, don't kill, don't steal, and so on) helpful. We could recite the books of the Bible and Bible verses as well as our alphabets — all with no ill effects I might add.

A typical school day would start with a prayer and a salute to the flag. Then the teacher would call the first grade up to sit in the row in front of her, and they would recite their lessons or she would teach them something. Then she would call the next group and repeat the procedure while we worked on our assignments at our desks. She would have one group doing math, another reading, and maybe another working on spelling. Often while working at our desks, we would be listening to her and catch the things we missed the first time around.

The summer I was twelve years old, I worked on a nearby farm in Boltonville for a lady who was crippled. She needed assistance getting meals for the workers and with housework. Her boys were musicians and played in the McClure Band. They would sleep late the day after playing for a dance, and I would have to be very quiet in doing my chores. I would walk the two miles there and stay for five days or so and then go home to visit my family. I also worked for a neighbor who liked to entertain and helped her clean up after her parties. My sister Charlotte and I picked raspberries and walked to South Ryegate to sell them. I used some of my money for clothes, but I saved most of it. I was always a saver.

Not all rural Vermont children got to go to high school in those days, but I think most of the children in our town did go on to high school. The Newbury High School was ten miles away in the village of Newbury so we had to board there. There was no school bus transportation then and twenty miles a day was too long for a horseback ride. We had a car, but the dirt roads weren't what they are today. They were too snowy in winter and muddy in spring for Dad to drive us. Plus, he was too busy

George Bailey and son John on the hayload, 1921.

with farm chores. So, as was the custom for rural children, we boarded in the village and went home occasionally on weekends and for vacations.

We were called "country hicks" by the village children because our ways were different from theirs and we dressed differently. It wasn't pleasant to have to put up with their teasing, but our parents were determined to have us finish high school. I think it was because they had been denied that opportunity that they wanted better educations for us.

During high school, I worked for my room and board. Madame Greer, the eighty-year-old lady I lived with, required me to get up at 6 a.m., build the fire in the kitchen stove, tend the coal furnace, and bring her a cup of hot tea by 6:30. My pay was $1 a week plus my room and board. I also had to work for her in the summer to assure a place with her in the fall. She paid me $3 a week during the summer. I did housework, mowed the lawn, weeded the garden, cared for the hens, and did other chores. I used the money to pay for my books, always trying to buy secondhand books because they were cheaper. In those days we had to pay for our school books.

I remember one day I got up the courage to ask Madame Greer if she stayed awake nights to think of things for me to do. Looking back I can see that was impudent, but she was a demanding task master and I was apt to speak out on those occasions when I felt ill-used. If friends came by to ask if I could go for a walk, Madame Greer would say sternly, "You're not here to walk the streets."

It wasn't that she was deliberately being mean. I think that she felt a responsibility for her boarders' welfare and worried that we might get caught up with the boys or into mischief. She was really being protective in her strictness because she felt other activities presented an opportunity to get into trouble.

But one year I played basketball and had a part in a play so that meant I had to change my living arrangements. Madame Greer would not allow any sports or other activities that might interfere with the work she expected to be done by her boarders.

There was no money for John and Lewis to go on to college so after high school Lewis stayed on the farm and helped father and eventually took over the farm while John got a job on a nearby farm. There weren't many choices for women in those days — you became a secretary, a teacher, a nurse, or a homemaker. I chose nursing because I didn't think I had enough knowledge to become a teacher, and I didn't like typing or shorthand so I didn't want to become a secretary.

I also was very impressed by my mother's stories of how well the nurses at the Hanover Hospital in New Hampshire (now Dartmouth Hitchcock Medical Center) had taken care of her when she was diagnosed as having gallstones. She never forgot the service they gave her or their kindness when she had to stay extra days because the Flood of November 1927 made it impossible for her to get home. I think her gratitude influenced me to see nursing as something good and important — a way women could make a difference.

I was accepted to the Mary Fletcher Hospital School of Nursing in Burlington in 1932, but I didn't enter right away. This was the time of the Great Depression and in order to be able to afford books and uniforms, which cost about $59, I first had to earn the money. I found a job doing housework for a family in the nearby town of Middlesex during the summer and fall of 1932. Then, with my savings and train ticket, I left for school in the big city in January 1933.

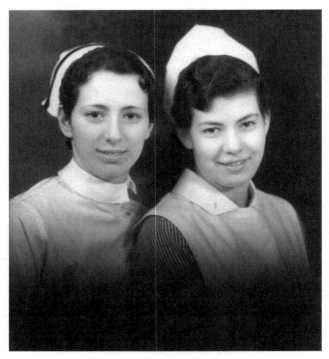

Madeline and Charlotte, 1936.

Madeline next to General Bayley's desk at the Oxbow D.A.R. in Newbury, VT, 1993.

Chapter Two

Nursing School

At first, I was very homesick at Mary Fletcher. But the long days of work and study soon did away with that. As new students, we were known as probationers and wore black shoes and stockings and denim-colored uniforms. We cleaned rooms, made beds, washed bed pans, did the dishes, and set up food trays along with attending classes. There was no pay for our labors during the three months we were "probies."

When we passed the probationary period, we became real nursing students. We received our caps and wore blue-and-white-striped uniforms with white aprons and white shoes and stockings. What a thrill it was to have responsibilities and patients to care for! I was very happy to have found my "niche" in life. I also liked the fact that we received $10 a month for the rest of our three years in training.

We were assigned to wards on a two- or three-month rotation. Sometimes we had night duty, which meant making adjustments to sleeping days. We worked twelve-hour shifts every day, seven to seven, with one-half day off each week. However, if classes were scheduled at that time, we had to attend. Most evenings were spent studying; occasionally, I would resort to hiding in the closet to finish my assignments after lights out. We took courses in dietetics, anatomy, pharmacy, psychology, urology, pediatrics, and nursing techniques among others. Most were taught by doctors, with some by graduate nurses. We had very little free time.

The ward nurses answered to the ward supervisor who was a Registered Nurse (RN). We all answered to the Superintendent of Nursing, Miss Hazel Berry, RN. Last came the Superintendent of the Hospital, Dr. Thomas Brown. He was Professor of Anatomy at the University of Vermont Medical College. He also taught anatomy to the nurses.

A few doctors tried their own anatomy classes out on the nurses, which advances were not always welcomed. I once slapped a doctor who tried to get fresh with me. Much to my surprise, he reported me to the ward supervisor who asked me how dare I slap a doctor? When I explained what he had tried to do, she let the incident go. Later, my sister was confronted by another doctor who tried to kiss her in an elevator. She had a laundry cart and played "checkers" with him, dodging his advances one move at a time.

Many girls didn't dare resist, though, as we all lived in fear of being dismissed for any infraction of the rules. Most nurses were in awe of the doctors. When they entered the nurses' station, we were to stop whatever we were doing and stand at attention to await our orders.

I received frequent letters from home while I was in training. Although we had a telephone at the farm, toll calls were expensive so we communicated by mail. I received a letter from my mother dated July 22, 1933, telling me that, "Yesterday, the house burned to the ground. We were only able to save a few things."

At the time, my uncle in nearby Woodsville, New Hampshire, was ill and dying so Mother had gone to help my aunt, Dad's sister Winn. My grandparents were living at our house along with Lewis, Evelyn, and Gerald. Lewis and Dad had been working in the barn but went in for the noon meal, which the family always ate together. Evelyn, who was twelve at the time, said she thought she heard someone walking around upstairs.

Since there was no one else there, Lewis teased her, saying, "Maybe it's the boogie man."

She insisted she heard someone, so Grandma asked Lewis to go up and look. When he opened the bedroom door, he saw the room filled with fire. He shut the door and raced downstairs, yelling "Fire." In a panic, they grabbed the tablecloth and carried the dishes, food and all, out onto the lawn where Dad proceeded to pass out. Lewis who had bought an electric water pump raced back into the house to save it.

After the fire, my folks moved into a house that they co-owned with my grandparents, and my father built another house. He cut the lumber from his own woodlot, took it to the sawmill, and waited for it to season before beginning construction. It took him five years to build an eight-room house in between his farm chores. He was the designer, carpenter, plumber, and electrician.

Receiving the news of the fire while at school was a shock. All my life's treasures had gone up in flame, and I knew I could never go home again. That night I put my mattress out on the third floor deck and slept outside in a kind of sympathy vote and expression of loss. The fire was doubly hard on me because the school authorities would not allow me time off to visit my family, and there was no scheduled vacation until September. Once again, I felt terribly homesick.

At this time in our training, we were learning "charting techniques" which include the times and reasons for medicines. The reasons had to do with pain, nausea, and anxiety. We were instructed to follow orders on time and exactly as written and, above all, to "always remember that the patient comes first." It struck me as strange that this consideration would not extend to the nurses' needs. I was disturbed by how its meaning was applied and that my own needs and anxiety over the fire were ignored.

My sister Charlotte also decided to become a nurse, so she joined me in training in September 1934. I was happy to see her, and the time between vacations became more bearable.

I was a timid and quiet person most of the time. When it came to following orders, I tried my best to do as told and to do it right. Sometimes, though, I made decisions that weren't "right" by others' standards. That got me into trouble on occasion — this was an era when you didn't question or ignore doctors' orders.

The physicians differed in their routine orders (instructions) on their patients. Because of this, all orders were written on the chart by the doctor and were to be followed exactly by the nurses — if we could read their writing, that is.

My first assignment to night duty was the Men's Ward. As I had worked days on this ward, I was familiar with the area. There were sixteen patients in the open ward (a curtain could be pulled around an individual bed for privacy) and seven to nine patients in the semi-private area. I thought it was an overwhelming responsibility for one nurse to be responsible for up to twenty-five patients.

Dr. George Sabin, a surgeon, had a standing order on his post-operated patients for codeine (one-half grain) and strychnine (1/60th grain) every four hours as needed for pain for two days following surgery and ending at midnight the second day.

One very busy night, a patient rang his bell at 1 a.m. and said he was in pain and unable to sleep. So I said, no problem and gave him a hypo, duly noting it on the chart.

The next morning the supervisor called me into the office and told me to report to Miss Berry. With fear and trembling, I obeyed her order.

Miss Berry had dark piercing eyes. One had a fear of her authority; those eyes told us "she knows all about you — you won't get away with a thing."

She ascertained that I had indeed given the medication after midnight and asked why I had done so. I explained that seeing the patient in pain, I didn't take the time to check the chart to see if the order had expired. She noted that I had broken the rules.

Fearing expulsion, my eyes filled with tears as she informed that this was a very serious mistake. She instructed me to stay up in the morning and report my error to Dr. Sabin. He was in surgery so I had to wait until 10 a.m. — all the while mentally packing my things in anticipation of being dismissed.

When I found him and admitted my error, he placed his hand on my shoulder and told me not to worry, that "strychnine 1/60th never hurt anyone." I could have hugged him! My fear of Dr. Sabin vanished, and he became my hero. I slept well the rest of the day and returned to night duty, resolving never to make another mistake.

But once again while I was on night duty, things went awry. This time I was working on maternity, my favorite duty. Patients were usually happy, and it was pleasant to work with the new mothers and their adored babies. At the 2 a.m. feeding, I was picking up a baby to return to the nursery when the mother asked about an insect she had seen crawling on her bedstand. I found the little creature and to her anxious inquiries as to whether they bite, I reassured her it was just a harmless cockroach.

The next morning the patient reported her encounter to the day supervisor. Soon I was reporting to Dr. Thomas Brown. This was deep trouble, I realized. Sitting in his office, I waited while he opened a letter. When he finally looked at me, I was trembling as I answered his question as to whether I was the night nurse on maternity. After opening another letter, he asked if I had told a patient there was a cockroach on her stand. I thought about lying but decided against it. I responded truthfully, and he opened yet another letter. His voice shook with anger when he finally said, "You might just have well gone down to Church Street and shouted that Mary Fletcher is full of cockroaches."

Dr. Brown was not around during the night when the cockroaches were most active. He just did not know. But I couldn't tell him that. So I sat in silence, waiting.

After his last letter, the head of the hospital glared at me as he said he was never so inclined to dismiss a nurse from training. "Don't ever, ever do that again," he ordered. Once again, I had learned a lesson. But so had Dr. Brown. The next week the exterminators began work at the hospital.

While that episode was unnerving, the hardest part of my training was to care for truly sick children. At one point, I cared for a sister and brother of ten and twelve in isolation. They had typhoid fever; and a brother at home had died from it. It was heart-breaking to care for such sick children.

Another difficult time was a three-month period of instruction at the Vermont State Hospital in Waterbury where we learned to care for the mentally ill. We were sent in groups of three to six and had lectures in psychology but lacked instruction in bedside care. While there, we were instructed not to enter a certain patient's room alone as she could be quite violent. One day as I passed by her door, I noticed that the patient was choking a nurse who just stood there holding a food tray. I entered and the patient let go of her.

Later, I asked Ruth why she hadn't dropped the tray and tried to get away. "I didn't want to spill the food," she replied, causing me to wonder what would have become of her had I not gone to her rescue when I did.

The State Boards were taken at the end of three years of training, after the course work was completed. You could graduate from nursing school, but you would not receive the coveted RN until you passed the much feared boards. The exams were held in early spring at the State House in Montpelier. They were an all-day affair for which we studied hard. I felt well prepared and thought I had done well, but there were a few questions that gave me some trouble, so like the others, I anxiously awaited the news.

I was very pleased and proud to learn that I had passed! Now I could look for employment as an RN. I loved nursing and was glad I had worked so hard. But there was another reason I was so happy at this time. I was dating a wonderful man, and I was in love.

Madeline and Clifford, 1935.

Chapter Three

Love and Marriage

I met Clifford B. Harwood in the spring of 1934. He was a premed student at UVM and was working as an orderly, in return for his room and board, when we met at the Mary Fletcher Hospital where I was in training.

For our first date, Clifford asked me to go to a movie. Nursing students were required to be in by eleven but were permitted one late night a month when it stretched to eleven-thirty. After the movie, we sat on the bench by the tennis court to talk. The moon was shining, but it seemed a bit cool. I sat there wishing that Clifford would put his arm around me. No such luck. Clifford Harwood was a gentleman from the old school and soon walked me to my door where he said good night.

Clifford had been raised on a small Vermont farm in the southwestern side of the state, over one-hundred miles away from where I lived. His family was a fifth-generation Harwood family in the town of Rupert, which is bounded by New York on the west and the Vermont towns of Pawlet, Dorset, and Arlington on the north, east and south.

Clifford was very proud of his ancestry and enjoyed telling his grandchildren about Bridget Harwood, his great-great-great-great grandmother. Her husband Benjamin died in Amherst, Massachusetts, in 1758, and three years later she migrated with her ten children to Vermont. The group she was traveling with stopped to eat lunch, but she continued on, thus becoming the first settler of Bennington on June 16, 1761. She planted a switch that she had cut from an apple tree and had used as a riding whip into moist, fertile ground, and it became a tree that produced apples for 107 years. The place, located in the shadow of Mount Anthony, later became known as the Harwood Farm.

Her son Zachariah (1742-1821) fought at the Battle of Bennington and had charge of the pest-house in Bennington (a place where persons suffering from smallpox were kept isolated from the community). His son Joseph (Clifford's great-great grandfather) settled in Rupert, Vermont and had a son Joseph B. Harwood (1809-1859). Both were farmers. Joseph B. had a son Charles (1833-1902) who became a doctor and surgeon. He moved to Dorset where he practiced medicine. Charles had three sons: Wayne, Burr, and Elmer. His three daughters all died of diphtheria in early childhood within two weeks of each other.

Charles' son Wayne (1872-1955) was trained as a penmanship teacher but

Charles Raymond (standing) Clifford (l) and Clarence Harwood (r), October 1917.

preferred being a farmer. He was a Vermont State legislator in the House of Representatives for the 1931-32 term. Wayne lived in Rupert and had three sons, Raymond and twins Clarence and Clifford, who were born at home on January 3, 1914. Rupert had a population of about 860 at that time, and the children went to grade school in Rupert and high school in nearby Granville, New York. The Harwood boys took the train for a year and a half before convincing their father to buy them bicycles. Then, they biked the twelve miles to school each day and home again for another year and a half. Their senior year they shared rides with students who had cars. When they graduated in 1930, Rupert had a population of 674 persons.

Clarence stayed at home to help on the farm and then went to Middlebury College but came down with polio just after registering. He returned home to regain his health and later resumed his studies and graduated from Middlebury two years after Clifford graduated from UVM. (He also studied medicine at UVM Medical College and became a pediatrician three years after Clifford became a general practitioner.)

Clifford wrote the following about his college years for a speech he gave in 1992:

> In September 1930, I started Academic College. I obtained a Senatorial scholarship from a state senator, and enrolled in the Agricultural Department. I also got a student loan from the Olin Scott Fund of Bennington. Later, I received a loan every year from the Wilbur Fund, founded by Honorable James B. Wilbur of Manchester.
>
> At that time, there were only eight students in the freshman Aggie class. Before the next semester, I changed to the Arts and Science Department and enrolled in the premedical section. I also started in cross-country that year. The first significant cross-country meet in which I participated was arranged by Coach Archie Post with Saranac (NY) High School. We went on the ferry to Plattsburgh. My group was in a car driven by Carlos Otis, later a classmate at UVM College of Medicine.
>
> I had two jobs during the next two years: one as a cleaner at the Home Economics Laboratory in Morrill Hall and another at the Home Economics Practice House on Summit Street (later to be owned by "Whitey" Palmer, a UVM basketball hero, prominent in the funeral service in Burlington).

During the summer of 1933, I took a job helping a farmer. I worked from dawn to about 8:30 p.m. for $25 a month and room and board.

Later that year, I obtained a position as a proctor at Converse Hall, for which I received a free room there. The winter of 1934 was the coldest in Burlington that I remember. I recall the thermometer being below zero for several weeks.

Economic times were severe. I largely subsisted on pancakes, cheese, and hot dogs and was nourished by free skim milk from the Aggie Department Laboratory. Other people who ate at the basement room included the late R.M. Peardon "Pete" Donaghy (later a noted neurosurgeon at UVM Medical College) and Rollaston Stiles (a student from Middlebury in the Engineering Department). Skim milk was good for my running ability, as I did well in the two-mile event. In May 1934, I ran the two-mile race in under ten minutes.

Clifford was the first UVM runner to break the ten-minute barrier for the two-mile run. He was also the captain of the 1933 Vermont Cross-Country Team and "Archie Post's top two-miler in the spring for two seasons," according to records at UVM. In the Canadian National Indoor Championships held in Montreal in 1935, he finished a respectable fifth. He was recognized for these achievements on October 3, 1992, at a UVM Athletic Hall of Fame induction ceremony, at which time his portrait was hung with other newly honored athletes.

The nurses often discussed their dates, so I learned that Clifford had dated a beautiful classmate from West Rutland. She could play the piano and was quite talented. I had never had the opportunity to learn music so I felt rather disadvantaged. I had never played tennis before, either, but Clifford taught me. We spent many hours on the tennis court. I guess I gave him a good game for he continued to ask me out.

Our courtship soon graduated to going places in Clifford's 1928 Chevy with a rumble seat. For our first ride, Clifford took me to meet his folks in Rupert. It turned out to be a harrowing experience — the drive that is. The ground was snow covered in some areas, and as we drove along I thought he was going awfully fast. I exclaimed about how curvy the roads were, hoping he would get the hint that I was a little nervous and slow down.

Wayne and Mary Harwood

"Most roads in Vermont are," he replied nonchalantly. No change in speed.

I sat there trying to think how I could get him to slow down without hurting his feelings. He was so good to me, and here he was taking me to meet his folks. I tried to take my mind off the situation by telling him about my exams and some difficult problems. I did pretty well but as we neared Rupert, he hit a deep rut and ripped off the muffler. Much to my relief, he finally slowed down.

Clifford's folks were wonderful, and we had a nice visit. I was glad I hadn't spoiled things by complaining about his driving.

As we went out more often in his car, I eventually got used to Clifford's driving. He didn't have any accidents at this point, but there were a few near-misses. I guess I would have to say that I never stopped worrying about his driving. It was kind of ironic that when it came time for me to learn to drive, Clifford undertook the task of teaching me.

We drove to Church Street in Burlington, where he taught me to parallel park. I tried stopping on a hill, then starting without sliding backwards. He was very patient as I stalled the car time after time. Eventually, I got the hang of how to manually shift gears as one foot worked the clutch pedal and the other the brake, and he pronounced me ready to take the test.

The written part of the test was a breeze, and I easily passed it. But the driving test was nerve wracking. Clifford had advised me not to touch the emergency brake as it was broken. He had propped it up with match sticks, he told me, warning that the officer would probably not pass me if he knew and that I might even be fined.

As we started out, the officer moved over, pointing to the emergency brake and explaining he would sit closer to it in case he needed to use it.

Worried, but trying to act nonchalant, I was driving around the block (with easy right-hand turns), when suddenly a large truck came into my lane. Instead of stopping, I drove up onto the sidewalk to avoid an accident. I was sure I would fail, but the officer said nothing, and we continued with the test. Afterward, when he told me I had passed, he added, "Remember, sidewalks are for pedestrians."

What a gentleman he turned out to be. Personally, I did not feel I was competent enough to have been given a license. I did become a careful and capable driver, though.

After Clifford graduated from UVM in 1934, he entered UVM Medical College. In spite of the Depression and additional debts for med school, we began to think about getting engaged in 1935. While visiting my home one day, Clifford decided to speak to my father about our plans. To his request for permission to marry me, Dad responded, "Well, do you think you can support her?"

I suppose that could have unnerved most men with times as they were, but not Clifford. With the possibility of an MD after his name in two years, he assured my dad he could.

Dad was a man of few words, so that was good enough for him. We had his blessing.

On Thanksgiving Day 1935, we became engaged, but there was no diamond ring to reveal our secret. This was necessary as I would finish my training the first of January and would need to work while Clifford finished his schooling and internship.

In those days, graduate nurses could pay a fee to have their names placed in a register that listed the names of nurses available for work. When a name reached the top of the list, the nurse was assigned the next available private-duty case. Private duty paid $5 a day and that was enough to pay for my room and meals for a week.

With the Depression on though, work wasn't plentiful and many nurses waited a long time, even weeks, to get work through the register. To make matters worse, a married nurse was not assigned a case when her turn came unless one of the doctors specifically requested her. Priority was given to single nurses; no one considered that discrimination which wasn't really in our vocabulary back then.

With my training completed and work opportunities simply too scarce to take a chance, we decided to keep our plans to get married a secret.

As we thought about setting the date, we determined that Clifford would have the weekend of the Fourth of July off. It seemed an ideal time for a wedding. We would never forget the date, and if lucky, we would have the day off for celebrating in future years.

We kept the engagement a secret until the day we went to City Hall to get the license. Dr. Clarence Henry Beecher, a highly respected diagnostician who was in great demand for consultations, was also Mayor of the City of Burlington at that time. When we got to City Hall, Clifford parked out back so no one would see us going in together. Then he walked in ahead of me, watching the corridors. As we were passing down one of them, whom should we meet but Dr. Beecher exiting his office.

"Right down the hall, last door on the right," he said, greeting us with a smile. His directions and diagnosis were accurate. But what about our secret?

"I doubt he'll tell anyone," Clifford said.

Clifford was a good planner and had gotten his brother Clarence to stand up with us. I had asked my sister Charlotte. But when it came to finding a minister, he just figured that the Reverend Tatum of the Burlington Baptist Church would marry us and left getting in touch with him until Thursday, July 2.

When the Reverend didn't answer his phone that day, Clifford drove over to see him. He wasn't home. "He will be back soon, I'm sure. He will have to prepare his sermon," Clifford had reasoned as he tried to reassure his worried bride-to-be. By Friday evening the minister had not returned. A neighbor said he was expected early Saturday, but at 9 a.m. on the day of our "wedding," the parson was still nowhere to be found.

Ever the good-humored, unflappable optimist, Clifford suggested we drive to Rupert and get the Reverend King to marry us. He would be glad to do it and wouldn't tell a soul, he said, trying to raise my spirits.

It seemed a good solution and Charlotte and Clarence were willing, so off we went. About fifteen miles south of Burlington, Clifford stopped and rented a room for that night, leaving our luggage there. Around noon, we reached Rupert and went straight to the parsonage. The Reverend and Mrs. King were not at home.

We drove to the Harwoods and informed them of our plans. Mother Harwood went off to find the minister, only to learn from a neighbor that they had left at ten and no one knew where they were going. But she felt sure they would return shortly.

Clifford was calm and practical. We would wait, and he would go over and check every now and then — a necessity as his parents did not have a phone.

Charlotte was still in nurse's training, however, and had to be in by 11:30 that night so as time passed on, I was beginning to get more and more concerned.

"No problem," Clifford continued to assure us.

But at 8 p.m. on July 4, 1936, there we were still waiting. No minister and our luggage was 85 miles away in a motel room.

As it grew to be 8:30, Clarence came to the rescue with the suggestion that a Methodist minister at the church in Poultney, where he had attended a youth group as a teenager, might be willing to marry us.

Without even calling ahead, we started out for Poultney twenty-five miles north. About ten miles into the trip, the car's lights went out. The two medical students taped some wires together, and we proceeded on our way.

Arriving at the minister's at about 9:30 p.m., I worried that he might be just a

Newlyweds Madeline and Clifford, July 1936.

little unhappy to be disturbed so late at night, but Clarence carefully explained our plight. After a few questions, including: "Do your parents know you are doing this?" he kindly agreed to perform the ceremony.

With the knot properly tied by the Reverend Paul Douglass, a handsome young man who lived with his two sisters, Clarence and Charlotte were speedily returned to Burlington, and we took possession of our motel cabin. Clifford had selected a cabin that looked like a birdhouse, so we became "love birds."

Clifford graduating, 1937

We managed to keep our marital status a secret, and, in due time, I got called to nurse a girl of sixteen. She was very ill with TB Meningitis, which was fatal at the time. Since this was a 24-hour case, I slept in her room on a cot. The dear girl lasted ten days. It was a heart-rending situation made even more difficult by the ward supervisor trying to talk me out of charging for my services. "The poor people cannot afford the $6 a day," she told me.

But I had already submitted my bill as they had requested. When the father came to the door to pay me, I felt guilty; but I, too, was poor and needed the money so I took it.

Our secret was soon out, however, so with no more calls I took a job at the hospital in Woodsville, New Hampshire, which was very close to my home. I worked there for four months during the winter of 1936-37, living in nurses' quarters there. Then I worked for a doctor in Burlington, a Dr. Gladstone, until he went on to graduate school, and I was once again in need of a job.

To my delight, I found work doing physiotherapy, electrocardiograms, and basal metabolisms at Mary Fletcher Hospital. Clifford had graduated from medical college in 1937 and was now an intern at the hospital, so it meant we could be together and even see each other at work.

Sister Charlotte Bailey and Brother Clarence Harwood

In February 1938 I realized I was pregnant, but since the hospital did not have a policy regarding any kind of leave, we simply kept that a secret, too, (or so we thought) and I continued to work.

When trout fishing opened in April, Clifford and I went to a brook near my home. Snow still lingered on the ground and it was cold out. I spotted a large trout in a pool and walked out on a log to try my luck. I soon had him hooked. But not wanting to lose him, I yanked too hard on my pole, lost my balance, and landed in the icy water. The trout landed on the bank, hook still attached.

I called to Clifford for help, only to see him go running to save the fish on the bank!

"Never mind the fish — why aren't you helping me?" I yelled to him.

"Well, if you went in there to get the fish, I thought I should save it first," he replied, perfectly serious. "Great thinking," I remember commenting as I sat shivering in the cold water.

Apparently Clifford recounted the episode to Dr. Beecher for the next time I met him at the hospital he inquired, "What were you trying to do Madeline, drown the little cuss?"

He sure was a great diagnostician, but so much for the secret of my pregnancy!

Chapter Four

Starting a Family Practice

With Clifford's internship almost over, it was time to start planning where he would "hang out his shingle." He had been advised not to settle in his hometown. "Those lovely neighbors and playmates you had when a child — of course you wouldn't want to charge them for your services," he was told. Rupert was too small anyway.

Clifford had always thought he would like to practice in Manchester, which was the nearest large town to Rupert. Doctors practiced professional courtesy in those days, so Clifford called on Dr. Campbell. Dr. Campbell was a very kind and considerate man, but he told Clifford that there was barely work enough for the two doctors already there. He was afraid it wouldn't work for a third to come in.

After visiting several other towns, Clifford stopped in South Royalton where a Dr. Munsell said he would welcome him with open arms. Royalton's population of 1,491 seemed large enough to support two doctors, and Dr. Munsell also told Clifford he wanted to take some time off and use his camp more. We found a place in the center of town just off the main street where we could rent first-floor living quarters large enough to convert the living room into an office. We moved in on September 1, 1938. A month later a local undertaker bought the building and moved in on the second floor. Not an auspicious sign, perhaps, but we were too busy purchasing furniture and medical equipment to worry about it.

To us, it seemed an ideal situation. The country doctor had a wife who was a nurse and also able to keep track of patients and billing (I had also taken bookkeeping in high school). Because our living quarters were adjacent to the office, I could help out as needed and also take care of our baby-to-be. It was a convenient setup that would allow me to be both a mother and a nurse.

The large living room was transformed into a splendid office and the hall into a waiting room. We had to take out more loans to buy the office equipment, but when the sign "Clifford B. Harwood, MD" went up on the door, we were proud and happy to be in business at last. It was just a little over two years since our marriage, and we were filled with great expectations.

I thought that Clifford looked very professional in his white intern coat and had suggested he wear it in the office. He agreed, but when he answered the doorbell and a patient asked if the doctor was in, he was a little disappointed. After the incident, Clifford commented, "Who did he think I was, the butler?" So much for the white coat.

As time marched on, business remained slow. But we knew it takes time to build a practice so we remained optimistic. We had another reason for our high spirits, the impending birth of our first child.

Clifford Jr. was born on October 29, 1938, at the Mary Fletcher Hospital, about fifty miles away. He kept me quite busy so I actually appreciated the fact that Clifford didn't need me too much at this point.

When Cliff was about four months old, he awakened us one night with the frightening cough of croup. We got a steam tent going, and his breathing became easier. Clifford had planned to attend a medical meeting in Burlington the next day so with the baby seeming better by morning he went on his way, telling me he would ask Dr. Johnson, a pediatrician, how to treat croup.

By noon, Clifford Junior was worse and I was getting worried. I recalled a treatment my mother had used for croup, so I phoned the drugstore and asked the pharmacist if he could give me a small bottle of Ipecac and one of glycerin. A neighbor picked them up for me, and I gave about a third tea-spoonful of Ipecac with a few drops of glycerin in it to Cliff. In no time, he coughed up a large amount of mucous and began breathing normally. What a relief and what a big hug he received from me!

When Clifford returned, he told me what Dr. Johnson had recommended. It was exactly what I had done. Old remedies still worked!

During the winter of 1939, we received a letter from Mother Harwood telling us that Clifford's father was not well and would we please

The Reverend King of Rupert, who baptised Clifford, baby Clifford, and later grandson Clifford, with Madeline and Clifford and their new son.

come. At this time we had a secondhand 1936, two-door Chevy. Children's car seats hadn't been developed yet, so we placed baby Cliff on a pillow in a clothes basket and put the basket on the seat beside me.

We were going down Mendon Mountain toward Rutland, a bit fast for the road conditions I thought, when we hit a patch of ice. The car went to one side of the road and then the other, out of control. We left the road on the right, rolled over, went down a slight bank, struck the right side, rolled over again, and came to rest on the driver's side door.

Baby Cliff came rolling out of his basket into my arms. Clifford was pinned down next to the driver's door by me as I held the baby. Fearing the car might catch on fire, he managed to turn off the ignition and asked if I could open the passenger door. I tried but could not budge it. Suddenly, the door came open and a stranger was offering to help. I asked him to take the baby from me so I could climb out and he obliged.

I then climbed up on the side of the car and slid to the ground, followed by Clifford.

At that point, the gentleman started to hand me Cliff and told me to go sit in the car with his wife.

Shaken, I told him "I can't. I can't stand up — my knees are too weak."

"Oh yes you can," he said, not unkindly. And to my surprise I did.

By this time other cars had stopped, including a big truck we had passed just prior to the accident. Clifford and the men tipped our car back onto its four wheels, and the truck pulled it up to the road. We were able to get to a garage in Rutland where they put oil and water back in, and we went on our way none the worse for our frightening experience. The only injury was a slight bruise to Clifford's cheek, which was caused by the sunglasses I was wearing. Our car registration was 3133. I never had liked the 13 in that number.

While living in South Royalton, Clifford joined the Masonic Lodge and also attended church. I mostly stayed home with the baby and awaited phone calls, which were none too frequent. Some of our friends told us that Dr. Munsell was not taking off enough time to go to his camp. However, we soon realized that Clifford's practice was made up of many patients who couldn't or wouldn't pay. We were able to afford food and rent, but that was all.

In mid-August 1939, a drug salesman stopped by and told Clifford that an elderly physician in Brandon had died and that he thought there would be a good opening there. Brandon was a larger town with a population of 2,891. So Clifford went to call on Drs. Esterbrook, a father and son team who were already practicing there. They were most kind. They did not discourage Clifford, but I had a feeling that they did not encourage him either. Nevertheless, Clifford was optimistic. We located a small house to rent for our residence and office and prepared to move.

Clifford had ordered many drugs from the salesman who called frequently, saying it was important to look busy. I carefully wrapped each bottle of medicine in newspaper and packed them in boxes. One of our patients who owed a bill came with his truck to move our goods. The truck was half loaded when another patient stopped by for a supply of medicine before we left. Having no idea where it was and knowing those boxes were in the front of the load, I asked if we couldn't just send it to him after we got to our new home.

But Clifford was firm, insisting the patient "wants it now." The patient always comes first was Clifford's motto, but under the circumstances — I was eight months pregnant and tending a one-year old child — I could not see the urgency and inquired as to what the emergency was.

When I learned that the medicine was needed for his potency, I lost all sympathy and patience (this was an older man who had a reputation for fooling around with a young girlfriend). But as usual Clifford won out. I climbed into the truck, searched box after box, unwrapping many many bottles until I found what was needed. By that time I was exhausted and felt like throwing it at him.

Once again, we settled into our new home with high expectations only to find that business was slow. Clifford had two or three patients a day for the first week or so. In his spare time, he sang in the Brandon Congregational Church choir. Choir rehearsals helped fill some of his time.

I joined one of the local cooking schools. I wasn't needed in the office much, but I was busy with little Cliff and domestic duties like washing and cooking. We didn't have a washing machine. I used two tubs set on stools and a scrub board. It was good back-bending exercise. Wringing sheets by hand also built up my arm muscles.

We received a lot of garden products instead of cash for Clifford's services. One patient kept us supplied with squab. Others, potatoes. But you can only eat so many potatoes, and we had no freezer for storing extra food. In fact, we had an ice refrigerator with a drip pan that had to be frequently emptied.

It was Friday the Thirteenth, October 1939, when we once again made a fifty-mile trip to the Mary Fletcher Hospital. But this time Clifford thought there was no hurry since my first labor had lasted twenty-four hours. He didn't even notify my obstetrician that we were on the way. It was duck-hunting season and he didn't want to disturb him in the event he was out hunting. He figured we had plenty of time to notify him after we arrived at the hospital.

On the ride I held baby Cliff on my lap with one hand and the inside of a double boiler in the other as I was feeling nauseous. For once it didn't matter to me how fast Clifford drove. My contractions had gone from every five minutes apart to three. When we reached the hospital, I left the car following a contraction, only to get part way up the steps when another struck. When another came in the office, they rushed me into the delivery room. I awakened to the cry of our daughter Catherine Ann.

Ten years later, I found out that an intern had delivered her. We were having dinner with our friends Betty and (Dr.) Richard Davis and both Betty, who had also been a nurse at Mary Fletcher, and I were expecting. "You know you two don't have to go all the way to Burlington to have a baby. We have doctors in this area who can handle deliveries just as well," Richard commented to us.

I responded that although the obstetrician who had delivered Cathy had since retired, I still felt at home going to Burlington. Dr. Davis started to laugh and when I asked what was so funny, he let the cat out of the bag. "No he didn't. He was out duck hunting and there wasn't time so Betty got me. I delivered Cathy!"

Now that we had two children to feed, a hospital bill to pay, and coal to buy for the furnace, I began to feel discouraged. Clifford's response was to go to the bank and secure a loan. But the reality was that the deceased doctor whom he had replaced had not had a big practice. Everyone loved the father and son team so there was no reason to change doctors. We had moved in with high hopes and expectations, but it was rapidly becoming apparent even to Clifford that something had to be done.

Sometimes prayers do get answered. I think that is what happened because one winter day, a Dr. Peterson and his wife stopped by to ask if we were interested in moving. They were leaving his practice in Whitingham as he was moving to Burlington to become a radiologist. One look at her beautiful new coat and his recent model car convinced us we were.

They told us that Whitingham had a large power dam, owned by the New England Power Company, on the Harriman Reservoir. It generated money for the town as well as power. At that time, taxpayers received a rebate on their property taxes, and the selectmen felt the town was rich. They had never had a resident doctor before, but they decided they could afford to pay a doctor to settle in town. Dr. Peterson had served them for two years.

The Town of Whitingham paid their doctor $1800 a year. In return, the doctor was to charge only $1 for an office visit and $2 for a house call, regardless of the distance traveled. A two-week vacation could be arranged if the doctor hired a substitute to cover for him while he was away. Each year at town meeting, the taxpayers voted to renew or reject the contract with the doctor.

In mid-February 1940, Clifford went to Whitingham to get acquainted with the area, and I began packing for move number three. As we drove over Woodford Mountain, the snow drifts were high on both sides of the road, and I felt as if we were headed for Siberia. But we made it to town and settled into the house Dr. Peterson had vacated.

When we accepted his offer, we thought we had found a gold mine. Soon we learned differently. It turned out that he was selling his practice to us, and we were to make monthly payments to him for his "good will." (We also got an electric refrigerator, a roll-top desk, and some office equipment. We didn't need the latter as we had our own but I appreciated the refrigerator.) Fortunately for us, it turned out to be a very busy practice compared to our past experiences, and for the first time my nursing skills were really needed. And we did have the annual salary, so things were looking up.

Cliff Jr. and Cathy.

Clifford, Cathy, and Cliff Jr.

Cathy, Madeline, and Cliff Jr.

Chapter Five

Our Year in Whitingham

Whitingham is located in southern Vermont, about thirty miles from Bennington, Brattleboro, Greenfield, and North Adams, the latter two towns being in northwestern Massachusetts. There was a small country store in nearby Jacksonville and one in the village of Whitingham; both supplied the basic necessities. But if a spool of thread was needed or a movie desired, it was necessary to travel those thirty miles to one of the larger towns. Whitingham was large in area size (23,040 acres) but only had a population of 734. It was a pretty, rural area. The people were very nice, and we were to be very happy there despite the threat of war looming over us and some rather unusual experiences.

For starters, just after moving into the house, I learned that a previous owner had hanged himself in the cellar. When I tended the furnace, I had visions of seeing his ghost flitting around the basement. Disconcerting to say the least.

Then about a week after arriving, the phone rang and a strange voice said, "I want the family doctor."

I asked who was calling but was told to "never mind — send the doctor now."

I asked where the caller was but received no answer, just the click of the phone being hung up.

I rang up the telephone operator and asked if she knew where the call came from. It was from the bar in Jacksonville and better to ignore it, she advised.

When Clifford returned, I told him about the strange call. Later, he had to go out on an evening call, and I asked him not to be long in case the man from the bar came by.

As I was preparing for bed, I heard a knock at the door. Sure enough it was the intoxicated caller. I showed him to the waiting room, telling him the doctor would be in soon. However, he kept returning to our living room asking for Clifford.

Fortunately, Clifford returned shortly and took charge. I went to bed but heard them talking until midnight. The next day I learned the patient was Swedish and was staying at the home of Peter Nachtheim, a German. Mrs. Nachtheim had died the day before and the Swede was concerned that he might have hastened her death. Clifford assured him that he had done nothing to cause her death.

A few days later, I was feeding Cliff in the high chair when our front door opened and in walked another stranger.

"Do you want to see the doctor," I asked.

"No, I came to see you," he told me.

Asking what he wanted, he told me, "You need my help. I have come to help you."

I told him I could manage very nicely. He walked over to the high chair and said, "I've come to take this baby away."

Frightened, I ordered him to leave Cliff alone.

"Then I will take this one," he said, walking toward the carriage where Cathy was lying.

Scared and worried that I was dealing with someone who was unhinged, I grabbed the chair I had been sitting on, raised it over my head as if to threaten him, and demanded that he leave her alone.

Seeing my fear and intent, he immediately said, "I am Peter Nachtheim. I mean no harm my lady." He then sat down to visit.

Pulling the carriage near me, I placed a bottle in Cathy's mouth while I fed Cliff Jr.

"That is no way to feed a baby. You should hold her," Mr. Nachtheim told me.

"She can manage this way," I replied, still feeling unsure of him.

"Put her in my lap. I can feed her," he responded.

Seeing he was insistent, I picked her up and placed her, pillow and all (so as not to contaminate her), in his lap, hoping for the best and wishing that Clifford were there.

Before too much longer, the kitchen door opened and in he came.

"What's going on here?" he asked me with a funny look.

"Your wife needs help," Mr. Nachtheim told him.

"She does not. If you want to see me, you come into my office," Clifford said sternly.

They went to the office and the intruder left shortly afterward.

Two days later, as Clifford was preparing to go to the Brattleboro Hospital, who should appear but Mr. Nachtheim. He had brought me two gifts.

Apologizing that he hadn't intended to frighten me, he asked me to accept some handiwork his wife had been working on and a cup.

As I turned the mustache cup over to admire it, I said, "Oh, this was made in Germany."

"That does not harm it, does it my lady?" came his worried reply.

Realizing I had possibly offended him, I assured him it was beautiful and thanked him.

He then told Clifford that we would never see the Swede again. They had had a fight and he had thrown him out, telling him if he ever saw him again, he would kill him.

Moments later, I looked out the window and saw the intoxicated Swede staggering between the snow banks as he made his way toward our house. As soon as he entered, an argument erupted with each using a few choice words. I stepped behind Clifford, telling him to kick them both out.

The Swede made a hasty retreat, promising, "You'll never see me again." Clifford took the German home on his way to his Brattleboro meeting. We never saw either man again.

We were told by neighbors, "Nothing like this ever happened in this town before."

About a year later, Clifford's twin brother Clarence was interning at the Mary Fletcher Hospital when the Swede was admitted with severe burns. He had been drinking, his clothes caught on fire, and he had rolled in the snow to extinguish the flames. Naturally, he mistook Clarence for Clifford and in his inebriated state found it hard to accept Clarence's explanation of being a twin.

That summer we decided to move to a house across from the general store. There was a lawn where the children could play and also better parking for patients. Moving day arrived and as usual, Clifford was busy elsewhere. Dr. Walker in Wilmington ten miles away needed an assistant during an appendectomy. So once again I packed and unpacked us — move number four.

Shortly after we had moved in, Mr. Jillison the storekeeper asked Clifford if he had seen the monument up on the hill behind the store. Curious, we walked up and found that it marked the birthplace of the Mormon leader Brigham Young. It was an average sized marker engraved with *Brigham Young born on this spot 1801. A man of much courage and superb equipment.* It struck us as a strange coincidence that in South Royalton where we had lived, there was a large granite shaft monument to Joseph Smith, marking his birthplace. Smith was the founder of the Mormons but had been murdered, and Young had taken over his leadership position.

That was but one quirk of history we were to experience in that town. It was in the spring when once again we decided to go fishing. Mary Coombs, a friend, and Clifford and I went to a very remote area and decided to separate, thinking we would have better luck that way. I went down stream, found a clearing, sat on a rock, and waited for the fish to bite. It was a beautiful, peaceful setting with the woods about 150 feet away.

Suddenly I noticed a large animal emerging from the trees. It appeared to be a German Police dog, and I wondered what it was doing so far from home. He was tan colored and had a long tail. As I sat there watching him, he turned toward me and I was startled to see a cat face that was now watching me. As he began to walk toward me in a low crouch, I screamed, got up and raced up the brook toward Mary.

When I screamed, the animal had screamed, too. As I ran, I felt sure he was on my trail and about to pounce on my shoulder at any second. As I reached Mary, I grabbed her, yelling, "Run Mary; he is after us."

Looking startled, she turned around and said calmly, "There is nothing after you," and called to Clifford, "Come fast! Madeline is white as a sheet."

Asking what was the matter and had I seen a snake, I assured him it was no snake. "I am certain I saw a Catamount [a mountain fisher thought to be extinct in Vermont]. He saw me and was coming toward me," I told them. Fortunately, I had probably frightened the animal as much as he did me and he had run off. Still, that was the end of my fishing for that day.

During our lifetime together, Clifford made a list of Catamount sightings that were reported in the newspaper. They were rare but there were several and some were verified by footprints in the earth. I guess I should have felt honored to have had such an encounter, but, at the time, I was just too frightened to have appreciated any part of it.

We had a most enjoyable social life in Whitingham. One evening while playing cards at the home of Ruth and Fred Carrier, I began to feel ill. I did not complain, but when we got home at 11 I went right to bed. Due to severe abdominal pain I was unable to sleep, so Clifford gave me a hypo to ease the pain. By 6 a.m., I had only slept a few winks and the pain was worse. Clifford decided to do a blood count. It could be handy having an office in the home. He hurried back upstairs, however, announcing a diagnosis of acute appendicitis.

Worried about the children and the need to have someone take care of them, we called Fred and Ruth and asked them to come over to watch them while we made the trip to the hospital. They arrived about seven. Just as we were about to leave, the doorbell rang. The milkman had fallen with a bottle in his hand and required stitches. Clifford's motto, "the patient always comes first," came into play once again. They disappeared into his office and I waited.

About a half hour later I was pacing the floor in pain, and Fred, concerned with my condition, offered to drive me to the hospital. I knocked on the office door and asked how much longer Clifford would be.

"What the hell ails her?" I heard the patient ask.

"She has acute appendicitis. I was about to take her to the hospital when you arrived," I heard Clifford explain.

"Good God, Doc! Get your wife to the hospital and forget about me!" the patient exclaimed.

The milkman's suturing was soon completed, and we were on our way. Luckily, Dr. Philip Wheeler was able to remove my appendix before it ruptured. Mother Harwood came and looked after the family while I was in the hospital.

On my birthday July 7, 1940, Mother Harwood and her friend Mamie Auman arrived for a visit and to help me celebrate. But before we could do anything, a man from an adjoining town came to get help for his wife who was in labor. Clifford did not know the family, but he assembled his obstetrical equipment and followed the husband. About noon, the husband arrived at our house in our car with a note requesting me to sterilize the delivery forceps and return with him to help Clifford.

As I arrived, so had the baby. I scattered the hens from the hallway as I climbed up the stairs. One of the neighbors who had come to help Clifford, seeing the patient begin to hemorrhage, panicked and beat a hasty retreat from the room. It was a serious situation and I gave intravenous ergotrate while Clifford tried to control the bleeding. Realizing the patient needed hospitalization and a possible transfusion, Clifford went down to tell the husband.

"We are on the town; you will have to get permission from the selectmen," the husband replied. Since there was no phone, Clifford drove off to find a town authority.

Meantime, the patient had passed out. Her pulse was weak, so I called downstairs for blankets and a kitchen chair. I had someone raise the foot of the bed as I slipped the chair under it, thus elevating her lower body and (in effect) lowering her head. She came to shortly.

Clifford returned with the permit, loaded the lady into our car, and took off for the hospital. In all the confusion and haste, he forgot to take the baby. A neighbor transported the baby.

Several months later, we had a mid-morning call to come see the baby. They said they had placed a bottle in the baby's mouth at 2 a.m. It was still there, and the baby was cold. There was nothing Clifford could do; the baby was dead.

I continued to use my nursing skills to assist Clifford, and he was pleased with my bookkeeping, too. Business was good. We could help people and most of the cases were more normal ones, the usual upset stomachs, broken limbs, and more routine home and hospital deliveries. Still, there were the exceptional and more challenging cases every once in awhile, and we felt good about using our skills to help people.

For the first time, we were making headway on Clifford's medical school loans and even saving enough to buy our first new car, a four-door Chevy. We bought it from Ray Roberts for $900, exactly one half of the annual salary paid by the town.

We had made some good friends in Whitingham and liked the area. On the first Tuesday in March, the townspeople voted to extend Clifford's contract another year. We were very happy. But that was Town Meeting Day 1941. Our happiness was to be short-lived.

In May, we received a letter from the United States Army. We knew from the newspapers that things in Europe had gone from bad to worse over the past two years and feared that war with Germany was inevitable. Clifford had taken ROTC in college and then attended regular Officer Training in Rutland and later in Brattleboro. He knew what was happening. On July 1, 1941, he was to report to Fort Devens for duty.

"We won't tell anyone. People won't pay their bills if they know we are leaving," Clifford said.

But it wasn't long before the news leaked out. I don't know if it affected collections or not. I was too busy planning and packing to know. Office furniture and equipment had to be packed separately from the things that we would take with us. We shipped them off to Jefferson Hill, 150 miles north, where they were stored in my parents' attic. Then we packed all our household goods and loaded up for move number five. We said many sad good-byes as we headed off for Ayer, Massachusetts, where we had located a small house on a nice, quiet side street.

Clifford and Clarence answering the call of duty in World War II.

Chapter Six

On the Move with the Army

Clifford entered the service as a first lieutenant assigned to the 16th Medical Regiment, which was not yet up to full strength. Most of the doctors were from the New England states; a few came from the Chicago area. The Chaplain was from Indiana. For the first few weeks, army personnel spent most of the time getting organized. Later, they went on maneuvers in the surrounding area.

In the meantime, I adjusted to our new life and located the stores and library in Ayer. I tried to create a homelike atmosphere for our children and for Clifford, but it was unsettling times to say the least. Of course, there were many other wives in the same situation. It didn't take too long to make their acquaintances and that was a big comfort for me. Being busy with the care of the children and setting up house also helped me make the transition to a new way of life. It was the first time Clifford was gone all day and doing work that was separate from our lives together.

The threat of war was looming over us and made life just a little more serious, but our adventures, which seemed to be part of our lives wherever we went, continued. It wasn't long before our good friend Chaplain Rowland Adams took Clifford aside and told him that the big house next to us on the corner of that nice side street was a house of prostitution.

We had noticed what seemed like a lot of activity but had figured it was just parties. How naive, I thought, as I recalled all the beautiful negligees that hung on the clothesline between our houses!

Then one afternoon, I had gone shopping and Clifford was home watching the children. A knock came at the door. As Clifford opened it, there stood a surprised soldier in uniform. "Whoops, wrong house," was all he said as he made a hasty retreat.

Dr. Ben Clark and his wife Bea, a couple we had known in Vermont, occupied the apartment across the street from us. One morning I noticed a police car parked by "the house." I phoned Bea, telling her to look out her window because it looked like a raid next door. This provided us with some real excitement .

We could see the girls nervously looking out their windows and an officer knocking on their door for what seemed an eternity. Finally, someone answered the door. With my own window open, I overheard the officer say, "Would you ask your visitors to park their cars on one side of the street only so they won't block traffic, please?"

Of course, I phoned Bea to tell her what he said. We had thought we would see girls lined up on the streets. What a letdown.

In September Clifford's regiment was assigned to North Carolina for maneuvers. They were to be located about forty miles from Fort Bragg. Many units from the New England states were involved. Officers were not allowed to have their cars while stationed there. Clifford went ahead and was to locate a place for us to live. We arranged to sublet our house, and I packed up our things for move number six.

Before we went to join him, I took the children to Rupert to spend time with his folks while awaiting his call. After a week, the call came that we were to live with a Mr. and Mrs. Henrick in Rockingham, which was quite close to headquarters.

At that time, Clifford's older brother Raymond was living in Boston. He told me he would check the condition of my tires if I would come by way of Boston, a distance of 150 miles. This sounded like a good idea as we could spend the night with him and break up the long drive.

As I was going up Peru Mountain, maybe twenty miles into our trip, I heard a thumping noise. Sure enough, I had a flat tire.

I had been told if that happened I should open the trunk and stand by the car looking dumb — someone would surely stop and help. Now was the time to try that technique. I unloaded the trunk, placed the luggage on the bank near the car, and sat Cliff Jr., not quite three, and Cathy, not quite two, on top of it.

Very shortly a man stopped to assist me. He changed the tire, then inspected the flat. It needs a blowout patch and the inner tube needs repair, he said. Then he offered to take them into town and get the work done.

We waited and he returned about a half hour later and put the spare in the trunk. Just as he was finishing, a car full of his friends pulled up offering to help. They also offered us some beer which was kindly rejected. The good Samaritan only charged me for the blowout patch, and soon I was back on the road to Boston.

Raymond, who worked for a tire company at the time, said he didn't think the spare tire was good enough for the trip. But I didn't have the money for a new one and his wife didn't want to part with the one he was going to give me, so the next morning I continued on my way without the assurance of a good spare. At 6 a.m. I left for Washington DC, a distance of 471 miles. There were no super highways and no seat belts in those days.

The children were well behaved, climbing back and forth between the front and back seats as children do, playing with each other, and sleeping for some of the time. I had no radio for company or to disturb me; no driver to spell me either. I didn't think much of the long drive, perhaps because I was young (age twenty-seven) and looking forward to being with Clifford so we could be a family again.

Clarence was stationed in Anacostia, DC, at the Bolling Field Air Force Base. He had a private room in the city but was on duty that night so the children and I were to stay in his room for the night.

As I got into downtown DC, it was getting dark. I asked Cliff for my map of the area. "I get it mummy," he said helpfully. He climbed into the back seat and got his piggy bank. "Here it is," he said as he tried to shake pieces of the map from the bank.

I was near a diner so I went in and asked for directions. The attendant was kind and helpful. He showed me my location on a large map on

Captain Clifford Harwood

the wall, and I located my destination. As I departed he wished me well, adding, "I gave up driving in DC some time ago. I was always getting lost."

Luck was with me, though, and I found the house with no difficulty. The children were restless and excited from the two-day trip, but I was exhausted. The three of us settled into the double bed but were unable to relax and sleep. I was beginning to worry about driving the next day when about 1 a.m. the landlady knocked on the door.

"Your husband is here," she announced.

Glory be, there he stood! He had taken a bus to DC to drive us for the rest of the trip. I was sure glad to see him, as were the kids, and the four of us slept soundly for the rest of the night.

Clifford drove us on to North Carolina the next day, and I enjoyed the scenery and catching up on the news while the children were happy to be with their Dad once again. As we approached Rockingham, I had to take over the driving as officers were not allowed to have cars there and, if caught, the keys would be taken by the Army Military Police.

After we arrived at the Henricks' home, there wasn't much for me to do as we simply had a large room with cots for the children and a bed for us and we took our meals with the family. Mrs. Henrick was very kind, however, and I helped her with housework and in return she watched the children for me occasionally.

One night we attended a dance at the Southern Pines Country Club. On the way home, we were told there would be a blackout test. We were to drive with no headlights. It was a beautiful, clear moonlit night, but I was scared and I doubt that I drove over fifteen miles an hour.

Another time there was a dance for officers and their wives. I wanted to go, but Clifford said his company was having a barbecue that night and he had to be with them. I was disappointed as there was not much excitement for me. Chaplain Adams came to my rescue and took me to the dance. I never did hear who gave the blessing at the barbecue, maybe Clifford did.

A moment of unwelcome excitement occurred one day as I stopped to say good-by to a friend who was leaving early. Knowing I would just be a few minutes, I left the children in the car. When I returned, I found that Cliff had taken a small bottle from the back of the glove compartment and opened it. There lay my codeine tablets on the seat in front of Cathy.

In a panic, I asked Cliff if Cathy had eaten any of them. "Only six or eight," he calmly replied.

I checked her saliva and realized she had put at least one in her mouth. But not knowing how many were in the bottle or if she had swallowed any (they are very bitter), I raced over to headquarters and got Clifford. I wanted to know if I should get her stomach washed out or what to do.

Calm as usual, Clifford figured that she wouldn't have eaten more than one due to the bitter taste and told me not to worry. When I asked what symptoms to look for, he told me to keep her awake and if she got sleepy to call him. I knew he was trying to reassure me, but I worried anyway. As it turned out, she was wide awake all afternoon and was more active than usual.

Still, I had learned a hard lesson — never leave children unattended in a car and never leave medicine in the glove compartment. (I had begun having headaches as a teenager during school and they had progressed to severe migraines as I got older. In those days, codeine was the medicine used for migraines. Afraid one would strike while driving, I had made sure to keep some pills in the car, never thinking the children could get at them.)

While in North Carolina, I had also begun having spells of severe abdominal pain that sometimes left me feeling faint. Worried that I might become ill on the return trip North, I asked Clifford if he could get permission to travel with us in the car when the time came to return to Fort Devens (I knew some officers were going home with their families). But he said he had to stay with his men, so the children and I headed back to New England without him.

Fifty miles into the trip, I stopped for gas and the attendant noticed my tire going flat. I asked him to put the spare on, but he said he couldn't because it wasn't safe to drive such a distance with a blowout patch. This was the tire the man back in Peru had gotten fixed for me. Adding that my flat tire was worn through and no good, he advised me to buy a new tire. I felt I had no choice and did so, and we were on our way.

I soon caught up with the long convoy of troops headed north and found myself going about 25 miles an hour. I'll never get home at this rate, I remember fretting when a military policeman who had seen my plight came back on his motorcycle and escorted me past the convoy to the head of the line. "That was great!" I remember thinking.

But a half hour later, Cliff had to go to the bathroom. That meant stopping and while I did so, the entire convoy passed me, the men waving as they went by.

Once again, the MP came to my rescue and we went to the head of the line a second time.

An hour later, it was Cathy's turn. Once more the convoy passed by. Before reaching DC, I had my third escort with more cheering and waving by the men. How delightful, I thought, as I made my way to Clarence's room, where once again we would spend the night.

Imagine my surprise, when I came upon the same convoy the next day about fifty miles north of DC. But this time we all were in for trouble. The entire East Coast was covered by a dense fog. I could not see two cars ahead of me. No one was passing. In fact, traffic was now moving about ten miles an hour. As dark closed in, reality also set in. There was no way I could make my parents' home in Newbury that day so I found a small hotel in Kingston, New York, where we ate our dinner and stayed the night.

Morning came too soon for this weary driver, who was now getting tense. The fog had not lifted and I had a long way to go to get to Newbury, where I had planned to spend a few days until our house in Ayer was ours again. By the time I reached Burlington, I was totally exhausted and my neck and shoulders ached with muscular tension. I made an unplanned stop at the Burlington Hospital, where my sister Charlotte was now working. I needed a diathermy (heat) treatment and a massage. How good it was to see her and to have someone pamper me with hands that kneaded away my aches and pains.

Feeling better, I made the last seventy-mile leg of the trip. When I stopped for gas in Barre, the attendant warned me to be careful going over the heights, cautioning me that it was very foggy and I had better drive with my lights on dim. Thanking him, I drove on undaunted. After all I had driven through, I was so glad to be close to home that a little fog could not scare me. I had driven over 900 miles and arrived tired but happy to see my family once again.

After a nice visit with the children's aunts, uncles, and grandparents, who were glad to see us, I was back on the road and headed for Fort Devens. I got home ahead of Clifford and made the house ready for his arrival on December 6.

When he returned, we discussed our respective trips. When I told him about the new tire, he exclaimed, "You mean to tell me you let him sell you a new tire?!"

Yes, I told him, noting it wasn't safe to drive on the one I had for a spare.

He was unconvinced. "He saw a woman coming so he sold you a new tire. You let him take you."

Knowing better, I let the conversation drop. There was no point arguing.

On Sunday, December 7, 1941, we learned the Japanese had bombed Pearl Harbor. President Roosevelt had declared it "a dastardly act." We knew war was imminent.

On December 8, President Roosevelt declared war on Japan. One of the many changes that came about the next day included the beginning of rationing. All tires for private automobiles were frozen. No more comments from Clifford about my new tire. The entire country began gearing up for wartime production. Troops were ordered on maneuvers as uncertainty prevailed.

Cathy and Cliff at Christmas

Family photo taken just before Clifford left to go overseas during WW II.

*A patriotic salute for dad. Snapshot Madeline
sent to Clifford during the war.*

Chapter Seven

The War Years

In late spring 1942, Clifford was sent to Carlisle, Pennsylvania, to attend Officers' Training School. We put our furniture in storage, and after a difficult search — most advertisements specified no dogs or children — found temporary housing in Carlisle.

Clarence was still in DC so we visited him there on his free weekends. On one visit, we were eating in the officers' dining room when four Russian officers arrived. They were very businesslike, but I what I really recall about them is that their boots squeaked with every step.

Six weeks later, we were back at Fort Devens, unpacking and once more getting settled. Only this time it was into officers' quarters. As the men were unloading the furniture, I overheard the boss telling his man to take one thing at a time as they were being paid by the hour. This made me so angry that I helped unload the truck.

Living in this area was enjoyable. There were many officers' wives with children so I found playmates for Cliff and Cathy, and I could share pleasures and concerns with the other mothers and didn't feel quite so alone with Clifford gone all day.

Our old friend Chaplain Adams offered Protestant services at the base chapel. He planned to hold Sunday evening services to accommodate the men. We attended his first and last such service. After waiting ten minutes, it appeared Clifford and I would be the only attendees.

"For where two or three are gathered together in my name, there I am in the midst of them," he began, citing Matthew 18, verse 20. It was a lovely service.

Although many troop movements were being ordered, Clifford never told me about them. One day I overheard his driver mention the name of an outfit that was moving out the next day. When Clifford joined me, I mentioned what I had heard. By his reaction, you would have thought that a top secret had been given to the enemy. (Needless to say, the driver heard more about that later.) "Loose lips sink ships" was the order of the day and every good service man was expected to obey the injunction to secrecy. Never mind consideration for their wives or families.

During the last part of July, my mother and sister Charlotte were visiting us when Clifford came home for lunch as usual. I drove to headquarters to pick him up while mother prepared the meal. As I sat in the car chatting with another wife, her husband and Clifford came toward the car. Clifford tossed some papers on the front seat, saying he would be right back.

Curious, I glanced at the papers and saw the words, Port of Embarkation. When Clifford returned I asked if it meant his outfit was going overseas. I knew the dreaded answer before he spoke it.

There was much discussion on the way home. Despite my tears, Clifford suggested we not mention the subject until after lunch.

We sat at the table to eat, but I was unable to swallow so I excused myself. Mother came to the kitchen and asked if something was wrong with the meal. I told her I just didn't feel well and went back to the table.

After lunch, Clifford closed the doors and windows so the neighbors wouldn't hear. I don't recall if he pulled the shades, too. He made his dramatic announcement, and they understood my distress.

Clifford also notified his folks and his mother came for a short visit. He shipped out on August 5, 1942. I awoke Cliff and Cathy and we drove Clifford to the base to say our good-byes. I drove back to the house feeling alone and utterly empty.

I had deliberately put off packing for our next move as I had been determined to maintain a homey atmosphere as long as possible. Now, I faced another move. This time would be different though, for now I was truly on my own.

Back in 1938, when things became noticeably hostile in Europe, Clifford had decided that if he ever had to go to war, it would be best if I were left with two children. I had not been consulted on that decision. But now here I was! I put our furnishings in storage and decided to head for home.

Once there, I realized I needed a way to pay the bills and care for the children. This time the decisions were mine to make. I also knew I needed to keep busy.

Fortunately, at this time there were no restrictions on married nurses working. Many nurses had joined the military so there were even some shortages. I drove to Burlington and called on Dr. Brown of the cockroach episode. Much to my surprise, he said that he needed a night supervisor. I hadn't worked there in a few years and asked if he felt I could do the work.

"I will take that chance. When can you start?" he replied.

I told him that with Clifford overseas I needed work right way, and he hired me on the spot.

I enrolled Cliff and Cathy in nursery school and made living arrangements for them in a home near the hospital. I was to stay in nursing staff quarters nearby. My duty hours were 7 p.m. to 7 a.m. and one night a week I could be off until 1 a.m. The pay was $55 a month. I stopped in to see Cliff and Cathy each morning when I got off duty and again at four when they got up from their naps. They were well taken care of and happy in their new situation. I was kept very busy. Miss Cleveland, the other night supervisor, disliked maternity duty so that was one of my many duties which was fine by me.

I thought I was well set to survive our separation, but I began to worry when I didn't hear from Clifford. He was always very secretive and took his orders seriously, never telling me much about what he was doing or where they would be sent next. Anxious, I made a visit to a fortune teller.

"I can see you are married but your husband isn't with you, am I right?" she intoned as she glanced into her crystal ball. (Considering world conditions, that was a good guess, I thought to myself.) "There appears to be a dark cloud! Can your husband be in Africa?"

"I doubt it, but I have no idea," I replied.

"He is either in Africa or to be sent there," she added.

I do not recall the rest of the visit. Clifford had taught me to be discrete so I reminded myself not to tell her anything I didn't have to.

Finally, a letter arrived from Clifford. He was in England — busy but safe. I had wanted to plan a code system whereby he could let me know where he was. "Too dangerous; some of our mail will be censored," he wrote.

Nonetheless, he did write often after this, sometimes telling me of church services he attended or people he met or homes visited. No army secrets, though.

On the home front, I was kept busy, too; gratefully so. One night when I went on duty at 1 a.m., I learned that there had been a delivery at midnight but was told everything was fine. I had established a practice of making rounds about two o'clock. For some reason, I started early that night.

First I checked the maternity ward and being assured everything was okay, I headed downstairs to the next ward. I had not gone far when something seemed to tell me to go back and check out the nursery. As I walked through the dimly lit room, I noticed the new baby's color wasn't normal. I turned on a brighter light and saw he was in distress. I called for the nursery nurse and got the suction machine going. While I held the baby upside down to remove the mucous from his throat, she administered oxygen. The baby gasped and started breathing again.

In the meantime, an intern had been called. He appeared and I asked him to take over. He told me I was doing fine and didn't need him. But I wasn't fine. My hands and knees were shaking.

While we were busy in the nursery, the mother rang her bell. She told the floor nurse she had dreamed something had happened to her son and asked to see him. The intern instructed the floor nurse to tell the new mother that babies weren't allowed out at that time of night, but she could see him for just a few minutes. The mother was satisfied, and the baby was returned to his bassinet, which was elevated. He was given oxygen until morning, and I gave the orders to watch him closely.

During my early morning rounds, I called on the mother. "What are you doing here, Billy (my nickname during training)," she asked as she recognized me. I hadn't seen her for several years and didn't know her married name so during the stress of the emergency I hadn't realized she was someone I knew. We had a short visit, but I did not mention the difficulties of the night. Only doctors could tell patients such things in those days.

In January 1943, Rita Cleveland joined the military, leaving me in charge of covering the entire 150 beds. My salary increased to $60 a month.

During this time, Chaplain Adams' wife Dora wrote to me frequently. Sometimes I learned of Clifford's whereabouts from her. He had been in on the invasion of Oran, Algeria (North Africa) the second week of November. He had even sent me a postcard, but the word Oran had been blotted out. So now I knew where the postcard had been sent from thanks to Dora!

Clifford did tell me that he had changed units and was now with the 261st Medical Battalion. On July 10, 1943, he went in on the invasion of Sicily. He narrowly escaped death as a buddy beside him was hit and killed by friendly fire while they were digging a foxhole. Later, he was sent into Italy before returning to England for further training.

After working for a year, my resistance was down due to the long hours, little sleep, and concern about Clifford. I contracted a case of measles and, being very ill, decided to quit my job. Dr. Brown was very understanding. His son had been in the same area as Clifford in North Africa so he knew what stress I was under.

I had also given Cliff and Cathy the measles, so off we went to my parents' home on Jefferson Hill. The children were very ill, and Cliff had also developed a bad cough.

One day mother said, "If that child doesn't have whooping cough, I'll eat my shirt."

I looked in Clifford's medical book. It said that if a child had whooping cough with the measles, it was apt to be fatal. I went to mother and told her I had looked in the book and that it said, "You don't get whooping cough with measles." I had lied, but we both felt better.

About a month later, well rested and ready to work, I was back in Burlington — this time working at the Elizabeth Lund Home for unwed mothers. The children, who had recuperated uneventfully, could live with me there and it was a very satisfactory arrangement as we were a family again — well, almost.

One day we needed to call a doctor for one of the girls in labor. Cliff was playing in the yard as the doctor arrived. He had picked some strawberries and offered them to the doctor as he went by. Being in a hurry, the doctor pushed his hand away and went inside.

I had been busy in the delivery room and was unaware of what was going on outside. Later I learned from my normally well-behaved, four-year old son that he had let the air out of the doctor's tires in retaliation for the rejection he had suffered.

My concern for Clifford's well-being went on alert when I didn't hear anything for over two weeks. I was aware he was involved in something but could only guess where. The newspapers said that southern France might be the strike area. Could it also be across the Channel? The Germans were guessing also.

I got my answer on June 6, 1944. It was D-Day, the invasion of Normandy by Allied Forces. Radios and newspapers gave details of the attack. I was certain this was what Clifford had been preparing for. I felt fearful and worried constantly. I tried to keep my overactive mind busy. It was difficult. Of course, they wouldn't send a doctor in on the invasion, the head nurse at the home had said, trying to reassure me.

Another long ten days passed before a letter came. Clifford wrote:

> June 11, 1944
> Somewhere in France. Safe and well. Wish you were here.
> Millions of hugs and kisses to you and Clifford and Catherine.
> Give my best to the others.
> Will write them later.
> All my Love Forever,
> Clifford

Knowing he was in France, Mother Harwood was very worried about Clifford. She had been having chest pains, so in August, I decided to quit my job and visit.

One night I found it very difficult to sleep. Father Harwood had hitched a cow outside my window. She had a new calf that he had put in the barn. All night the cow bellowed for her calf. Come morning I spoke to Mother Harwood about it, asking if she thought father would be upset if I were to ask him to hitch his cow someplace else since I hadn't slept all night.

"If you didn't listen, you wouldn't hear it," came her no-nonsense reply. The cow stayed. I'm not sure, but I think I still heard her.

Although Clifford wasn't one to reveal what he was doing, the press did. On December 19, 1944, the Burlington Free Press ran this story.

Captain Harwood Tells of Great Demand Upon Medical Battalion.

Captain Clifford Harwood, a graduate of the University of Vermont College of Medicine in 1937 and a former intern at Mary Fletcher Hospital, is a member of the Medical Battalion of the First Engineer Special Brigade which was recently writ-, ten up in the *Stars and Stripes*, distributed to the western front. The article, date-lined Paris, reads in part:

You can't rightly call them forgotten men. They'll never be forgotten by the men they treated on the blood-soaked sands of the Normandy beaches. The stories they tell are the stories of men found everywhere — about the medics, armed only with a Red Cross arm band and the kind of guts combat men mention in awe. The battalion landed at H-hour plus 120 minutes in the face of heavy enemy artillery fire. Within sight of the retreating enemy, the medics set up their tents while medical officers and EM technicians gave immediate emergency treatment to hundreds of casualties, established clearing stations, and were performing major surgery.

For five days this battalion was the only installation in the entire area performing definite surgery. It supported an entire corps. The first company to land was commanded by Major Raymond Skinner of Greenwich, New York. Shortly thereafter, two other companies arrived, commanded by Major John Burns of Milford, Massachusetts, and Captain Clifford Harwood of Rupert, Vermont. Treatment left nothing to be desired — blood plasma, sulfa drugs, penicillin — every lifesaving drug known to medical science which could possibly be brought in was there for all who needed it, including wounded POWs.

During the first few days when casualties were high and medical units few and far between, officers and men worked night and day until they themselves were ready for medical treatment. But these men, veterans of Africa, Sicily, and Italy knew, as medics always know, that theirs was a job well done.

By January 1945, Clifford had joined the 93rd Evacuation Hospital and had moved into Alsace-Lorraine. He was able to assure me he was in no danger — that he was far away from the front line. Home, too, I thought. It had been over two and a half years since I had last seen him.

On April 12, 1945, we learned that F.D.R. had died. Soon after I received a letter from Clifford dated April 13. He was in Germany.

Dearest Madeline,

I was just turning in after I finished the letter to you last night when at 5 minutes to 12 the news came on with a mention of President Roosevelt's death. Of course, all day today the news has been full of tributes and telegrams of sympathy to Mrs. Roosevelt. All the officers and men were discussing it all day, too. Everyone was very silent, thoughtful, and respectful at the newscasts and discussions, and there was not one unfavorable word mentioned about him, even from those who did not vote for him.

My feeling is still the same as when I voted for him last fall. I do not think that any other American will be able to bring America's ideals into the Peace as effectively as he. On the other hand, as far as the Senate and House are concerned, he may well exert more influence on their voting, through his proclaimed ideas, as a figure from History than he would have in person. It was only a few days ago that Congress turned down his proposals on manpower, which he had several times stated were necessary.

On May 7, all forces of Germany were unconditionally surrendered. What rejoicing!

A letter from Chaplain Adams, telling us "they may all be home in a matter of months" was followed by one from Clifford. It was written on June 24 and said the same thing!

I was living in West Rupert at this time because I had enrolled Cliff in school there the previous fall. It had been a difficult decision on where to live, but I had prayed on it and decided that the children would benefit from living near their grandparents. I knew I wouldn't get as much work as I would in Burlington, but I felt better being near the family. My sister-in-law Ruth Harwood (Raymond's wife) owned a vacant house in West Rupert and rented it to me so we were only two miles from Mother and Father Harwood — walking distance in those days.

Young Cliff was entered into the first grade, but there was no kindergarten class for Cathy. Cliff was generally an obedient child, but one day he forgot the rule to be quiet on the way to visit the bathroom and sang in the hall. When he returned, the teacher said, "All right Cliff, you like to sing, come up front and sing to the class."

He did and sang "Jesus loves me this I know, for the Bible tells me so. . . ." The other kids started raising their hands asking if they could go up front and sing, too.

I counted my blessings that it was his only serious misstep at school! I also was lucky to get some nursing cases, so it was a generally pleasant time even though I worried fairly constantly about Clifford.

With school letting out and Clifford's homecoming to look forward to, I decided to spend some time at Jefferson Hill with my family. My brother Lewis was living on a farm in Peacham and wanted me to spend some time with his family, too. I was enjoying my visit there and the change of scenery when a call came from mother. Clifford had called to say he was in Fort Dix, New Jersey.

It was July 16, the day the first atom bomb test occurred. I had no idea he was coming home that early. He reached me later that day. What a joy to hear his voice again! He told me he was leaving for Fort Devens the next day and to meet him there. I immediately drove to Rupert to tell his folks, deciding I could leave from there to drive the hundred miles to Fort Devens.

The children were excited, although Cathy did not remember her father well. He had been gone just two weeks shy of three years. Cliff was not sure he wanted to go with me. He was afraid his Dad wouldn't look like his picture. It was his way of telling me he wondered if Clifford had been wounded.

We left early the next morning. When we saw him, we ran to meet him and to get our hugs and kisses. "Daddy, you look just like your pictures," exclaimed Cliff.

I thought he looked more handsome than ever!

Clifford had to sign some papers before he could leave the base. To my worries that he might be sent to the Pacific, he assured me that the war was nearly under control, and he was home for good. Those wonderful papers held our future. He would be discharged on November 14, 1945 — there was still some time to go.

Grateful that he was back and safe, we drove to Boston to spend the night with his brother Raymond and his family. The next day we attended church in Boston to thank the Lord for all His blessings. Then we drove on to Rupert to be with his parents.

On August 6 the atomic bomb was dropped on Hiroshima and on August 9 on Nagasaki. The Japanese government agreed to unconditional surrender on August 10. We were still in Rupert when the news came, and Clifford joined the local residents in ringing the church bells. It was a time of heartfelt rejoicing.

The formal surrender was signed on September 2 on the battleship *Missouri* in Tokyo Harbor. For the first time, we could be sure that Clifford's formal discharge from the service would come through. Our prayers were answered. It was time to start our life together again.

The names of Clarence and Clifford Harwood were placed on the World War II Memorial at the Rupert Congregational Church, where they were baptised.

Clifford's notes about his war experience.

In August 1942, the 16th Medical Regiment embarked from Brooklyn, NY on the Pacific and Oriental Company liner *Orcades*. It landed in Liverpool, England and from there we moved by train to Swindon, Wiltshire, England. We received equipment, vehicles, etcetera and prepared for the mission to North Africa. We landed at Oran, Algeria two weeks after initial North African landings, November 1942.

Because of loss of our supplies (due to torpedoing of our supply ship by a German submarine), our Battalion was given other equipment and stayed in Oran for several weeks. Later [we] moved to Constantine, Algeria where we took care of less severe casualties from the fighting with the Germans at Kasserine Pass. The 16th Med. Regiment changed to the 161st and 162nd medical battalions.

After [the] Germans were driven from Tunisia, I was transferred to the 261st Medical Amphibious Battalion and participated in the invasion of Sicily on July 10, 1943. Later [we] moved to Caserta, just above Naples. Soon our Battalion was put aboard the Mariposa (an old ship later sunk by the Germans) en route to England, preparing for Normandy, France invasion to be held the following summer. The Mariposa was resupplied in Oran, and I was there for Thanksgiving, 1943. [I] Went to see some doctors I had known before, who were still stationed in Oran at that time.

Arrived in Glasgow, Scotland, early in December 1943, and we were quartered in an old estate in Probus, Cornwall, England with part of our men living in Quonset buildings on the grounds of the estate.

The next few months we engaged in practice landings on the English Channel coastline to prepare for the expected Normandy landings. Afterward, [we participated] in the invasion of Normandy June 6, 1944. Went on into Germany, and was a member of the 93rd Evacuation Hospital near Munich at the time of the German Surrender. I had no injuries while in the service.

The house as we bought it on Maple Street in 1945.

Our house after we made changes. The street was eventually renamed Main Street. Roger and Ricky are by the snowpiles. Doc's office was on the right.

Chapter Eight

Manchester at Last

After the war, the University of Vermont Medical College offered refresher courses for service men. We lived near the school in the Queen City Park area of Burlington for the month Clifford attended classes. Then it was time to resume our lives. Clifford felt that because he had signed a contract with the selectmen before the war that we should return to Whitingham. The town had been unable to obtain a physician while we were away, and he thought abiding by the contract would be the honorable thing to do even though they were placing no demands on him.

The house we had previously occupied had been sold, so once again we went house hunting. Clifford had heard of a plumber in Jacksonville who wanted to sell his home so we checked into it. It was a well built house but had no front lawn and abutted a river in the back. This was no place for young children to play outdoors, but I felt we could stand to live there until March when the contract expired.

However, as we stood talking in the kitchen, we were told we would have to buy the built-in refrigerator. I objected as we had our own. That doesn't matter you will have to buy this one, we were told. Then the owner added, "There is over a ton of coal in the cellar. When we went to oil, we didn't need it. You will have to buy that also."

I left the house and went to the car. Clifford came out and inquired as to what was bothering me. "Clifford, you went overseas to fight dictatorship. We will not buy this house," I declared.

He had to go back in and tell the man, we would think it over. But there was no thinking needed on my part. My mind was made up.

The next trip to Whitingham was just as unrewarding. We found a place that had been a creamery. It still had a sour-milk smell, but we thought we could make do until March. Then we learned a selectman had bought the building the week before. He didn't want to fix it and rent it to us. He wanted to sell it for $1,000 more than he had paid for it.

This time it was Clifford who said, "No way."

Frustrated but feeling we had made a good attempt to honor the contract, we decided it was time to look elsewhere.

There were many possibilities, but Clifford decided he wanted to open a practice in a larger town. Once again, we began to check out a town's need for a doctor and the availability of housing.

We explored Lyndonville, a beautiful college town. We learned the town could accommodate another doctor and found a lovely home being sold by a widower. I made the fatal error, however, of saying aloud that we could convert a room to an office and another area to a waiting room. The widower did not like the idea that we might change his beloved home and decided he didn't want to sell after all.

Next we visited Randolph. We found a house that had beautiful bird's-eye maple woodwork. I fell in love with the house. It was on a side street near the hospital, which was convenient. Unfortunately, we discovered another doctor, who had also served in the war, had his eye on the house with right of first refusal. Of course, we wouldn't think of moving in if another service man was coming to town.

Wallingford wasn't far from the Rutland Hospital so we looked there next. We made an offer on a house, but it was low and was refused.

Clifford had always wanted to live in Manchester, so he paid another visit to Dr. Campbell. This time he felt there was enough work to accommodate another doctor. Someone told us that Mrs. Lottie Cook, a Civil War veteran's widow, owned a house on Maple Street in Manchester Center that she might be willing to sell. She was living with relatives in Granville, New York, so on October 1, 1945, we called on her there.

Since she was interested, we offered her a ride to Manchester so she could show us the house. It had four bedrooms upstairs along with a large attic. The main floor had six rooms plus a bath — plenty of room for our family and an ideal location for a doctor's office.

She said she would sell to us if we could wait until spring since she needed time to have an auction to sell the home's contents. We decided to offer her extra for her furnishings since we could use some of them ourselves and were eager to move. We also offered her the use of a bedroom to store things of sentimental value that she wanted to keep until she could arrange for them to be removed. She liked the idea, and we agreed on a price. It was a most pleasant experience.

A few days later, we returned with Mrs. Cook and made a list of things we were to purchase. She had a large beautiful braided rug for which she had no use and therefore offered to us. Then she decided that the picture of Manchester on the wall belonged with the house and offered it. Brass candlesticks, two bedroom sets, some chairs, a dining room table, and a few dishes were to go to us, too. Then we obtained a lock for her to put on the bedroom door where she was to store the things she was keeping.

One day we returned to the house to find a local antique dealer's van backed up to the house. My first thought was he was helping her with some of her things. Instead, he was helping himself to our things. There in his van were the picture of Manchester, the braided rug, and the candlesticks.

"Clifford, he has the things she told me I could have. He can't do that," I protested.

Clifford tried to quiet me, telling me to let him have them. He didn't want to make a scene the first thing in our new home.

Being the obedient wife, I held my tongue and my temper. But I never forgave the antique dealer.

By October 13, we had moved in and Clifford's shingle was once more hanging from our home. Only this time, it was really ours. While Clifford was overseas, the government had sent me an allowance from his salary; with that plus the wages I had earned, I had paid off his college loans, finished the payments to Dr. Peterson (for his Whitingham practice), managed our living expenses, and saved enough for the down payment on a house.

Here we were, finally able to start with a clean slate in our own home! We had much to be grateful for and an opportunity to build a practice where Clifford had always wanted to live.

"Couldn't you find anything better than this?" Clarence asked when he came to visit for Thanksgiving.

Brothers can be devastatingly frank with each other, so we didn't take offense or let him dampen our enthusiasm. Besides, we knew there was work to be done. There was no central heating system (a potbelly stove in the dining room burned soft coal; the waiting room had an oil-burning stove; an upstairs bedroom had a small stove; and the kitchen had a large iron cook stove for heat and food preparation). The only bathroom was in the room that became the office. But no one in the family was allowed to use it during office hours!

We had a reason for our optimism though. Clifford was already seeing patients by the time his family members joined us for Thanksgiving dinner. Dr. Campbell had gone to visit his daughters for the holiday so Clifford was busier than ever. Most importantly to us, he was being accepted and recommended to others, a key to building a good practice. When Clarence made his observation, we knew we would soon be able to afford the necessary renovations.

Cliff Jr. and Cathy were enrolled in the Manchester Elementary School. However, we quickly learned that the sight method of reading (See Dick. See Spot. See Jane.) used at his former school didn't measure up to the progress made with the new Phonics Method. Cliff would have to repeat first grade as his reading ability was not up to second-grade level. He was mortified to be in the same grade as Cathy. But other than the hurt to his ego, he survived the transition and both children made new friends and enjoyed their new school. (Many years later when working at a Firestone plant in North Carolina, Cliff discovered some symptoms of dyslexia. Dyslexia was something unknown when he attended school, however.)

We were about fifteen miles from the Harwoods in Rupert, something his folks appreciated as it made more frequent visits possible. I was happy to be really settled with my family and to have one set of the children's grandparents so close by.

There was much work to make the house livable, though, so in the spring we consulted Clifford's second cousin Harold Harwood. Harold, who lived two houses away, had built many homes in the area. When we asked about putting in another bathroom, he informed us that it would be necessary to raise the roof in the attic to do so.

"I'm afraid I'm going to raise the roof myself if we don't get one soon," I replied, explaining the inconvenience of the family not being able to use the bathroom during office hours.

We also consulted a plumber to arrange for a furnace and learned a new chimney would be needed. These renovations were quickly adding up, but the Factory Point Bank gave us a loan and we lined up the workmen.

Just prior to their coming, I had the duty of cleaning out the attic. I had loaded several old stove pipes in my arms and was descending the narrow stairway when my heel caught, and I tumbled all the way to the kitchen. I ached all over and was quite concerned when I saw how black my knee had become. I got to the sink and began to put cold water on it to prevent swelling when miraculously the black came off. It was the soot from the stove pipes! However, I did sprain my ankle so when we left for a vacation a few days later, I was on crutches.

The house was slowly but surely fixed up, and we were happy and proud of the progress being made. When the work was finally done, we were quite comfortable and glad we had bought the place. With the kids in school during the day, I was busy helping "Doc" when needed or taking care of household tasks. Some of his patients had taken to calling Clifford "Doc" while others always used the more formal Dr. Harwood. Since we also had a son Cliff and I was forever mixing the two names up, I too, began to call Clifford "Doc."

Our adjustment to the community was a good one. Manchester was a larger town with more services, businesses, and people. That was good for Doc's business — it kept growing and Doc was becoming known as a dedicated general practitioner. It also made more work for me. My nursing and bookkeeping skills were increasingly in demand.

By the summer of 1948, Doc felt it was time for us to take a long vacation. He wanted to go by freighter to visit England and Normandy. I wasn't too keen on the idea as I get seasick just looking at water. He insisted I would be all right and that we would save money by booking passage on a freighter instead of going on a big ship. Luckily for me, he was unable to secure guaranteed return reservations on another freighter.

The backup plan was more to my liking. We bought camping equipment and headed for the West Coast for what we thought would be a relaxing vacation. Cliff and Cathy were excited, but they soon tired of riding long hours in the car each day. Sometimes Doc and I — we always took turns driving — would drive as many as 500 or 600 miles in one day. I bought comic books for the kids, and we made stops at filling stations to eat and break up the long hours of riding. We saw some nice parts of the country, but our vacation also had some rather "iffy" and exciting moments.

My most unusual experience came one day as we were driving through South Dakota. Unable to locate restrooms, Doc drove up beside a gravel pit. An ideal place for relief, I thought. Suddenly I heard a strange noise beside me. Glancing down, I saw a diamondback rattlesnake curled up and looking at me. My needs were instantly forgotten as I made fast tracks to the car.

When we reached Yellowstone National Park that evening, Doc and the children began pitching the tent while I got the camp stove going and started frying hamburgers.

You better put that cooking away, or you will have every bear in the area here for dinner, another camper warned me. I glanced up and saw a bear up on a knoll sniffing the air. It didn't take me long to unlock the trunk and put stove and hamburgers away. During the night, a few bears sniffed around our tent and the car, and Doc and I didn't sleep much. The next day we rented a cabin in the park.

Our adventures became a little more serious while fishing off the coast of Washington on Puget Sound. Doc rented a rowboat, and we were fishing for salmon when our rowboat got caught in an outgoing tide. We had visions of ending up miles out in the Pacific Ocean. Doc rowed as hard as he could and when he tired, I rowed.

We weren't making much headway toward shore, and I was beginning to become very worried when he had the idea to row toward an island and then back to land from there — less of the tide to get through, he reasoned. Again, we took turns rowing until we were both exhausted. But his suggestion worked, and, after reaching the island and resting, we were able to row back to shore. So much for some quiet fishing.

The oddest occurrence came as we drove south in Oregon. Unable to find a motel one night, we drove up a side road on the outskirts of a

Yosemite Park, CA

Glacier Park, Montana

Columbia Ice Fields

Mount Rushmore, Back Hills, SD

Scenes from our vacation out West

town. Soon we were on a dirt road. Doc told me to stop the car so we could get out and pitch our tent. It was a very quiet spot and no one was around. As our eyes adjusted to the dark, we discovered we were in a cemetery by an open grave.

Naturally, we headed back to the main highway and drove on until we found a turnout. We pitched our tent there by the side of the road. That was a safe thing you could do back then.

On the way home, we had car trouble in Salt Lake City and spent a few extra, unplanned days there — days marked by anxiety over how much car repairs would cost. We arrived back in Manchester six weeks later, tired but happy to be safely home. And glad to have survived encounters with bears, tides, and snakes. The children had much to share with their friends, and Doc enjoyed hearing me recount our adventures.

It was to become a trademark of his to relive our experiences by having me retell a story. "Tell them about the time we almost went to China," he would say. That is how I learned to find humor in our near catastrophes. I enjoyed becoming the family raconteur. Friends laughed and often said I should put our stories into a book — but living through them in the making was sometimes anything but funny.

The time we went to New York City was one of them. We were driving through the theater section of the city on the way to the Taft Hotel when Cliff spied a marquee announcing a movie that he wanted to see. Could he and Cathy please go, he asked.

Doc stopped the car and gave Cliff, then age 10, and Cathy, age 9, money for the show. He told them to call a cab to take them to the Taft Hotel when the show got out.

I told him I didn't think it was a safe thing to do, after they were gone. In those days you did not countermand your husband's actions in front of the children, but I was very worried so I dared to voice my concern after the fact.

He assured me that they could hail a cab and find the hotel okay.

"But this is New York City, not Vermont," I had protested.

"Don't worry, they'll be all right," came the nonchalant response.

We went on to the hotel, registered and after watching TV for a while Doc fell asleep. I couldn't sleep; I was too worried about the kids. It was getting late and they should have been out by nine.

Finally, at about 11 p.m. there was a knock on the door. There stood Cathy and Cliff. They had forgotten the name of the hotel a very tired Cathy explained. They found a policeman, who called around until he found where we were registered. I was grateful for the policeman and very relieved that they were safe. But I wasn't too happy about the worry Doc had put me through!

As Doc's practice grew, he became so busy that the only way to truly get a break or time off was to get out of town. In addition to more distant getaways like travel to New York, he planned to take Thursdays off as a midweek break, but we usually didn't get away till noon because he had so many patients to see or emergencies to tend to.

As a country doctor, Doc made house calls in the mornings, kept afternoon office hours from one to five, usually managed to eat dinner with us (sometimes he had to make house calls during supper), and then had evening office hours from seven to nine four days of the week. He also worked on Saturdays and was always on call on Sundays. Eventually, when another doctor arrived in town, he was able to be on call every other Sunday.

Doc saw patients of all ages and with all kinds of complaints, from common childhood illnesses to automobile accidents, heart disease to cancer. Of course, he delivered quite a few babies, too — some at home and some at the Putnam Memorial Hospital in Bennington. Many times he would be out on a visit when it was necessary to call him home for an emergency. Throughout his career, the patient always came first. This was something people appreciated about him and made note of when they honored him with a community-wide party (celebrating his first twenty-five years of being a family physician in Southern Vermont) in 1970 and again upon his retirement in 1983.

I did the "books" for Doc's practice. It was time consuming what with many different insurance forms in various formats to fill out. I usually worked on the books evenings, sometimes until very late. During the day, I was needed in the office when a woman needed examining or disrobing; a small child needed holding for restraint; or when suturing was done. In addition, it was my duty to answer the phone.

On May 7, 1949, our third child Richard David was born. We drove back to Burlington for the delivery, but luckily with no hitches this time. Cathy and Cliff were very pleased with their new brother and became attentive baby-sitters. With three children, we now made summer vacation plans for a few weeks at Lake Dunmore, north of Brandon. It would be much more relaxing than traveling with small children we decided.

Cliff and Cathy had learned to swim at the Manchester town pool and loved the water. One day while at the lake, Cliff noticed an inner tube floating away from shore and decided to swim out to get it. As we watched him, I realized he was not gaining on it fast enough and was getting quite a distance from shore. I could also see he was getting tired. Concerned he would get in trouble, I asked Doc to get the boat and go out after him. But Doc thought it better to wait and see if he could make it on his own. We stood and watched. Finally, Cliff threw his arm over the tube. He was exhausted and so was I.

"Yup, he made it," Doc commented.

I ended up with a bad migraine headache.

When Doc was around seventeen years old, he and his older brother had been allowed to hitch hike out to the World's Fair in Chicago. They went out together with each having just $10. On the return trip, they figured they would have a better chance of getting rides if they separated, so they did. Doc told me about hopping on the backs of trucks only to find the pickup he had chosen would then head down a road he didn't want to be on. He finally got home by riding with a truck driver who needed help unloading his cargo at various stops. Both he and Raymond got home safely, so he had a different understanding of what a young person needed to do and could do.

That is probably why Doc could let the kids go to a movie alone in New York City or swim out too far in a lake. He was more open to the concept of "spreading one's wings" and being able to do things that entailed some risk.

Over time I had become somewhat accustomed to Doc's more carefree attitude when it came to the children. I had learned during our visits to his parents' home in Rupert that he had been brought up this way. One day when I was telling Cathy and Cliff not to go near the road, Mother Harwood commented, "Not to worry." She added that her children had played there and never got hurt.

"But that was long ago, and there are more cars now," I had protested, to no avail.

Another time, I worried that the kids might remove the stone from the cover over the well and fall in. Again, she replied that her kids never did that, and there was "no need to worry."

She had raised her children to be independent and unafraid. I am not sure what caused her to be less fearful than I, but I do think that the world was a less busy and safer place back then.

However, since Clifford wasn't brought up to fear doing anything, the common refrain became "Don't worry." And since it was a time when the man was still clearly the boss, I did not question his authority. I just worried about the consequences!

As a young mother and a nurse, I knew the harm that could come to children and adults (I saw plenty of evidence in the examining room). Not worrying was much easier said than done.

Sometimes, I didn't get tense, though and on some occasions I even enjoyed the humor of the situations Doc found himself in as a result of his carefree attitude. One of those times happened when I suggested we take a medical student, who was working with Doc as part of his training, up Equinox Mountain. He was leaving in a few days and I thought he might enjoy the view. Doc agreed.

We reached the top and spotted the new hotel that had just been completed. As we pulled in, we saw a girl in a full skirt coming down the fire escape. The wind caught her skirt, and Doc joked, "See Cedric, I told you we would have a good view up here."

Doc parked the car and we proceeded to take a walk. We went to the lookout rock and took in the grand view toward Manchester Village. As we returned, we walked behind the hotel and came to an area where several people were gathered, looking down over the bank. "Oh my, look at that car," exclaimed a woman.

As we got nearer, I saw it was our car and started laughing. The lady remarked that it wasn't funny — that the people who owned it had gone off for a walk and didn't know it had rolled away.

I told her it was our car. Doc had forgotten to put the brake on. In fact, he had left it in gear while distracted by the "view" and his joke.

We called a wrecker to pull the car back on the road. The frame was sprung, but Doc managed to drive the car down the mountain. A few days later, we had a new car — the first of many.

Doc was very fond of cars. He thought it necessary to trade every year, if not every other year. He told me it was more profitable that way, and it was necessary for a doctor to have dependable transportation. But the way he drove always concerned me, and in bad weather I would worry that he wasn't cautious enough. Of course, I had reason to be concerned. I never forgot the time I caught baby Cliff when the car rolled over on Mendon Mountain. It would take many more years and several wrecked cars before Doc would heed my pleas to slow down and be more careful.

In 1952, I was pregnant again, and on May 5 we took a drive up to Rutland to interview a woman for the job of caring for the children when I would go to the hospital. When we got home, the baby-sitter who had been watching the kids, told me she had knocked over the bird cage and the parakeet had escaped.

"No problem," I assured her. I closed the kitchen door and climbed up on one chair, then another, in an effort to catch the bird which flew wildly from window to window. I finally caught it as Cathy arrived home from school.

She needed food for a Brownie picnic so off we went to the store. As I entered the car, however, my water broke. So much for catching birds by climbing chairs!

After we returned with Cathy's food, I told Doc about my situation. We hadn't had supper and he had office hours scheduled for the evening, but I told him "not to worry" as I was not having any contractions yet. But I did tell him I was anxious to find someone to look after the children for when we would have to drive to the hospital.

I was seeing to our supper when the phone rang. It was Mrs. Taylor. She had promised she would come to work for us when her current job was over and she was calling to say she was now available and when did we want her? I was relieved to find that she would be available that evening. The Lord does provide!

By nine thirty, Mrs. Taylor had come, Doc had seen his last patient, and we were off to Burlington. Doc drove as far as Wallingford, about fifteen miles, when he asked me to drive as he was getting sleepy and didn't want to drive off the road. He knew my contractions, which had started at nine, would keep me awake. I drove the remaining eighty-five miles in active labor.

Two hours after arriving at Mary Fletcher, our third son Roger David was born. I had told Dr. Slavin that Doc was awfully tired so he found a room where Doc could sleep. I also asked the doctor not to disturb him unless he was needed, so Doc slept through the birth. He was right — I really could handle myself.

Chapter Nine

The Ups and Downs of Family Life

The 1950s and 1960s were times of major change in this country, of postwar prosperity and rapid economic growth. Vermont was slower to change, but the interstate highway system and economic progress of the early 1960s eventually speeded up a transformation that had begun as early as the 1920s.

It was during the 1920s that summer travelers from out of state began to rediscover Vermont in great numbers due to the popularity of the auto and the many tour books that came out promoting the state, its scenic beauty and recreational assets. Manchester was highly touted on the Ideal Tour of 1920. Like Woodstock, Manchester was included in all the guide books as a place of fine accommodations and outdoor recreation. Southern Vermont was closer to major cities and had improved roads and a reputation as a fine tourist region. As a result, Manchester was one of the towns that city guests visited more frequently. Many also bought property, becoming summer residents. Some, like Robert Todd Lincoln, eventually became year-round residents.

At the same time, the auto which made its debut in Vermont villages around 1915 contributed to a slow but steady transition away from an agrarian way of life. Subsistence farming, country stores, taverns and inns, and other hometown industries (blacksmiths, hoopers, shoemakers, dressmakers, some twenty to thirty small tradesmen in all) formed the economy for rural towns. With the exodus of workers from the farms to the cities, many towns that had once flourished as independent communities became "bedroom" towns. The self-sufficient rural way of life where townspeople did business with each other disappeared as more people found jobs in nearby towns and cities or left the state to find work and better paying jobs in the manufacturing centers. This trend of out migration had actually begun in the 1800s but it continued in the 1900s and picked up steam in the 1940s and 1950s.

As a result of farming's continued decline, Vermont was becoming more dependent upon manufacturing and tourism to bolster a sagging economy. Manchester was one of the better established towns that had historically reaped the benefits of summer residents and tourists, beginning in the mid-1800s with the era of the railroad bringing city guests to the mineral springs, the Equinox House, Mount Equinox, and the Battenkill River. So while over 200 Vermont towns suffered from declining populations and dwindling economies in the first half of the twentieth century, Manchester was not one of them. Although it did suffer a gradual decline in its farms, Manchester with its picturesque villages, railroad station, and summer trade continued to flourish. It also began to reap the benefits of winter tourism from the Big Bromley Ski Area which opened in 1939, one of the first five commercial ski centers in the state. Later, in the 1950s and 1960s, the second-home winter industry also added to the more vibrant economy found in Manchester.

With Doc's practice firmly established, we had reason to be optimistic about our future in Manchester and that of our family. We had four healthy children, owned our own home, and lived in a wonderful town. The community was still growing and had good schools, active churches, a library, support for the arts, and the tourism that the many shops, inns, and restaurants depended upon.

Of course, bringing up four children had its delights and its moments, its good times and challenges. Like most young parents, we were learning as we went.

We had heard that the children of ministers and doctors had a difficult time growing up. "Too much is expected of them by the public," we

Cliff, Cathy, Doc, Madeline, Ricky and baby Roger

were told. We tried to keep them out of mischief as best we could, keeping them busy and active with school, church, jobs, and Scouts, but some high jinx just naturally went with the territory.

In the eighth grade, our oldest son Cliff, who was something of a jokester, was prone to mischief. One day, Chief of Police Munson Nelson came to the house to see us. He had a fifty caliber bullet he had taken from Cliff at school. Shocked, we told him we had no idea where it came from. It turned out that a classmate had gotten it from her father's World War II souvenirs and sold it to Cliff. He and a classmate had built a fire out in a field during recess. They were about to put the bullet in the fire to see it explode when the police arrived.

Cliff was not the only one to cause mischief in our household. When he turned fifteen (in 1953), Doc thought he should take him for a driving lesson over Rupert Mountain to see his grandparents. He insisted on taking little Ricky with them, too. The mountain road wasn't paved, so I was a little concerned about Cliff's driving it for a first lesson. Doc maintained that he had to learn to drive on dirt roads.

About forty minutes after they left, I got a phone call. It was Doc wanting me to go and get them. The car was upside down on a stone wall. Everyone was all right but the car was wrecked, he told me.

I hurried over the mountain in my car to see if they were really okay. The boys were shaken up but not hurt.

Asked for an explanation, Doc told me that, "Cliff was driving and I thought he was getting too near the ditch so I grabbed the wheel. He lost control and we went over, landing on the roof. That's all."

Cliff had to fill out an accident report form. He wrote, "I was doing real good until my father grabbed the wheel."

"We can't let him send that in," Doc had protested.

I told him I didn't see why not as that was what had happened.

Doc sheepishly admitted we had a point. The report went in "in the driver's own words" as requested on the form.

Father and Mother Harwood were married fifty years on October 26, 1954. We planned a celebration for them, including a dinner party to be served by Fredericka Hilliard, a local caterer, at the hall at the Manchester Congregational Church where we were regular parishioners.

Relatives from New York, Connecticut, and Massachusetts arrived at our home to change before the festivities. There were Father Harwood's brothers and their wives, the Harwood children and their respective families. We had a house full of confusion, but Doc was out on a "home delivery."

When he returned at four, he told me he was in pain, but that it was in his left side so he knew it wasn't appendicitis. We called Dr. Harrigan who said he might have a kidney stone and should get down to the Bennington Hospital to have it seen to. Doc didn't want to miss the anniversary party so at his request he was given a shot for the pain. We attended the party, and Doc even managed to smile for the family photo. Immediately afterward, I drove him to the hospital. His problem turned out to be a kidney stone as diagnosed, and he was hospitalized for three days before he returned home.

By mid-November 1954, my office bookkeeping was piling up and the family seemed busier than ever. Cathy, who was now fifteen, was a great help with the housework and watching the two little ones (ages five and two) when she wasn't in school. At times I had help from other baby-sitters, but still there just didn't seem to be enough hours in the day to get things done. Christmas was just a month away, and there were bills to get out and too many insurance forms to fill out. I was feeling the pressure. My migraine headaches got worse, and some nights I even had difficulty sleeping.

After ten days of headaches and medication that didn't work, I told Doc I thought I had a brain tumor. His response was that I should take a few days off — that I might have been working too hard.

"But I couldn't enjoy time off with this constant pain," I protested. "Time off won't cure a brain tumor, either," I added.

Doc didn't think I had a tumor but seeing how upset I was, he suggested going up to Burlington to have a specialist check me out. I agreed.

As we entered the admitting desk area of the hospital, I recognized Dot Pettit, a nurse I knew from working there. As she filled in the form, I noticed that she had written migraine headache. "Dot," I said, "It isn't migraine; I have a brain tumor."

She looked up at me, smiled sweetly, and said, "I like the sound of migraine better."

After Dr. Schumacher, a neurologist, had seen me, Doc left for Manchester. He had to get home to arrange for someone to take care of the children during my absence.

I was put on a strict diet. My allergies were acting up, my head felt full, and my eyes and nose were running. I was miserable. They put me in a whirlpool to help me relax. Instead of having the desired effect, I felt so tense that I could hardly wait to get out.

Doc came up on his day off to see me. I still had the pain in the back of my head. "Very little relief," I told him.

They had not mentioned a brain tumor to me, and I wondered why. At Dr. Schumacher's next visit, I told him I had to know if it was a tumor.

He told me I did not have a tumor. He believed I was a perfectionist, who expected one-hundred percent from myself. He suggested that I learn to settle for seventy-five percent. He also suggested that I learn to relax, telling me that he saw I was busy writing my Christmas cards. He advised me to put them away, saying it didn't make any difference if I sent them or not.

He sure gave me something to think about. Mother had taught us, "All that you do, do with your might; things done in halves are never done right." Now I had to think about reforming. Or, doing fewer things.

I had been there ten days when Doc arrived again, hoping to take me home this time. It was late afternoon before Dr. Schumacher came in. But to Doc's inquiry, he responded that I could not go home until I was fully free of headaches. He also told Doc that he had asked me if I would rather do the office work or care for the children and the house. Since I preferred to care for the children, he told Doc to get an office girl and to do so "before we let her go home." Then he loaned Doc a book on headaches.

We didn't know much about the relationship between the mind and the body and the need for relaxation or moderation in those days. Type A personalities, Yoga for stress reduction, and the benefits of regular exercise/recreation hadn't been heard of yet. We were simply a generation who worked hard, as our parents had done, in the pursuit of the American Dream. It had not occurred to me that I was overdoing it. My illness was a learning experience for both of us, and we agreed to take the doctor's advice.

But by now, Doc was going to be late for his evening office hours. He had a maternity patient who was due, and she had an eight o'clock appointment. He had to get home!

I asked Doc to drive carefully, reminding him that the car wasn't his now that he had agreed to trade it in for a new one.

He kissed me good-by and left. At eight, the night nurse came in and told me I was wanted on the phone. It was Doc. "Hi Honey, I thought I better tell you I've had an accident."

He had come upon a patch of road in New Haven where blowing snow had caused a whiteout. He had hit a telephone pole and turned the car over. He gave me a detailed account of how he had been trapped inside and had to crawl out through the broken windshield. He had started up the road to call the police when he remembered the loaned book and went back to find it in the snow. Now he was calling from a garage in Middlebury.

Concerned that he might have internal injuries and could have trouble during the night if he went home, I asked him to let me call my sister

Charlotte. I wanted to see if her husband Dick would pick him up and have him spend the night with them in Burlington.

As I was phoning my sister from the hall phone, Dr. Upton came by and asked what I was doing in the hospital. I told him I had been having headaches and that I was phoning for a ride for Doc who had just had an accident.

"Hell of a good treatment for migraine headaches," he commented.

At about midnight, Dick Amidon came into my room with Doc. "Here is that son-of-a-gun husband of yours," he said. "Take a good look at him. He is all right." It was just what I needed to see.

A week later I was discharged. We had another new car. Doc had an office girl, his cousin Olive Dern. She would work four days a week. That would give me more time for the family and less stress. I would work weekends. I guess that gave me my seventy-five percent reformation.

Having office help was indeed a luxury. In addition to working from nine to five, Olive took care of the bookkeeping and billing. This allowed me more time to be a mother and housewife and also to be a useful citizen in the community. The doctor had suggested that I find a recreational outlet, so I took up golf, too. That was somewhat frustrating at first as the pro insisted I learn to play right handed even though I am left handed. Eventually, another pro told me it was all right to play left handed, and I took to enjoying the game regularly.

With four children in school, I attended a PTA meeting only to learn that the group was going to have to disband for lack of someone to serve as its president. Under those conditions, I volunteered my services, noting I wasn't sure if I could do the job. However, they were stuck and I was duly elected. After conducting my first meeting, someone complimented me, saying I had done a good job.

Such praise encouraged me to work on other committees and in various other volunteer positions. I had really been a quiet person, listening to others but not one to speak out during my early years. Now, once encouragement was given, I was not afraid to dig in and go to work. Of course, when people realize you are a hard worker, lots of volunteer opportunities come your way.

I became a member of the Order of the Eastern Star and of the Daughters of the American Revolution in the 1950s and later served as officers in both. I also was a director for the Mt. Laurel School for the Mentally Retarded and served on the committee that worked on building a new school.

We went to church regularly, and I tried my hand at Sunday School teaching but keeping rambunctious children in order was not one of my fortes. I did better on committees and volunteered in various capacities for the Ladies Aid, Mission Committee, and Ladies Benevolent Society. I worked on church suppers and once made all the apple pies for the annual fall dinner. We took the children to Sunday School and confirmation lessons, and all four were confirmed in the Congregational Church. Years later, I also served as Church Moderator.

Being in the medical profession, Doc became an active member of the Vermont Medical Society (president in 1964). I was in the Auxiliary to the Vermont Medical Society, eventually serving as its president. We attended many state meetings as well as national meetings of the American Medical Association. Later, I joined the Vermont Heart Association and served on its board.

Doc was interested in current events, our government, and world affairs. He read the paper and frequently wrote letters to the editor to express his opinions. We both became active in the local Republican Party. I eventually became a campaign worker for various local and state elections. Later, I would work on national campaigns but during the 1950s when the children were still young, my political work was kept closer to home.

I enjoyed the opportunity to be a volunteer and found the various committees and organizations interesting. I could participate in events and activities around the children's schedules and liked both being at home for them and working with other people for various causes. I was never bored. There was always something to learn.

Of course, there were the children's many Scout, school, and church events that kept me busy. One child or the other always had a game or a competition, a parade or concert, or a special event like a Court of Honor to attend. The boys played in many, many Little League games, and Cathy played field hockey in high school while Cliff played football. I tried to get to all their games while Doc attempted to make Cliff's home games because he could be on call then.

Weekends, I was still "on call" to work for Doc so I didn't lose my nursing skills either. Winter weekends were especially hectic when skiing was at its best. Then there were many skiers on the slopes and more accidents. Often times that meant other patients had to wait while we treated the casualties.

Injured skiers usually started piling in late in the afternoon. [Ski accidents happen in greater numbers toward the end of the day when skiers are tired. Since serious injuries can lead to shock, prompt treatment is necessary.] By the time they reached us, it would be an hour or more after they had been injured so by then they had often become emergencies, or thought they were. Some weekends we would treat ten to fifteen skiers a day. Each patient usually had a friend or two (or three) along with them so our waiting room and office often became overcrowded, sometimes to the point of becoming "a zoo."

Doc had an x-ray machine. Leg fractures were usually obvious, but ankle injuries always needed x-raying. If a fracture was found, arrangements were made to have the patient see an orthopedist as Doc did not set broken bones — he did not welcome the possibility of a lawsuit. Sometimes there would be two patients being seen at once with one on each examining table.

My biggest dread was a patient with a dislocated shoulder. They were usually large muscular men in great pain. It took a great deal of effort to reduce the dislocation and it was exhausting work.

As a teenager, Cathy was a big help around the house. On the really busy winter weekends, she would help prepare the evening meal so the children could eat on time. Many times it would be nine or ten o'clock before Doc or I would get a chance to eat.

One busy Saturday afternoon, a patient arrived with a cut on his leg. He appeared very upset. As we x-rayed his leg, I learned that another skier had run into him, knocking him down. I knew that Cliff Jr. was up on the mountain skiing that day and hoped he hadn't been the one to run into him. Fearful, even though I knew there were many skiers on the slopes and that it didn't have to have been Cliff, I asked if he had gotten the other skier's name. He hadn't but the skier did stop to help him and called the ski patrol.

Doc was suturing the cut with my help when a loud knock came at the door. Thinking it was yet another emergency I went to the door. There stood Cliff.

"Mother, I ran into that man and must see him," he said. Before I could stop him or warn Doc, he marched into the room.

"This is the fellow who ran into me," exclaimed the patient. Poor Doc looked like he had seen a ghost.

Cliff apologized, telling the patient that he had gone to the first aid room to see if he was all right, but the patrol wouldn't allow him in. He had come to our office to make sure he was okay.

Doc made the best he could of an embarrassing situation and introduced his son. The man did not appear to hold a grudge and thanked Cliff for trying to help him. Needless to say, there was no charge for the office visit, and we were greatly relieved that the leg was not broken! We were also pleased that our son had not avoided his responsibility and had checked on the man's condition. But what a way to find out that he was an honorable person!

Cathy, Cliff, Roger and Ricky

Father Harwood passed away at age eighty-two on February 8, 1955. This was hard on all of us for we loved him dearly. After the funeral, Mother Harwood went to Boston to be with Raymond and his family. Doc was very busy and I could see that his father's death had taken its toll and that he was getting fatigued more easily.

Two weeks later, he came home from making house calls to face a waiting room full of patients. Before going into his office, he said we should take a week off and go to Bermuda.

"How and when?" I asked with surprise — and relief that he would get a break.

He suggested flying down and told me to go to the Rutland Bus Station and make the reservations that afternoon [we didn't have a local travel agency back then]. Soon after, the two of us traveled to New York City where we boarded a plane for Bermuda. It was my first flight, and I liked it much better than my previous boat excursions.

We had left the children in the care of a trusted baby-sitter, Mrs. Georgia Dulac. It was our first vacation without them, and I thought it would be a well deserved rest for Doc.

Naturally, we had registered at the hotel as Dr. and Mrs. Harwood. No sooner had we gotten to our room than the manager paged Doc. Ever the dedicated physician, he went to the rescue of a woman who had had too much to drink. She was in great pain because she couldn't void. Doc prescribed a hot bath to relax and that did the trick.

Doc had become a greatly admired and much loved "family doctor." People knew if they called him, he would always attend to their needs, no matter the time of day or night. He never refused to make house calls. If he needed my help, I was there, too.

Many times a patient would come to the office during the night. The household was awakened and it would be some time before Doc could get back to bed, especially if there were injuries due to an automobile accident. Sometimes, he would spend the entire night at the hospital or at a home on a delivery. Although he didn't get much sleep, he was always ready to go by nine in the morning.

One night when he was gone, I was awakened by the sounds of a crash and thought someone had gotten into the house. Doc never locked the kitchen door when he went out at night so he would have a way back in without fumbling for a key. Now, I was sure there was an intruder downstairs.

Knowing I would not get back to sleep without investigating, I got the German bayonet Doc had brought back from the war and went to check things out. After looking into every room and finding nothing amiss and no one hiding in the shadows, I went back upstairs to check the boys' rooms. Ready to fight or at least threaten anyone near my kids, I found that Roger had knocked the lamp off the head of his bed. So much for Mom and her bayonet — and my racing heart!

Through skiing, Cliff Jr. had met a girl named Marty Dean from Ridgewood, New Jersey, and they had corresponded some.

One deer hunting season, he asked us if he and his friend Richard Brownell could take the car to go hunting in the Rupert area for a weekend. Permission was granted along with use of Cliff's folk's house for sleeping. (His mother had since gone to live with a very close friend Jesse Harwood, Doc's second cousin, in the village.)

Telling him I would worry about their safety in the woods, I asked him to call in on Saturday night. He reminded me that because there was no phone there, he would not be able to call but not to worry.

Sunday, Doc and I went to church as usual. On the way home, I said, "Doc, during the sermon I got to wondering if those boys could have driven to New Jersey to see their girlfriends."

Doc responded that he doubted they would do such a thing, but I noticed he was quiet for the rest of the ride. As we got home, he announced he was going to Rupert to see if they had slept at the house.

He drove off and as I started dinner, it occurred to me to check Cliff's closet to see if his good clothes were there. They were gone along with his dress shoes. Doc returned and confirmed that they had not slept in the beds at the house. I told him about the missing clothing.

We discussed the situation over dinner and decided to phone the New Jersey residence to see if he was there. I got the address off an envelope and placed a person-to-person phone call to Cliff.

Although the girl who answered told the operator that Cliff Harwood wasn't there, my mother's intuition made me insist that he was and that it was urgent that I speak to him. The girl said just a minute, and Cliff came to the phone.

"Just checking in to see if you got your deer. I mean a four-legged one," I said lightly.

Catching him off-guard, he meekly replied, "No."

Then I ordered him to return home immediately. He indicated he couldn't because Richard was over at his girlfriend's. I told him to go get him and that we would expect him to start home in exactly one hour.

An hour later the phone rang. Cliff said that they hadn't gotten much sleep the night before and didn't have any money. Could they wait till morning?

Telling him that would not solve their money problem, I insisted he be home by 11 p.m. or we would call the police and report they took the car without permission. I asked if he understood, and he said yes.

When they showed up at 10:45 p.m., Cliff explained that they had taken the slower back roads to avoid paying tolls on the highway. He added, "Mother, I can never get away with anything with you." He even confessed to disconnecting the odometer cable so we wouldn't know how far they had traveled.

Later, I also learned that they had smoked cigars on the way home to keep awake. We decided to withhold car privileges for a while. Cliff knew we meant business.

Doc sometimes promised the children things without consulting me. Cliff had diligently saved his money from his paper route (he was the first boy in town to deliver the *Rutland Herald*), and Doc had told him he could use it to buy a motorcycle if he passed all his courses through high school.

In view of the recent infraction, I suggested to Doc that Cliff should not be permitted to purchase the bike. However, Cliff responded that if you promised something for ten years and then changed your mind, that "you might upset a kid mentally." Doc and I could see where he had a point, so he got his wish.

Besides being helpful around the house and baby-sitting for her younger siblings and other children, Cathy participated in Girl Scouts and was active in school sports like field hockey and basketball, played

Cathy, 1961.

clarinet in the band, and sang in the Glee Club. She was in the church's Junior Choir for several years and taught Sunday School. Dependable and hard working, she never got into trouble (at least none that I was aware of). She was very loyal to Cliff and never told on him, either.

Following her Junior year at Burr and Burton Seminary (an independent high school now known as Burr and Burton Academy), Cathy was accepted to the University of Vermont, Middlebury, Bates, and Colby. After visits to all four campuses, she chose Bates in Lewiston, Maine, liking its smaller size and friendly atmosphere.

When it came time to leave home in September 1957, she was worried about being homesick and purchased a small balsam pillow in a local store, thinking it would be a touch of Vermont to take with her. Imagine her surprise when she discovered it was made in Lewiston! She took it with her anyway and soon settled in at Bates where she majored in psychology.

Cliff, on the other hand, had told us he wasn't interested in college and that we would be wasting our money if we insisted on his going. He wanted to join the Navy. We didn't object and soon he and his classmate Harold Waters were off to see the world.

It was difficult to have two children leave the family at once. We were happy to see them grow up, but we missed them, too. I was thankful to have two more at home. We were putting off the empty-nest syndrome for the time being.

While Cliff was in the Navy, we drove out with the two younger boys to the Great Lakes Naval Base to visit him. On the return trip, Doc decided we should take the all-night ferry across Lake Michigan, saying we could sleep on the boat and save time. We had a cabin with four bunk beds. Doc and I took upper bunks, and in no time Doc was asleep. I became very seasick, however, and, thinking there would be less roll on the bottom, decided to switch bunks with Rick. All three slept soundly, but no such luck for me.

At 5:30 a.m. we vacated our rooms so they could make them up before we docked. I commented to Doc that it had been an awful rough crossing. He disagreed, saying he thought it was just average.

When we went out on the deck, it became evident from the odor that I had not been the only seasick passenger. I asked one of the attendants if it had been an ordinary trip.

"Oh no," she replied, "I have been crossing this lake for many years and this was the roughest I have ever seen. It was so bad that most of the passengers spent the night on the deck."

Cliff Jr.

So much for my old sea captain's opinion!

In late February 1959, we found out that Roger, who was in the first grade had an adrenal tumor. Our new office nurse Genevieve Bell, who had replaced Olive, moved into our home to take care of Ricky while Doc and I took Roger to Mass General in Boston.

Dr. Talbot spoke to us the night before surgery. He told us that two out of three cases he operated on turned out all right. That didn't sound too reassuring to me, and I did a lot of praying. A few days later, Roger was recuperating nicely, and Doc was able to go home by bus while I stayed with Roger until he was able to travel.

About a year later, Roger complained of a pain in his side. Doc detected a lump and wondering if his tumor might have been malignant, we fearfully went back to Boston. Dr. Talbot told us he would operate the next day. The lump, however, turned out to be a hernia. Roger had tried to push the car away from the basketball hoop so he could play ball and had strained himself in doing so.

We were relieved but following the surgical repair, the doctor notified us that he had ordered a chest x-ray and found a spot on Roger's lung. He asked Doc not to leave for home, and we did some serious thinking and praying once again.

An hour later, the doctor called us in. Not satisfied with the x-ray, he had ordered another and discovered the lung was clear. The spot turned out to be an artifact on the film. Our prayers were answered once again.

Rick was ten years old during the presidential campaign between Jack Kennedy and Richard Nixon. He had become so interested in the campaign that he scratched Nixon's name in the leather on our coffee table. He certainly had listened to our discussions and knew our politics.

On November 23, 1963, the day after President Kennedy was shot, Rick was very upset and asked if his classmates would say a silent prayer for President Kennedy. One of the students spoke up to remind him that they weren't supposed to pray in school. Rick responded that no one had to do it if they didn't want to. There was silence as he got his wish.

Later that same day, as a parent picked up her son, she called to Rick and said, "I suppose you are happy that the President was shot." He came home in tears. It was difficult to explain to him that sometimes people could be cruel and get carried away, even at times like this. It was harder still to know that adults could be so mean to such a young person.

Rick was a studious boy and a Boy Scout. One winter the Scoutmaster planned an overnight. To test his equipment, Rick decided to sleep in a snow cave in our back yard behind the garage. During the night, it snowed hard and the wind howled. Worrying about Rick, I could not sleep. Finally at 4 a.m., I put on my coat and boots and went out to his cave.

The opening had blown full of snow. In a panic, I pushed the snow aside, flashing my light into the cave. I could not see him. I called to him but got no response, so I got down on my knees and crawled inside only to find it was empty but had a tunnel that led to another chamber. I crawled through and found Rick sound asleep. After I shook him, he woke up.

"What do you want, Mother?"

"Rick, we are having a blizzard and I want you to come into the house."

"What time is it?"

When I told him it was four in the morning, he said, he hadn't spent the whole night outdoors yet and protested against coming in. I persisted, noting he had proven he could do it and would he please come in for my sake.

Reluctantly, he came into the house, dried off, and went back to

Roger and Ricky with their paper routes.

sleep. He really had been prepared and was a good Scout, but sometimes a mother just has to do what she has to do. Worrying comes with the territory, and that night I needed to know he was safe inside.

But hard as we try to protect our children, sometimes things just happen that you have no control over. I found this out the summer Doc had a AMA meeting to attend in Chicago. We decided to drive out and take Roger and Rick with us. When we stopped in Buffalo, Doc informed me that he hadn't made reservations at the Drake Hotel where the meeting was to take place and would now call ahead to do so. I told him that they never book full and I didn't think he needed to call, so he didn't.

When we pulled up the next afternoon, Doc went to check in but they were full and had to make reservations for us at a place on the Loop. It wasn't a place I wanted to be all day with kids, but the reservations had been made so off we went. As we arrived and the doorman opened the car door for me, I paused to undo my seat belt. Just then we heard a crash of glass and a thump.

The doorman exclaimed, "Oh my Lord!" and left. As I looked out the window, I saw a man's leg lying on the sidewalk near the car. Doc went to see what had happened while I stayed with the boys, telling them not to look. We soon learned that a man had jumped out of a thirteenth story window and in hitting a glass marquee, his leg had been severed. The boys were so upset that they wanted to return home immediately. I told Doc we couldn't stay there now and he agreed.

We drove to the North Side and found accommodations near Wrigley Field. While Doc attended his meetings, I took the boys to various parks and museums. They enjoyed many interesting hands-on exhibits and explored history through replica coal mines and even a captured German submarine. It helped to take their minds off the suicide and eventually they got over the trauma.

Rick had the same paper route that Cliff had before him. He also worked at the IGA store after school and on weekends. He enjoyed his job and the customers liked him because he was always willing to help them. He saved his money and bought his own motorcycle just as his older brother had. But somehow Rick had also gotten Doc to promise him that he could drive it out to the West Coast. Needless to say, I had not been consulted about this.

Rick ready to go out West.

The original intention was for Rick's cousin to go with him, but for some reason that plan did not materialize. Rick, who was then seventeen, arranged to go by way of North Carolina so he could see his older brother Cliff for a few days. After he left, I phoned Cliff with the request that he talk

Rick out of the trip if he appeared the least bit saddle-sore or hesitant.

A few days later, Rick called us from North Carolina to say he was on his way. Cliff told me that Rick was so well prepared for the trip that he didn't have the heart to talk him out of it. That left me with no alternative but to hope and pray that he would be all right.

Rick called us collect every other night to let us know his plans for the next two days. He visited our friends in Arizona and California and came back by way of the Boy Scout Jamboree in Idaho, where he saw Bob West, the leader of his troop. Some nights he slept on picnic tables in parks; if it rained, he slept under the table. He was well prepared and easily survived his trip. We were proud that he could handle himself so well. Still, he was a welcome sight when he returned home, and I slept a lot better with him back under our roof.

Roger also was a Boy Scout, who enjoyed many summer camp experiences. But his first summer, he wrote us indicating he was quite homesick. It was the first letter we ever received from him and I still have it. He also had a paper route and saved his money to buy his own motorcycle.

Nicknamed "Wombat" by his friends, Roger was a very social youngster and was always busy doing something with them or playing on the soccer team. One of his activities as he got older was to become the first president of the reorganized state chapter of the Children of the American Revolution (C.A.R.)
He had been approached by a Vermont Chapter President of the Daughters of the American Revolution who wanted to get a C.A.R. chapter going in Vermont. He became president of the Vermont chapter in 1971-72 and treasurer in 1972-73; later he ran for treasurer of the national C.A.R.

Roger and his motorcycle.

While our children were growing up, we enjoyed family vacations and trips, but Doc and I also occasionally took trips without them, especially as they got older. One summer I attended a medical convention with Doc in Atlantic City, where one of the diversions was to visit the auction house on the board walk. The two of us had always enjoyed going to auctions but this one proved to be very different.

We noticed that the daily auctions followed a certain pattern of selling small articles like cheap watches on the board walk to get the attention of the passersby and entice them inside for the actual auction. Often the auction would start with a setup of some sort — perhaps a prearranged question where the auctioneer would recognize a "plant" in the audience and get a little chitchat going with him or her in order to establish a rapport with the audience.

Many doctors and their wives attended the auctions, which as they progressed featured more valuable items. Often the auction ended with diamonds up for bid. We noticed that a discussion with someone in the audience (probably another plant) would precede this bidding. It was a way to establish credibility and up the ante. It also wasn't long before someone in the front row started raising the bids and the diamonds went for thousands of dollars.

We watched what was happening, and we observed people going into a side room to discuss payment afterward. We felt badly knowing that some had probably been taken in and could not afford to pay what they had bid or else had bid too much.

Nevertheless, on the last day at the auction, we decided to buy a flat iron which I needed. We were told to pick it up in a new box when we left the auction area. Upon reaching our room, I checked on the iron and discovered that bare wires were visible. We finished packing, and Doc drove me back to the auction place so I could get our money back.

When I reached the gallery, a worker inquired as to what I wanted, and I explained my mission to return the faulty iron. He told me to wait, went out back, and reappeared, saying "Follow me."

He led me past a crowd of auction attendees to a small room with a bare light bulb hanging from the ceiling. "Wait here," he instructed and disappeared.

A burly looking man came in and asked my problem. I explained and he said, "Wait a minute," and left. Soon another large man entered and asked what the problem was. Again I explained and politely requested a refund.

"Don't come in here shouting at me about it," he ordered.

I told him I wasn't shouting, but that I wanted my money back as the auctioneer had said everything was guaranteed. I also told him if I didn't get satisfaction that I would report them to the Chamber of Commerce.

"Don't you come in here threatening us, you hussy," he snarled at me.

Tapping my foot to show my impatience, I told him my husband was waiting for me in the car and could I please have my money so I could leave.

He turned to a man in the doorway and shouted, "Give her her money back and get her the hell out of here!"

As the attendant began to lead me out of the windowless room, I was tempted to rip open my blouse and yell HELP in front of the audience as we passed by. It would have served them right, I thought, indignant over the rude treatment I had received.

When I described my encounter to Doc, he said, "For heavens sake, weren't you scared? They could have dropped you down a trap door or something and no one would have ever found you."

I told him I guessed I was too angry to be frightened. The flat iron was just a little thing, but between their rude treatment of me and knowing they were taking advantage of people, I just found the whole thing so disgusting that I held my ground. I wasn't going to let their racket get me, too. It was the principle of the thing, I told Doc. He just shook his head and laughed.

Vermont Delegates to the 1964 National Republican Convention.
Madeline is second to right in front row.

Chapter Ten

From Patients to Politics

In 1964 I turned fifty. Some people like to joke that you are "over the hill at fifty." Maybe, but I was enjoying life and was too busy to be worried about a downward slide or hitting bottom just yet. After all, it had taken me a long time to get to this point, and although I was certainly a little older, I did not feel old.

In fact, as far as I was concerned, I was still climbing up the hill. Our children were less dependent on me now with just Rick and Roger, who were 15 and 12, still at home. (Cliff, 26, was married and living in North Carolina; Cathy, 25, was married and in Burlington.) I now had more time to pursue the other things that I cared about at this stage of my life.

When Doc was overseas, I had vowed that I would get involved in politics some day. The war had bothered me. I felt it was terribly wrong and that too many people suffered, including those at home. I felt that there must be a better way to settle differences than for men to have to kill each other. In Vermont alone, 49,942 men served in the armed forces during World War II. [The state's entire population was 359,231 in 1940 so that was a sizable percentage.] Of these Vermonters, 1,233 died and 3,870 were wounded. That meant a lot of hardship and heartache for thousands more.

I sensed that part of the solution was to work through the problems that lead to war. I was curious about politics, but as a young nurse and mother with a growing family, I hadn't had much time to pursue this interest.

That slowly changed during the 1950s as both Doc and I became active in the Republican Party. It had started with Doc writing letters to the local newspaper, expressing his views on what was happening in local, state, national, and international affairs. Doc was against Communism because of what he had seen in World War II. He knew the threat to freedom that totalitarian regimes pose. He had brought home photographs of the bodies he had seen at Dachau at the end of the war. He never forgot the atrocities, and he was willing to warn others of the similar danger that he saw in Communism and particularly in the threat of Soviet Russia.

Having lived through a time in history when one faraway dictator had caused our country to go to war, Doc was truly worried that the Soviet Union was the next threat. Both dictators and Communists had a mutual interest in stifling and eradicating democratic influences and governments. Doc was keenly aware of this as were our government leaders and many Americans in the 1950s.

Doc read extensively, following the spread of Communism throughout the world in the 1950s and particularly its foray into Latin America (in our southern hemisphere). North Vietnam's invasion of Laos was another concern with fear that country would become Communist. The *Communist Manifesto*, a product of a Congress of about 80 Communist parties from around the world was released by Moscow in December 1960. It set forth in detail the aggressive objectives and plans for conquest of the world, much as Hitler had done in *Mein Kampf*. (In the *Communist Manifesto*, the United States is labeled the main obstacle in the path of Communist world domination, and Communists are directed to center their fire on the U.S. and the American way of life.)

In the year 2000, when the political entity of the United Soviet Socialist Republics is no more (but the situation in Russia is anything but stable) and the Berlin Wall has been torn down, that threat seems laughable, but in 1960 the United States was very concerned about the Communist gains in Latin America and particularly the possibility that Latin

American countries would turn toward the Soviet Union. The rise of Fidel Castro and his seizure of American property in Cuba during 1960 along with the breaking of diplomatic relations between the U.S. and Cuba fueled a fear that he would seek an alliance with the Soviet Union. Khrushchev's offer of military assistance and the threat of Russian missiles (with nuclear capability) being deployed on Cuban soil and aimed at the U.S. created serious problems and increased tension in all the Americas.

Taking Khrushchev's threat to "bury" us seriously, Doc vocally joined in the concern about Castro's Cuba. At the time of the resulting Bay of Pigs Invasion and the missile crisis in Cuba (April 1961), our son Cliff was stationed on a mine sweeper off Guantanamo Bay (where the U.S. had had a naval base). It was a scary time for our country and for us personally. Along with the ongoing Cold War, it fueled our mistrust and fear of Communist governments.

Doc was also profoundly influenced by John Noble's book *I Found God in Soviet Russia*. The America author, who had been captured by the Russians in Dresden during WW II, told of being imprisoned in Russia. Russian leaders denied that they had him, however, and it took the persistence of Noble's Congressman to secure his release. Doc met the author and learned firsthand of his horrible experience and treatment. It left an indelible impression upon him and on top of everything else caused him to support a strong defense system for our country, a view that I shared.

With our particular concerns and interest in politics, we became more active in the Republican Party. Doc was elected chairman of the Manchester Republican Committee, serving in that capacity for many years. We joined the Bennington County Republican Committee, also, and Doc became finance chairman for the county committee, which automatically made him a member of the state committee. He was quite a fundraiser and had a special way of nicely asking people to donate to the Republican cause (although he would never ask his patients who owed him money to pay their bills). With his wide-ranging interests, Doc served as a delegate to the White House Conference on Aging in 1960 and joined the Vermont Educational Medical Pac (VEMPAC), an organization that raised money for candidates, becoming its chairman in 1968.

One of my earliest memories of working for the Republicans is of stuffing envelopes for the Eisenhower elections and of calling people for fundraisers. I remember that Abraham Lincoln's great-granddaughter Margaret Lincoln Beckwith also helped us solicit funds during one of the elections. Like Doc, I joined many different groups. I was elected secretary to the Vermont Republican Party and became president of the Vermont Legislative Council (1963-65) and joined the Vermont Federation of Republican Women (serving as its president from 1965-66).

We still had to juggle our duties and work around family needs and commitments, however. In March 1964, Doc was working for the nomination of Senator Barry Goldwater for President. Before he left to campaign and fundraise in Bennington and Readsboro one day, I reminded him to be home by seven as it was Maundy Thursday and the night that Roger would be joining the Church. Doc assured me he had not forgotten and would be back in time.

As a director of the Vermont Heart Association, I attended a VHA meeting in Springfield that day. It had been snowing and the roads were very slippery, but I made it home by four. When Doc failed to show up, we ate supper without him. The service was at eight and I was beginning to worry. At seven-forty, the phone rang.

It was Doc. He was at Ray Crosier's in Heartwellville. I admonished him that he hadn't planned his time very well and could never make it in time for the service.

He agreed and then dropped the bomb that he hadn't planned on something else either. His car was upside down in the river.

To my anxious inquiry if he was all right, he noted, "You've changed the tone of your voice." Then he told me he had called a garage in North Adams and that I should go on to the service without him. He would have the garage tow the car home and ride with the tow truck.

It was rollover number four for Doc. It occurred to me that he led a charmed life, for which I was very grateful at that moment.

Following the service, we had been invited to Dr. Edwin Treat's home. I went there, expecting Doc to arrive at any moment. At nine-thirty, Mrs. Miller (a woman who stayed at our house to take calls or watch the kids when we were away) called. Doc had telephoned to say that he had been unable to get a ride home. He would be waiting for me to pick

him up at Crosier's. He had also asked her to tell
Woodford Mountain, which is steep and windir
but safer route of North Adams.

Somehow I did not receive the last part of his m
was concerned about my driving alone and offered to go
declined, telling him I did not want the responsibility for anyone
life going over that treacherous mountain. After thanking him for his
polite offer, I left.

When I arrived sometime later, following a most gut-wrenching drive
down the mountain on ice and snow during which I had to avoid fallen
trees and branches, Mr. Crosier greeted me, saying, "Well, I am glad
you didn't drive over the mountain. I would have needed to go to your
rescue if you had."

"But I did. No one told me not to," I replied to his stunned amaze-
ment.

Needless to say, we returned home by way of North Adams. All was
well, but when we arrived safely home, I admonished Doc, sternly telling him, "You know the Lord has others to watch over as well as you.
Someday He will not be with you. You better take it easy."

For me that moment of anger and concern and speaking my mind
was an emancipation of sorts — I had dared to tell my husband what to
do. The modern reader may laugh, but for a woman who returned a
dress if her husband didn't like it, or got his approval before buying a
hat, that was a pretty daring thing to do. I guess I got through to him,
though, for he never rolled a car again.

In 1964, the Manchester Republican Caucus elected me a delegate
to the Republican State Convention, which was held in May. The delegates at the state convention elected twelve delegates and twelve al-
ternates to attend the Republican National Convention, which nomi-
nates the Republican candidate for president.

Supporters for Goldwater, Scranton, Rockefeller, and Margaret Chase
Smith were in attendance. I was pledged to Goldwater and although
there were many of his supporters present, I was elected one of the
three Vermont Goldwater delegates to the National Convention. Doc
was elected as an alternate.

llowing the election of delegates, we met to select one man and woman to each of the committees: Rules, Credentials, Permanent organization, and Platform (Resolutions). Attorney George Cook and I were elected to serve on the Platform Committee. That meant we would meet in San Francisco a week before the convention started. We were sent reading material to familiarize ourselves with the tasks before us. I chose to go to California by train, thus giving me more time to study the material.

On July 4, while changing trains outside of Chicago, I helped an elderly lady with her luggage. After I was settled back on the train, a conductor appeared asking for our tickets. Looking for my pocketbook, I realized I didn't have it. I explained my plight to the conductor, who said that without a ticket, I would be put me off at the next station!

Fearing I had left the missing purse on the bench at the last station and not having a dime to make a phone call for help, I began to panic. Resting my head in my hands with my eyes cast downward in despair, I sensed something telling me to look under my seat. There was the pocketbook. What a great sense of relief I felt.

Little did I know then, that the train was speeding me to a whirlwind adventure for which I would feel similar great relief and jubilation when it was over. For the time being though, the rest of the trip proved uneventful and delightful. The scenery was pretty and made me happy and proud to be living in this beautiful country.

That ride was to be my last experience with normalcy for the next two weeks, however.

Shortly after I had arrived and checked into my hotel room, I received a phone call telling me I was wanted at the Hotel St. Francis right away. The person was calling from my hotel lobby so I asked him if he could take me there as I did not know the address.

The page escorted me to a most impressive office about a block away. There, an attendant notified Congressman Melvin Laird of my arrival. He introduced himself as the chairman of the Platform Committee and told me I was needed to serve on the Drafting Committee. He explained that I would need to work late and lose sleep and then asked if I would do it.

What a challenge. Of course, I would do it!

The truth was that often when I had joined a new group I felt in over my head. I was not always confident that I could do the task, but I worked hard and soon felt more comfortable with whatever lay before me. This time I was excited and looked forward to the challenge!

The whirlwind began that very evening at seven with the announcement of the subcommittees and Drafting Committee. Fortunately, Congressman Laird had warned me that as the only member of the committee who wasn't a past or present member of Congress that the press would be after me. He also asked me not to tell them of my assignment until after the meeting and that I could refer them to him for questions I didn't wish to answer.

So I was prepared when reporters from *Time*, the *New York Times* and the *Philadelphia Inquirer* descended upon me with their rapid-fire questions. They were after information from this amateur, thinking I might spill the beans on who was committed to whom. When they realized I was not about to give them news, they thanked me and left. I was glad Mel Laird had warned me so that I hadn't committed a *faux pas* out of my greenness.

There were nine members of the Drafting Committee and we did work long hours. Each day began with a meeting of the entire Platform Committee where announcements and important information was circulated. This was open to everyone. At ten, the subcommittees (civil rights, economics, environment, medicine, education, etcetera) met and took testimony from the public. At the closing, they would summarize the results and report to the Drafting Committee, whose members also served on subcommittees.

The Drafting Committee met at six in the evening in Executive Session to begin their work. We often met while having sandwiches for our dinner and worked until 2 a.m., knowing we had to attend the morning meeting at eight.

It soon became apparent that there were many different personalities to deal with and that not everyone was a Goldwater supporter. The interests of many candidates were at stake. Our meetings were serious affairs that dealt with major issues.

The media also had interests. They would stop me in the hallway and try to extract information. Their special interest was the Civil Rights

Madeline and Mel Laird

Plank, also the interest of all who were present. Each time I referred the reporters to the chairman and eventually their questioning stopped.

I also had a special interest. As President of the Auxiliary of the Vermont Medical Society, I saw a great opportunity to be of help to them and the American Medical Society by getting a plank in the platform addressing their concerns.

This wasn't hard to do because there were a few doctors at the hotel who were officials of the AMA. They had contacted me, and I had been using a back elevator to get to the tenth floor where I was able to talk with them and get their suggestions. The day finally came when it was appropriate to introduce my proposed plank. I went to Chairman Laird and told him I was interested in doing not only what was needed for the Republican Party but also in helping the medical societies.

He placed his arm on my shoulder and said, "We know all about you, Madeline. What can we do for you?"

This surprised me for I felt sure no one had seen me use that back elevator. I explained the plank which was as follows:

> We pledge:
> tax credits and other methods of assistance to help needy senior
>   citizens meet the costs of medical and hospital insurance;
> a strong, sound system of Social Security with improved benefits to
>   our people;
> continued Federal support for a sound research program aimed at
>   both the prevention and cure of diseases, and intensified efforts to
>   secure prompt and effective application of the results of research.
>   This will include emphasis on mental illness, drug addiction, alco-

holism, cancer, heart disease, and other diseases of increasing in-
cidence;

full coverage of all medical and hospital costs for the needy elderly
people, financed by general revenues through broader implemen
tation of Federal/State plans, rather than the compulsory Democratic scheme covering only a small percentage of such costs for
everyone regardless of need.

"No problem, introduce it," Chairman Laird said.

It became the Harwood Amendment and was passed in its entirety.

It was a high point and a real source of pride to be able to use my
experience in such a productive way. Whoever would have thought that
a lifetime of collecting urine specimens and helping Doc sew up cuts or
serving on medical association committees would have ever led to such
important work? Suddenly, I appreciated my life and our lives in a new
and different way. I guess you could call it the thrill of public service.
Whatever it was, I was glad to be useful and make my experiences count.

What I didn't appreciate, though, were the many phone calls that
would start at 6 a.m. with someone asking for my support for one of
their candidates. We were lucky if we were able to get a few hours
sleep, and such calls were most unwelcome.

Finally, our work was done. We met at 8 a.m. one morning with
copies of the completed draft placed on each table. Any time a member
left the room, all papers were to be left behind. When we recessed, all
papers were locked up. All of this secrecy was new to me. But the press
was not to know anything until all our work was completed.

We broke for a quick lunch, then resumed our work. All afternoon
we listened to proposed amendments and voted them up or down. I had
never realized there were so many ways of saying the same thing.

A half hour was allotted for dinner. The committee met over sandwiches as we discussed programs.

By ten that night, many members had left their seats to walk around
the room to avoid cramps and battle fatigue. Aspirin was available as
were coffee and soft drinks. The walking went on intermittently all night.

At about 2 a.m., Senator John Tower turned to me and asked if I
would promise to stay with them no matter how long it took. "We are
going to need your votes," he told me.

I assured him I would, provided he would explain to my husband why I looked so awful when he arrived. I had lost ten pounds and many, many hours of sleep since I had last seen Doc.

The meeting lasted until 7 a.m.— twenty-three hours of work! The final hour had been spent discussing a news leak by Senator Hugh Scott of Pennsylvania, a member of the Drafting Committee. The leaked information was a matter of great concern to (former) President Eisenhower, who was on his way to the convention by train. He had received news of the incident while en route and had phoned his displeasure to the Chairman. A most unpleasant hour was spent in reprimanding the leaker and extracting an apology from him.

By 7 a.m. Sunday, July 12, we were free to go to our hotels and sleep. A quick breakfast and by eight I was out cold. The phone rang at ten. It was Consuelo Northrup Bailey, Vermont's National Committee Woman, inviting me to join her at one for a trip to a winery — the last thing I needed at that point.

"This is a special function of the National Committee," she explained as I tried to tell her that we had worked all night and I needed my sleep.

Connie was insistent so I went to her room at one. Her driver proceeded to get lost. We drove around San Francisco and the Richmond area for several hours. No winery was found; I lost an additional four hours of sleep.

When Doc arrived, I introduced him to some of the doctors with whom I had worked on the medical plank. One of them said, "I sure enjoyed your wife all week." Poor Doc, he wasn't sure he understood what was meant.

As a reward for my efforts, however, the doctors took me to a five-hundred-dollar-a-plate reception for the benefit of the Republican Party. What an elegant affair! And what an honor!!

The Convention started on Monday, July 13 at 10 a.m. with National Committee Chairman Congressman William Miller presiding.

Clifford and I were invited to attend a luncheon meeting of the Southern California Medical Society on Tuesday at noon. When I was introduced, they asked me to be their speaker. I was taken by surprise, but they were all interested in the procedures of a national convention so it was my privilege to oblige them.

The third session was long and tedious. It began at 4 p.m. There were many speakers, including President Eisenhower. Rules Committee reports were given and, after a few attempts at amendments, were adopted. Next came the Platform Committee report. Each section was to be read by a delegate. I had been assigned the section that dealt with "Faith in Limited Government."

As I sat at the back of the podium awaiting my turn, I watched Governor Archie Moore of West Virginia deliver his speech in great oratory style with arms waving and voice booming. In a sudden moment of absolute stage fright, I turned to the person beside me and said, "I can't do that. If I faint on my way to the podium, will you just step over me, pick up my paper, and read it before you read yours?"

After that moment of panic, I got hold of myself and decided not to faint! I told myself it was not necessary to be an orator. Once I reached the podium, my fears left me. I was able to do my part.

Following the reading of the entire Platform, Senator Hugh Scott, a Scranton supporter, made many attempts to amend it from the floor. This was a real surprise to me as he was a member of the Drafting Committee and had voted its approval in committee. He failed at each attempt, however, as did other delegates' efforts to do so. But they succeeded in making it a long session that lasted well after midnight.

The following day was devoted to nominating the presidential candidates. The names placed in nomination were: Senator Barry Goldwater, Governor Nelson Rockefeller, Senator Hiram Fong, Governor William Scranton, Governor George Romney, former Congressman Walter Judd, and Ambassador Henry Cabot Lodge. Lastly, Senator Margaret Chase Smith from Maine was nominated by Vermont Senator George Aiken. She was the first woman ever to be nominated for President of the United States. Even though I was committed to Goldwater, I felt a tingle of pride and excitement to be present at such a moment!

Each nomination was presented with three or more speakers who had five- or ten-minute speeches. Following his nomination, Lodge withdrew his name, leaving seven candidates. Balloting of each state by roll call was then ordered. The tally was 883 for Goldwater out of 1308 ballots cast. The remaining candidates withdrew.

On Thursday, Congressman William Miller of New York was nominated to serve as the Vice Presidential candidate. It was considered advisable to establish geographical balance in selecting a president and his running mate.

Senator Goldwater's acceptance speech was followed by exuberant floor demonstrations. Delegates marched around the hall, cheering and blowing noisemakers in celebration while the two candidates posed at the podium for photos.

As if this pandemonium were not enough to cap the events, we were told that there were protesters outside who had threatened to stop all buses from leaving the area by lying on the ground in front of them. Not able to locate Doc, my good friend Dr. Roger Mann escorted me from the hall.

Once outside, we saw no demonstrators and I inquired of a policeman of their location. "We ordered the cameras to stop photographing them, and we have them inside a barricade out back. They will not bother you," he assured us.

This was the last day of my introduction to the national convention process. What an exciting and eventful course in Politics 101!

Once we got home, there was work to do to explain Senator Goldwater's position and get him elected. He was a true conservative whose desires for less government were not always well understood. The Vietnam War was an issue, and soon the opposition began using commercials to discredit our candidate.

They produced a one-minute film that appeared during prime time television on NBC. It showed a little girl in a field of daisies. She was plucking petals from a flower as a voice in the background started a countdown. Then the scene exploded and the girl disappeared in a mushroom cloud.

The results were devastating. The message told viewers that Goldwater was a trigger-happy hawk who would blow up the world if he were elected. This was my first lesson in negative campaigning.

The Liberal GOP Eastern Establishment was anti-Goldwater, also, so I worked hard on the local level to try to get his true message across. We had been told it was better to have a backache the day after an election than to have a heartache. I had both. Our candidate had been roundly defeated by Lyndon B. Johnson.

I found myself exhausted and deflated, great conditions for a post-election cold and flu to set in. I was lying on the couch at home feeling totally miserable when a knock came at the door. Thinking it was a patient for Doc who had come to the wrong door, I called out for the person to enter, ready to add, "next door, please."

Much to my surprise it was Dean Slater of the UVM College of Medicine. He had a dozen red roses in his arms. "Gee, I didn't know I looked that bad," I said, stunned to see him.

My unexpected visitor went on to express appreciation for all Cliff and I had done to facilitate their contact with a Mrs. Larson. It turned out that through our introduction to her, she had donated $2 million for a new medical building at UVM.

We had lost the election, but I had helped the medical profession with a plank in the platform and now a new medical building. Such small victories were a sweet reward at a time of major disappointment.

Politics might have its "ups and downs," but I was definitely hooked.

In 1965, I was elected president of the Vermont Federation of Republican Women (VFRW). This was a time-consuming position that required attending New England regional and national meetings as well as local and state committee work. Attending the annual meeting in Washington DC in 1966 gave me one of my most unusual experiences.

I chose to drive to the meeting and after parking at the Sheraton Hotel garage, I entered the lobby where I bumped into a friend from California, Joyce Wenger. She was

Richard Nixon was a guest at a National Federation of Republican Women meeting (in NY.) where Madeline represented the VFRW on the national committee.

waiting for a cab. While we were talking, a lady came up and said, "Joyce what are we going to do about the room?"

As her cab had arrived, Joyce answered, "I must go, maybe Madeline can help you."

I inquired as to the problem and discovered they were in the same room with one double bed. I had a room with twin beds so I offered to have Joyce stay with me.

"Why don't I move in with you, as I have no idea when Joyce will return," the woman suggested.

I acquiesced, thinking a friend of Joyce's should also be a friend of mine.

After we were settled in, I told her I was going to the dining room and asked if she cared to join me. She said no, that she was expecting an important call and would order room service.

When I returned, she told me that Congressman Robert Stafford's wife had called and wanted me to come see her at the Shoreham Hotel. She and Senator Prouty's wife were preparing a luncheon to be held the next day for Congressmen's wives.

The Shoreham was just one street behind the Sheraton. I thanked her for the message and said I would walk over to see her.

"No, you must not walk there alone. I'll go with you," my new room-mate said as she opened her pocketbook and pulled out a gun. "It isn't safe to be alone. I have my Derringer and it is loaded."

As she said this, she checked the chamber. "No S.O.B. is going to rape me and live to tell about it," she added.

Somewhat surprised, but not wanting to precipitate an encounter with that gun, I said I had better phone to see if they were still there. Thankfully, they weren't.

She told me her name was Fowler and that she and Joyce had been on the plane together. She also said she was knitting a sweater that she planned to drop from a plane to her boyfriend, who was in Arizona on location with a movie crew.

When it came time for bed, I noticed that Miss Fowler had put the gun under her pillow. Since it was still loaded, I was concerned lest I have a bad dream and talk in my sleep.

The next morning she informed me that she wouldn't be attending the opening meeting as she had an appointment to meet the Ambassador of Mexico. Later, when she returned, she described what a charming man he was and then announced she would not be staying for the Convention, for she had to leave.

When I checked out the next day, I discovered that she had left me her hotel bill, including the charges for her expensive dinner. Later, I told Joyce of my experience with her friend.

"She is no friend of mine," Joyce replied. "I met her on the plane from California."

So much for being a friend to "a friend" of a friend.

My gun encounter not withstanding, the real excitement of 1966 was our decision to build a new home. After twenty-one years of living on the main road with Doc's office in the house, we began to think about our need for more privacy. In fact, I was getting very tired of accepting urine specimens at the kitchen door while preparing a meal. There were many times when Doc could not finish eating without someone coming to the office and asking for immediate service.

Finally, it occurred to us that we could build a smaller home nearby, and we could keep the office at its present location while renting out the house part. It seemed a perfect solution. By spring 1966 we had purchased two acres of land about a mile and a half away from the office on a quiet road where we would be the only residents. We hired a contractor whose wife helped us with planning the layout of the rooms.

It turned out to be a most interesting venture. Many decisions had to be made at different stages, and we appeared at the construction site almost daily. When it came time to drill the well, we realized that maybe we should have hired a dowser as they had to go some three hundred feet, some of it through hard quartz, before they struck a water vein.

Our house on Village View Road, 1966-2000.

But by fall, we were able to move into our six-room home with its pretty view of the mountains and the village below. We had a sit-down dinner party for everyone who had worked on the house and their spouses. We were pleased with their work and our home served us well. Doc really enjoyed the quiet and privacy, too. Rick had his own motorcycle by now so even though we were farther away from the high school, he had his own transportation. We took Roger, who was only fourteen, to school until he was old enough to ride his motorcycle.

Having become used to travel, I attended a meeting of the American Heart Association in San Francisco in June 1967. While there I met a girl from Haight-Ashbury who was on a street corner hawking magazines. I stopped to chat with her, curious as to why she was selling magazines for a quarter. She explained that it was the way her group made money. I then discovered that she was from the Mid-West and had not seen her family in several months. When I asked if she wouldn't be better off going back to them and making something of her life instead of standing on a street corner selling magazines, she wistfully admitted that she wished she could. Feeling sorry for her, I suggested she think about doing so, telling her, "Your life is worth more than this."

As I handed her a quarter, her eyes filled with tears as she said, "Thank you. I think I will."

As I took the magazine and turned to leave, I noticed several people gathered behind us, listening. As I walked away, I could only hope that the girl would leave the group. The *Berkley Barb* was crude and pornographic!

It was 1968 when the political bug bit me hard. I had been asked to run for the Vermont Legislature. Thinking it would be easier to run for the House than the Senate, I asked the House incumbent if he would consider running for the Senate. He was not interested. So after consultation with my family and many politicians, I decided to run for the senate seat, realizing it would be a difficult uphill venture.

Bennington County was entitled to two senators. Senator Allen Angney of Arlington had decided not to run for re-election. The other Republican, Senator Sal Santarcangelo would run again. By the time I announced, four other Republicans were seeking the office. Three of them had legislative experience. They also lived in the Bennington area, which was the largest voting district.

The first order of business was to locate supporters, raise money, and get fliers printed. Once the fliers were in my hands, I was ready to campaign.

One day Doc and I stood outside one of the mills in Bennington to pass out fliers as workers left the building. We were covering two different exits. As I passed a flier to one worker, he looked at it and said, "Madeline Harwood, who in hell is she?"

"I am sir," I replied. He did not stop to speak but walked directly to his car.

Soon Doc came up to me and commented that we were wasting our time there. "They are coming out of here like a dose of salts. They don't want to be bothered." He was right. No more campaigning at the mill.

A few days later, I returned to Bennington and visited the merchants. Some of them did take time to talk with me and ask questions. As I went into what I thought was a restaurant a bit on the dark side, I discovered much to my chagrin that I was in a bar. My first impulse was to turn around and get out. But realizing that I was already in and that people had seen me, I got up my courage and went over to speak to some patrons. The customers were not in a hurry. No one was going anywhere. They were very considerate as they took my fliers, and they even asked me questions. Suddenly, someone asked where I stood on gun control.

"Well, if you fellows want your guns to go hunting, you should have them," I said.

That did it. I was their friend. Campaigning in a bar was easy after that. I was very cautious not to enter or leave with anyone, or to stub my toe when exiting. Some time later a good friend, who happens to be a Democrat, told me that bar campaigning had helped me win the election!

Bennington is a large county. It was impossible to call on all the voters, but Doc helped me when he could. I campaigned in the rural areas alone. Often no one was at home and I would leave a note, saying I was sorry to have missed them.

During the campaign, the League of Women Voters held a forum. They asked us many questions. Some of the answers I gave were not to their liking, but I tried to be honest in all my answers. For example, I was opposed to the Equal Rights Amendment. I was not opposed to equal rights and opportunities for women but I was opposed to making changes to the Constitution. I have always felt that that document should not be tampered with lightly. I thought that the goals of equal rights could be accomplished without such an amendment (as people worked through the various issues — something history has proved possible). That is not what many women wanted to hear, however.

It was tough when they didn't like your stand, but from the beginning I tried not to tell people what they wanted to hear but what I stood for and why. I learned that you would not necessarily lose votes that way. People in Vermont tend to respect a person's right to have a different opinion. As long as I listened to the views of others and explained myself when our views did not match, they seemed to be satisfied.

Apparently people appreciated that about me for when we faced the voters in the September primaries, I was the top vote getter. Since there were no Democratic candidates that year, Garry Buckley, the other top vote getter, and I faced no opposition in the November elections. We were on our way to Montpelier. The campaign seminars I had attended had paid off. Now it was time to make plans for living in Montpelier.

Although it had been a busy summer campaigning for the Vermont Senate, I still found time for the 1968 National Convention, which was held in Miami. Once again, I had been elected to serve as a delegate and Doc an alternate. I was also chosen to serve on the Platform Committee again.

Imagine my surprise when I entered the organizational meeting and Senator Everett Dirksen greeted me with, "Where have you been? I've been looking all over for you. I want you to be my secretary."

"I'm sorry, Senator, I don't take shorthand," I replied.

"You won't need to. You just have to help me keep my papers straight," he answered.

It turned out to be a very interesting and challenging assignment. There were many amendments to keep in correct order of introduction. I also acted as timekeeper for different speakers.

At one of the Platform meetings, Senator Jacob Javits introduced a very long amendment. Since he was the only one proposing it, Senator Dirksen allowed fifteen minutes for discussion with Javits given seven minutes and two opposing speakers four each.

As the debate was ending, Senator Javits sent me a note asking how much time he had left. I spoke to Senator Dirksen, saying, "He has less than a minute. What do you wish to tell him?"

"Tell him he has all he needs," came the reply.

When debate ceased, Javits requested a division of the House. Senator Dirksen said, "All in favor of the Javits Amendment, please rise." Senator Javits rose. "All opposed, please rise." Senator Javits turned to count — all ninety-nine delegates were standing.

Senator Dirksen was a well-seasoned politician. He knew what he was doing by allowing Senator Javits extra time.

This was a more relaxed Platform Committee than my previous experience. We met daily for a week. Congressman John Rhodes of Arizona was chairman of the plank on Economics and I was vice chairman. Things went smoothly and it was a satisfactory experience.

The Convention began on August 5, 1968 with the usual announcements and introductions. Governor Kirk of Florida welcomed the delegates and there were several other speakers. On August 6, the Platform was read in part as everyone had a copy. Senator Dirksen gave an inspiring speech, introduced delegates who summarized portions of the Platform, and it was adopted without any attempt at amendments.

On Wednesday twelve names were placed in nomination with many lengthy speeches. Among them were former Vice President Richard M. Nixon and several governors, including Nelson Rockefeller, George Romney, Winthrop Rockefeller, Ronald Reagan, and a few perennials like Harold Stassen.

It was a very noisy and rowdy convention. The delegates were milling around, often not listening to the proceedings. Some were holding their own mini-conventions in the aisles. At one point when Nelson Rockefeller tried to use his microphone to address the Chair, he discovered that someone had cut the cord. It was an incident that caused great consternation.

The television media of NBC, CBS, and ABC had workers with large cameras on their shoulders, followed by one or two other workers carrying long cords. Whenever they received a signal from their base stations, they would push through the crowd in the aisles as they headed

;ignments. Some of the delegates would then follow them to
:xcitement, hoping to be seen on television.

The Chairman of the Convention and presiding officer was Congressman Gerald Ford. He frequently called for order, but to no avail. Delegates who remained in their seats to listen to the proceedings found it
difficult to hear the speakers. With twelve nominations, there were many
important votes at stake.

Finally, Consuelo Bailey, who was Secretary of the Republican National Committee, called the roll for the election. On the first ballot,
Nixon had 692; Reagan 182; and Rockefeller 277. Governor Reagan
called for making the vote unanimous for Nixon; it was so voted.

The next day, Governor Spiro T. Agnew of Maryland was nominated
for vice president and Nixon gave his acceptance speech. Once again, it
was time to go home and work for the election of Republican candidates. This time we met with success at the polls in November when
Nixon narrowly beat Senator Hubert Humphrey. As already noted, the
voters in Bennington County also chose to send me to the Vermont
Senate in 1968 so I was one busy and happy, budding legislator.

*Serving on the University of Vermont Board of Directors proved an interesting
experience and provided an introduction into how our laws work in the courtroom.*

Chapter Eleven

Senator Harwood Goes to Montpelier

By January 1969, my plans to serve in the Vermont Senate were in place. Rick was in his second year at Champlain College so that left just Doc and Roger to be home alone while I was in Montpelier from Monday afternoon until Friday afternoon. I would prepare their dinner for Monday night, and then drive up to the capital where I rented a room Mondays through Thursdays at the Montpelier Tavern. Doc would go to Rotary for his dinner on Tuesday night. Roger, our wonder cook, would prepare the meal on Wednesday. Wednesday evening after office hours, Doc would drive to Montpelier to spend Thursday with me. He would leave for Manchester on Friday morning at six. I would return Friday evenings for a three-night stay at home. Roger was seventeen now and had his own motorcycle so our plan worked admirably well. Since the legislative session ran from January to May, it only meant four months of living apart on a regular basis. Of course, when I was home weekends I was still on call for Doc.

On Doc's fifty-fifth birthday, January 3, 1969, I took the oath of office. My profession and life had changed. I was now one of the thirty senators serving the State of Vermont.

There were two other women, Margaret Hammond and Dorothy Shea, in the Senate that term. They were very helpful in showing me the ropes. I had the impression it was my duty to study every bill that was introduced, but they set me straight. I learned it was the duty of the committee members who received the particular bill to study it.

Each senator served on two committees with one meeting in the morning and the other in the afternoon. I was assigned to the Health and Welfare Committee and to the Institutions Committee — both interesting assignments. As the appointed clerk of the Health and Welfare Committee, it was my duty to keep the minutes and to arrange for witnesses and administration personnel to testify on bills. Senator Christowe, the chairman, had served many years. He expected me to know all there was to know about making contacts so I had to learn fast.

The legislative process seemed very complicated to this freshman. We were to work within the confines of a specific opening date and a target adjournment date for a total period of fourteen to sixteen weeks each year. We were elected to a two-year term, so that meant we needed to pass any bills in our committee during that first or second session. Bills could carry over to the following January (second session) but not the following term. If they didn't pass during our the term, they were dead; if someone really wanted to enact that legislation, they had to start all over again. The first sessions tended to end by the May 1 target date, but the second sessions tended to run over or well into May.

The first day we found notebooks on our desks and a pile of about thirty-five bills. Intimidated and somewhat at a loss, I asked my seatmate Richard Mallary what I was supposed to do with them. He was a considerate and experienced senator who was glad to explain. The bills were originated by individual legislators. The idea for each bill was submitted to the Legislative Council, which consists of four or five lawyers who put the idea into legal "bill" form. I learned that the majority of bills poured in during the first two or three weeks of the session and were placed in notebooks for future reference.

After committee assignments are announced, the lieutenant governor, who presides over the Senate, assigns the bills to the appropriate committee(s) for study. Some bills are never seen again; others are amended after due consideration. When the committee votes to send a bill to the floor, one committee member is assigned to "report the bill." This person's job is to explain it and be able to answer any and all questions. If voted on favorably, the bill is also reconsidered the next day before passing. After passage, the bill is then sent to the other chamber, the House, where it goes through the same process.

The first bill I was to report came from the Institutions Committee. It addressed the problem of young people escaping from the Vergennes Training School for difficult and troubled youth. Senator Hammond came to my rescue by helping me with the proper reporting procedure. I told the members of the problem of frequent escapees and the recommendation to send the offenders to a correctional center after a third escape. I gave the names of people who had testified regarding the need for stronger punishment and outlined their concerns. I also reported that no one had testified in opposition to the bill.

No one questioned this very nervous freshman and the bill passed.

A few days later, however, a letter appeared in the *Rutland Herald* and castigated me for introducing the bill. The writer also questioned "the need for such drastic measures."

That night I received a call from Doc, who was clearly upset.

"Why did you introduce that bill," he asked me.

I told him that Senator Gay had introduced it.

"But the paper says it was your bill," he responded..

I explained that I had reported the bill.

He advised me to call the paper and set things straight. Trying to reassure him, I told Doc I would speak to the chairman about it.

It just so happened that I was eating dinner with Senator Gay when Doc's call came. When I explained Doc's concern, Senator Gay said, "Tell him not to worry. If they are criticizing you, that means you have arrived; they know that you are here and working."

Poor Doc. He was so supportive of my activities that he found it hard to think that I was being criticized. I think it was harder on him than it was on me.

For my own part, bill reporting was not always that easy. I found it a challenging part of the job that must be endured.

Someone told me that a freshman legislator doesn't usually speak from the floor for the first month. I certainly didn't want to make a fool of myself, so that was fine by me and I kept quiet for the month.

Senator Hammond introduced a bill in favor of allowing horse racing on Sundays. She had become a good friend, so I went to her and asked her if my need to speak against it from the floor would upset her.

If you feel that way and don't speak against it on the floor of the Senate, I would feel more upset, she said, reassuring me that our relationship could survive a difference of opinion.

When the bill was reported out of committee and placed before the Senate for action, I rose and said, "Mr. President, I hope I have passed my probationary period, for I wish to speak against this bill."

"Senator, you have fulfilled your obligation, proceed," came the reply of Lieutenant Governor Tom Hayes.

At this point, I spoke of the need to strengthen the family by keeping members together on Sundays instead of attending horse races. I ended my speech by adding, "We made the first mistake by letting the horses out of the barn to race on weekdays."

Later, I learned that Senator Hammond had introduced the bill allowing racing on weekdays. It appeared I had added insult to injury. But she remained my friend and her bill passed.

During the summer months, Senator Olin Gay, chairman of the Institutions Committee, made arrangements for the committee to visit the prisons in the state. The tour proved to be an eye opener for us.

We first visited the Woodstock Correctional Center where the inmates at that time were all women. Their quarters were small and crowded. Senator Smith was surprised to see that women needed to be imprisoned.

Next, we visited the State Prison in Windsor. This was one of the oldest prisons in the country (constructed in 1809, the year Lincoln was born). After a tour of the grounds and buildings, the warden invited us to dinner. We were to eat in the employees' dining room.

It was a very hot summer day. The windows were open, but apparently there were no screens for the flies were plentiful. The table was set family style. There was a large bowl of hot boiled potatoes, a dish of vegetables, and a platter of beef. As I sat down, I thought they were serving raisin bread. Closer inspection showed the raisins were flies.

I had already been offered potatoes, vegetables, and meat when the warden passed me the bread, saying, "We make our own bread here; will you have some?"

"It looks good," I said, "but I have a potato and I don't eat both at a meal." Yes, I got out of that one. The warden took a slice and our chairman was able to have the second slice with no "raisins."

From there we went to St. Johnsbury to visit a small lockup. Then we traveled across the state to St. Albans to visit the new prison for youthful offenders where we visited with some of the inmates. We stopped next at the prison in Vergennes and then ended our long day with a stop at the Rutland Correctional Center. We were mentally and physically exhausted, but we all had a better understanding of the correctional system and the condition of our state's facilities.

At the time the St. Albans facility was built, the residents of the area had been promised that only youthful offenders would be sent there. However, it later became apparent that the facility was needed for older prisoners. Sometimes it is necessary to act against the taxpayers' wishes, and knowing that promises cannot always be kept makes it hard on an elected official who strives to be honest with his constituents. Becoming aware of such hard decisions opened my eyes to one of the more painful realities of politics.

I was most struck by the fact that the decision to build a correctional facility is such a difficult one to make. The legislature must establish the need, obtain a location, hire an architect, and determine the cost. The Finance Committee is charged with figuring out how the State will pay for it, and the Appropriations Committee must appropriate the funds. All of this takes a great deal of time, and it isn't made any easier when people do not wish to see a prison built in their neighborhood or town.

I had never before realized the true nature of the responsibilities placed on each member of the legislature. Working on that assignment made me see more than just the issue of correctional facilities and needs. I saw our role as a senator or representative as that of being a public servant who must do the best we can with the information we have. There is the responsibility of representing those who elected us, but also those who did not. We really were charged with working for the good of all the people of Vermont and the State itself, not just our own towns and constituents. I was also struck by the thought that I was no longer a nurse tending to a few persons' health needs but rather a legislator, who was looking after the health, welfare, and needs of many people.

I saw this as a very big responsibility. Even though we were considered "part-time" legislators due to a four-month session, we really were on call to help meet the needs of our constituents at any time during the year. We could also be called back during the summer to study an issue, as we had done with the correctional facilities. Many legislators had other commitments and jobs as well. They were teachers, mothers, business owners, professors, farmers, lawyers, shopkeepers, medical workers, etcetera. We all came in contact with different people in our work and personal lives so we truly could represent all of Vermont's citizens.

This was brought home to me when I visited my sister Evelyn and her farmer husband in Groton. He was also a lister [a townsperson elected to evaluate the worth of property for tax-roll purposes] and told me that the requirement that farmers pay an inventory tax on their livestock was a burden. The listers found it difficult to count the livestock, he said, wondering if I could do anything about it.

I told Herman that I didn't know but inquired as to what the difficulty was with counting the animals. He said that when a farmer knows the listers are coming, they sometimes put their cattle in the back pasture. "We never know for sure how many he has in hiding," he explained.

I asked if this practice would include horses as well as cows.

"Oh yes, most of these farmers rely on their horses for the heavy work. Many don't have tractors. Some are having difficulties making ends meet. An exemption of this tax would help the farmer, and it wouldn't make that much difference in income to the towns," he added.

I told him that I would try to introduce a bill, but that he might have to come and testify. Herman wasn't sure he would want to do that, but I explained that it would be necessary to have expert witnesses to present the reasons and answer questions.

This was my first attempt at introducing a bill. I went through the appropriate channels — giving it to the Legislative Council for drafting into correct form, finding supporters to co-sign it, getting it to the Finance Committee for revenue analysis, and to the Agricultural Committee for study and action. Herman testified before the latter committee, telling me later that, "I was so nervous I forgot where I parked my car." But he did a good job and convinced them. The bill passed the Senate and later the House; the inventory tax on horses and cows was dropped.

When I won re-election in 1972 to my second term in the Senate, I was once again assigned to the Health and Welfare Committee, but this time I was made chairman. There were two lawyers, two college professors, and two women on the committee — a most congenial group. Senator Dorothy Shea of Montpelier was a Republican veteran, having served in the House before joining the Senate in 1966. At age seventy, she was a great help on the committee where her experience, common sense, and warm personality made her a pleasure to work with. Senator Russell Niquette, an attorney and a Democrat, had served many years in the House before joining the Senate in 1941. His experience and knowledge made him a valuable member; he was also the vice chairman. Republican Senator Robert Bloomer of Rutland was the other lawyer. He served as clerk. He had been a pilot in the U.S. Army Air Corps and had served in the Senate for some time. His father Asa Bloomer had been in the Senate in the 1950s and Bob succeeded him when he died (in the Senate for three years, then taking a break and returning in 1972).

Frank Smallwood was a Republican freshman senator from Norwich. He was a Dartmouth political science professor who was on sabbatical during the first session of the term. [He later wrote a book entitled *Free and Independent* about his term and his introduction to state politics.] The other professor was Democrat William Daniels of Burlington. He taught history at UVM and was also a freshman senator. The two professors spent a lot of time together and gave us some long-winded seminars on occasion. But they also took their jobs seriously and were a true asset to the committee.

At the first meeting, I announced that we would all be even partners on the committee. The prior chairman had made decisions as to when we had heard enough testimony even when some of us wanted to hear more. At times, he also would announce that we were all in agreement on a bill when in fact we were not. I wished to be more even handed and to treat the others as equals.

Setting priorities on bills was also necessary as we had to review testimony on many bills. I tried to assign reporting to the member of the committee who seemed to show a special interest in it, thinking that member would be more attentive and do a better job.

During this term, we had several difficult issues facing us. One of them was a multitude of revisions of licensing bills. Many trades and professions wanted more authority in granting licenses to members of their group. We were inundated with requests from well-drillers, bartenders, hearing-aid specialists, doctors and nurses, funeral directors, and many others. One rather unusual incident occurred with a bill that dealt with the licensing requirements for funeral directors. It became entangled in a web of standards which the funeral directors felt were necessary before an applicant could be licensed. We spent a lot of time discussing it and listening to testimony.

Finally, Bill Daniels introduced the bill to the Senate: "I am pleased to report S. 117, the licensing of funeral services," he intoned. "This bill has been buried in the Health and Welfare Committee for so long that many of you may think it is a dead issue. Let me assure you, though, that it raises a number of grave questions."

Despite his lighthearted approach, a long debate over the "grave questions" followed, during which there was some vigorous objection to a last minute amendment by the funeral directors. It provided that "no body could be released for cremation less than forty-eight hours after the time of death." Senator Graham Newell pointed out that funeral directors had been after that provision for years, saying it was a thinly disguised attempt to line their pockets with more burial business. We had already debated this bill in committee; now the Senate voted to send it back to us for further study. In the end, we laid S. 117 to rest.

When it came to the licensing of nursing homes and S. 124, we used our allowed summer meeting time of six hearings to further study what was a most complex issue. We visited several different homes to become knowledgeable about the care of our elderly. Not only are there different size facilities but they all offer different levels of care and different kinds of services, from those who offer assistance with daily living in small homes to larger facilities where highly skilled nurses are needed to deliver services on a daily basis.

To complicate matters, we had to deal with federal regulations like the national Occupational and Safety and Health Act (OSHA) as well as establish safeguards of our own. But to make things even worse, the law governing nursing homes in Vermont had been amended so many times that the very definition of a nursing home was now unclear (there were many contradictory definitions of facilities) and federal guidelines defined care in yet other ways as Levels I, II, and III.

We ended up with a bill that called for the registration of small homes which were in essence boarding homes with no direct medical supervision required and the licensing of larger ones where medical services and treatments were rendered. By reclassifying the facilities into two categories, we created a system whereby the registered homes would be subject to informal state inspections (and not to OSHA and other requirements that might put them out of business) and the licensed facilities to the more stringent regulations. Thanks to the brainstorm of Senator Niquette, the hard work of the committee, and the capable reporting by Senator Smallwood, this dual system passed muster in the Senate and later the House and was voted into law as Public Act 153.

Many of the other bills we considered concerned a diversity of needs: commitments to mental institutions, sale of beer on college campuses, state general assistance programs, employment security benefits, fees charged at state hospitals, inspections of restaurants and food establishments, and ambulance services and certification to name just a few. One of the bills that was passed was the Tooth Fairy Bill, which allows for needy children to have free or reduced-cost dental care. Since so many of life's problems can fall under "health and welfare," we sometimes felt like we were a catchall committee. But we did accomplish passage of some significant legislation.

Other times we became hopelessly muddled in a mire of technical terms and technology. When it came to a bill permitting the substitution of less expensive generic drugs for brand name drugs providing they were "chemically, biologically, and clinically equivalent," we were in never-never land. The idea behind S. 150 was to reduce the escalating costs of medical care, particularly for low income and fixed-income elderly who use a lot of prescription drugs. However, coming up with a list of authorized substitutions for each drug (a formulary) was so difficult that even the experts who testified disagreed. The result was our committee split three to three, and we never got the bill to the floor for discussion despite having spent long hours on the issue.

The second bill that I introduced was not as simple or easy as the first, but it did lead to some pretty exciting times. It dealt with making the possession of marijuana a criminal offense. I was asked to testify on the bill. Senator T. Garry Buckley, who was chairman of the Judiciary Committee, asked me about the need for the bill. I told him that it was needed to address the pusher who was selling the drug. I noted there are young people in high school who are being encouraged to smoke marijuana, but if we make the fine for possession high enough, we may be able to discourage the use of it.

There were four long-haired young fellows waiting to testify. They snickered each time I answered a question.

Undeterred, I stated, "Senator Buckley, if we can discourage the use of this drug, we will also prevent our youth from going to harder drugs." More snickers.

"Okay you folks, you will have your turn to testify. No more interruptions," Senator Buckley ordered.

I didn't stay for their comments, however, as I was needed back at the Health and Welfare Committee meeting.

A gentleman from Montpelier also testified in favor of my bill. He told of how he had lost a son who went from marijuana to hard drugs, left home, ended up in Oregon, and died of an overdose. His testimony was very persuasive, and I was gratified to learn from the chairman several days later that the bill had passed in committee. Next, there was passage by the Senate, which occurred after some opposition and debate.

It went on to the House where it stalled in committee until the last week of the session. It finally passed in April 1973.

In 1974, House member Michael Silver of Bennington introduced a bill to decriminalize the personal use of marijuana. The House Judiciary Committee decided this was a bill that required a public hearing.

Representative Silver received much publicity for his efforts and had many contacts to testify as experts. When the media learned about the "experts" who were coming to speak, they asked the gentleman from Montpelier who had supported my bill in 1973 to appear with me on television to give an opposing view. We agreed. The interview was held the night prior to the public hearing.

As we entered the studio, we were introduced to a woman doctor from Washington and Mr. Hugh Hefner from NORMAL (National Organization for the Reform of Marijuana Laws). The two experts were to speak first, which they did at some length. Then the Montpelier gentleman told of his son's experience. The doctor immediately started telling him that he had presented no proof that it was the marijuana that caused him [his son] to experiment with other drugs. No matter how hard he tried to explain, they both kept interrupting him.

When it was my turn to speak, I received the same rude treatment. At last I tried to quote from a book I had read in preparation, *Marijuana, The Deceptive Weed* by Gabriel Nahas, holding it up to the camera. They both chimed in that Mr. Nahas's works had been discredited. There was little we could do as we were outmaneuvered by these two who had commandeered most of the TV time.

The hearing was held the next evening at 7 p.m. in the House Chamber. When I arrived at 7:20, there was standing room only. Television crews with cameras and bright lights were everywhere.

The first four speakers were from out-of-state. They included a professor from Harvard Medical School and three persons from Washington: an elderly female doctor, a former official with the Federal Bureau of Narcotics, and Hugh Hefner. They presented reams of statistics in an effort to prove that marijuana is not a harmful drug as the cameras rolled. They had not been given a time limit so they went on for well over an hour stating their case.

As I stood listening, I felt we were being sold a bill of goods by high-pressure salesmen.

After they finished, the chairman called for the next speaker, who was to speak in opposition. As he approached the table, he said, "I am a Vermonter. I didn't come here to sit under these hot lights and listen to a bunch of experts from out-of-state tell me how to live my life."

Turning to the previous speakers, who were now seated in the balcony, he asked who had paid for their trip to Vermont. At that point, I noticed that the camera crews got a signal to cut. They apparently didn't want to record any opposition.

Mr. Hefner answered, saying, "We are sponsored by some medical groups, mental health associations, and Playboy."

"Are you telling us that Playboy paid for your trip?" the Vermonter asked.

The question went unanswered and after a short period of silence, the audience broke into laughter.

The Vermonter turned to the chairman and said, "That's all I wish to say, Mr. Chairman," and returned to his seat.

There were several other speakers who spoke against the bill. None were as dramatic as the first speaker. The hearing ended with no one else wishing to speak in favor. The "experts" had given the fatal blow to the bill to decriminalize the personal use of marijuana.

As a mother, nurse, and a Senator who had worked hard on the 1973 bill, I was relieved and pleased that common sense had prevailed.

Public hearings could be very interesting. One stormy night, there was a public hearing regarding a snowmobile bill. There was such a large crowd that they moved the hearing to a nearby high school auditorium. The place was packed with snowmobilers, many of them dressed in their snowmobile garb as they had arrived on their machines. They feared government control as the bill tried to regulate the use of snowmobiles on private property and government land. The bill specified that they would need to get permission to drive over private property, thus creating a concern that they would be restricted and not able to go places as freely as before.

The hearing became vituperative and nearly got out of hand. The snowmobilers were adamant. You would have thought the legislature had planned to take their machines away from them. At one point, Dr. Schumacher (the nice doctor who had treated me for migraine headaches) started to speak about the possibility of back injuries. He was booed so loudly that he was unable to speak. One representative, fearing there might be a riot, left the hearing.

There are times like this when people through their own behavior defeat their position. But they have their say and the system works. In the case of the snowmobilers, they were granted permission to ride on designated trails in the state forests so they did not lose as much as they feared they would.

During these years when I was becoming familiar with how the Senate operated and my role as a senator, I was most impressed with the political process and the role that individuals play. I could see that there were many good public servants who took their responsibilities seriously and worked hard for their constituents and for the welfare of Vermonters throughout the state. I tried to be one of them, carefully doing my homework before weighing in on what would be best. I thoroughly enjoyed my job and I guess I did okay by my constituents as they returned me to the Senate for a total of seven terms or fourteen years.

My public life was not limited to the Senate, however. In 1969 I was appointed to the Governor's Council of Civil Defense, a six-year term. This was another new experience for me. We dealt with national catastrophes such as train wrecks or riots, natural disasters like tornadoes, floods, and hurricanes, and other emergency situations. Many programs on preparedness were given throughout the state. In fact, a tornado touched down in Manchester the very day the Council members visited the town.

Governor Deane C. Davis appointed me to serve on the Vermont Bicentennial Commission, a term that ran from 1970 to 1976. The members planned for the State of Vemont's part in the nation's Bicentennial

Celebration. We also assisted Vermont towns and the state in planning their respective celebrations.

I was also elected a trustee of Champlain College in Burlington in 1970. Our son Rick had graduated from Champlain in 1969. I was the first and only woman on the Board until Ruth (Mrs. Norman Vincent) Peale of New York City joined us. (I doubt that I have ever met a more charming lady. She radiated joy and good common sense.) Champlain College President Bader Broulette was a personal friend of Dr. Peale and was able to engage him as a graduation speaker. (Dr. Peale served for fifty-two years as minister of the Marble Collegiate Church in New York City. He became widely known for his preaching and inspirational writings, particularly *The Power of Positive Thinking*, which became a bestseller.) He held the audience spellbound with his philosophy for living. Getting the opportunity to hear such inspiring speakers was a wonderful bonus to serving on this college's board.

In 1971, I was elected by the Vermont Legislature to serve as their representative on the Board of Trustees at UVM, where Roger was then a pre-med student. At the time I was the only woman on this board, but I wasn't the first (Lucia Ladd, Mildred Burbank, and Hazel Wills were all trustees before me). This experience was much different from serving on the board of a smaller college. In fact, it offered another most unusual and unexpected turn of events.

At the December 4, 1971 meeting, we were required to vote on the retention of faculty members whose contracts were up for renewal. One of these persons was Michael Parenti, an Associate Professor of Political Science. In June 1971 he had been convicted of assaulting a police officer two years earlier at the University of Illinois during a campus protest. While at UVM he joined a student anti-Vietnam demonstration, marching through downtown Burlington carrying a North Vietnam flag to protest the Vietnam War in front of the Draft Board. When confronted by other citizens, he shouted obscenities. On another occasion he had refused to salute the American flag. The Trustees felt it advisable not to renew Mr. Parenti's contract. The vote was fifteen to four.

In doing so, the Board of Trustees went against the recommendation of the President of UVM, the Academic Council, the UVM Student Association, and the entire political science faculty who all supported Parenti as an "outstanding scholar, nationally recognized in his field, and a stimulating teacher." (*Rutland Daily Herald,* December 6, 1971.) The faculty and students also set up a defense fund on behalf of Parenti.

As a result, Mr. Parenti took legal action against the University and its trustees. This action was the subject of many subsequent trustee meetings.

On September 6, 1972, I received a notice from the United States District Court summoning me to appear for a deposition. UVM President Dr. Edward Andrews, UVM Trustee Francis Peisch, and another newly elected trustee, Senator Robert Boardman were also called. Dr. Andrews and Mr. Peisch had both supported the retention of Dr. Parenti while Senator Boardman had run for his position as a trustee on the promise to fire Parenti.

Mr. Parenti had engaged Thomas Hayes as his attorney. He was to take my deposition. This was rather awkward as I knew Tom Hayes. He had worked in Washington in Senator Prouty's office. He came back to Vermont in 1968 and ran for lieutenant governor; I had helped him with his campaign. He was elected and served during my first two terms in the Senate. He was acting as governor the day after four students at Kent State were shot and killed during anti-Vietnam protesting there. He had ordered the flag at the Vermont State House to be flown at half-staff. (Governor Davis was notified and returned immediately to Montpelier and ordered the flag back to full staff.)

So here I was in an extraordinary situation. Tom Hayes, a friend of mine, was representing Mr. Parenti, and calling me for a deposition.

Attorney Douglas Pierson of Burlington was the attorney representing the University. He met with me an hour before the deposition to explain the proceeding to me. Besides telling me to answer truthfully and as best I could, he said he would speak up if Hayes line of questioning seemed unreasonable. This was a bit of comfort for I had never dealt with lawyers as lawyers before and was a bit apprehensive.

After being sworn in, I answered simple questions at first like my name and when I became a trustee and when I heard about Mr. Parenti. Then the questions went on and on. I soon knew what he was trying to get at. He was wondering if I ran for the position of trustee with the intent of getting rid of Mr. Parenti. He kept giving me different time spans to identify my knowledge of Mr. Parenti.

Having established what my knowledge had been, he pressed on and on as to what motivated me to vote against him. What was my state of mind? What incident did I think was enough to cause me to vote against him? Was I instructed to vote as I did? Did I consider Mr. Parenti a good American? What did I think constituted a good American?

Finally, after over an hour of drilling, Mr. Pierson objected to the repetitive questions, and Tom said, he had no further questions.

Of course not, I thought, he has asked them all.

As I got up to leave, Tom looked up at me and said, "That wasn't so bad, was it Madeline?"

"Not if you're sitting on your side of the table, Tom," I answered truthfully.

I had no interest in the case before I joined the board. I had voted against Parenti's retention based on reports of his conduct, both for the obscenities which seemed out of place for a professor and for his disloyalty to his country. What I really objected to was the poor example I felt he was setting for students and for that reason I had voted with the majority not to renew his contract. To be called into court for exercising that judgment was both intimidating and unsettling, but to have a friend question my motivation and integrity was most maddening and a little insulting.

However, I realized the interrogation was a part of the law and what lawyers do to protect the rights of their clients. Tom was simply doing that to the best of his ability. Still I was glad when Mr. Parenti was not reinstated. I felt justice was served.

The case itself was settled out of court. I think that was an indication of both Mr. Parenti's recognition of the university's position on standards of conduct and UVM's awareness that these were turbulent times where freedom of speech issues conflicted with public policy and personal rights — as was manifested by some through acts of civil disobedience.

Certainly, having had this experience made me more familiar with and appreciative of the political process and how the laws we make affect real citizens, including trustees serving on boards!

Coffee hours were sponsored at Kitchen Cabinets around the state for Madeline's 1974 run for the U.S. House.

Chapter Twelve

Exciting Times and A Run for the U.S. House

In the summer of 1972, there was another Presidential nomination (Richard Nixon for a second term) and thus another national convention, which was held at Miami Beach in August. As twice before, Doc and I were elected alternate and delegate respectively. I was to serve on the Platform Committee again so I went down a week early. The Platform activities were less hectic and after we completed our work, I moved out to the Newport Hotel which had been designated for the Vermont delegation.

The real excitement came when the Convention was in session. There were anti-Vietnam demonstrations throughout the city, some of them led by Jane Fonda, who had recently returned from Hanoi. Many times during the Convention, demonstrators ran rampant in the streets and on the sidewalks, interfering with the delegates getting to social functions. They were a noisy, rowdy, and at times destructive bunch. In some areas they would stop delegates' cars, slash tires or raise the hoods and slash wires and hoses. A woman alone was at their mercy.

Buses loaded with delegates were also under attack. If a bus stopped at a traffic light, a gang of demonstrators would pry up the rear bus hood, slash wires or hoses or pour molasses onto the motor. Because they were everywhere, the police were unable to control their actions.

The last night of the Convention we were advised to be at the Hall at least an hour early. Some of the streets had been closed off by buses parked so as to block the entire street and prevent gangs from entering. We loaded as many Vermont delegates as we could into our car and headed for a restaurant a block from the Hall. Doc was to drop us off, park at the Hall, and then join us for dinner. As I got out, I noticed that the street ahead was full of demonstrators. I went around to all the doors and locked them, and watched as he pulled away.

To my great dismay, instead of turning right at the corner and thus avoiding the gang, he drove straight ahead and into the group. As I watched, I could see them trying to stop him. There was much yelling and cheering as he drove along and then I could no longer see the car. Worried, but realizing there was nothing I could do at that point, I went into the restaurant to join our group. They ordered dinner, but I was too worried about Doc to eat. I sat and waited.

After twenty minutes, I went outside and looked in all directions but there was no sign of Doc. Frank Mahady, an attorney and delegate that year (who later became a judge on the on the Vermont Supreme Court) came out. I told him I was going down the street to find my husband.

He offered to go for me, gallantly removing his suit jacket, handing it to me, and telling me to stay because he looked "more like one of them than you do" (a reference to his long hair).

After walking the length of the street through the crowd, he returned. Having not seen any sign of him, he tried to assure me Doc was probably all right and that I had better go in and eat.

I still didn't feel the least bit hungry, but I went in with him to wait. An hour after he had left us, Doc reappeared. In his usual calm manner, he told us that he had decided to get gas before parking the car and, because so many streets were closed off, it had taken longer than planned.

Just as I was about to vent my pent-up worry and tell him about the anxiety he had caused me, he turned my tirade to grateful relief, as he proceeded to tell how the protesters had tried to stop him and tip the car over. They had kicked great dents in the sides and had thrown water soaked magazines on the windshield so he couldn't see.

"One cuss climbed on the hood and was hanging on. One of them threw one of those rectangular trash cans in front of the car to stop me.

Doc was snapped driving through the protests in this UPI photo that got large play in the national press in 1972. (United Press International)

They even bent the wipers off. Someone came and pushed the trash can away so I kept going. I wasn't about to let them stop me," he said.

The police had found it necessary to use tear gas to disperse the crowd, so as we were leaving the restaurant the considerate proprietor gave us napkins to place over our faces for the walk to the Hall. They came in handy as the air was still heavy with the stinging gas.

Despite the attempts to disrupt the convention, President Nixon made it to the Hall, and the festivities concluded on a more normal note with the acceptance speech and usual celebrating.

The next morning we left early for Vermont, leaving all the confusion behind. When we stopped many miles north of town to get new wipers, I noticed some of the protesters standing nearby, trying to thumb rides home. I asked one girl where she was from. She told me she was from Ohio. When I asked if she had been at the convention, she beamed brightly and replied, "Oh yes, we were there."

When I inquired as to why they were protesting, she said it was because "There is no work for us. We are all out of work."

Disturbed by that answer, I told her there was plenty of work. I added that even if she had to scrub floors or make beds, jobs could be found.

"I wouldn't be seen doing that kind of work," she retorted with great indignation.

Bothered by the senseless rowdiness and damage they had caused and her own unwillingness to do work that I myself had done, I told her, "Manual labor never hurt anyone. I hope you have a long walk home."

The next morning we stopped in Georgia for breakfast. Doc, as usual, bought a newspaper. As I was reading the second section I spotted a photograph of a familiar looking car with a demonstrator on the hood, a trash can in front of it, and magazines plastered on the windshield. A *Hackett for Governor* sticker confirmed that it was indeed our car.

I had been co-chairman with Dorothy Shea's son Charles of the Hackett for Governor Committee that year. Luther F. Hackett (we called him Fred) had served in the House and was also a UVM Trustee. I felt he was well qualified to be governor. [Attorney General James Jeffords of Rutland defeated Fred in the primary, but Democrat Thomas Salmon defeated Jeffords in the 1972 election.]

Although we got away on vacations and to conventions occasionally, Doc had kept up his hectic schedule of working long hours throughout the years. He still took Thursdays off and kept to working on Saturdays and being on-call on Sundays. He also maintained his evening office hours and continued to make house calls. He loved his work and never complained.

However, I noticed that many days he would skip his lunch or be very late for dinner. One day I phoned the office at about 6:30 p.m. and asked him how long before he would be home for dinner.

"I can't say. I still have two patients here. I have to make a house call and office hours begin at seven," he answered.

"But you should eat," I insisted.

"Will you get off my back? I may not be able to get home to eat."

"Doc, you can't keep this up; you are going to have a heart attack if you don't let up," I warned.

I knew we followed a hectic schedule and that our life pattern was putting strain on Doc. He was almost sixty years old and should be slowing down, but instead his patients were still coming first.

On Doc's day off, November 27, 1972, we decided to take our grandchild Debbie to the mall in Albany to see Santa Claus. We returned her to her mother Cathy in Bennington and got home around eight in the evening. We had been in bed for about an hour when Doc woke up and took a pill.

I was reading and asked what the medicine was for.

Doc answered that his arm felt numb.

I asked if he had any pain and he said no, that he had probably slept on it. So what did you take, I inquired.

"Just a nitroglycerine pill," came the answer.

To my inquiry of any chest pain, he said, "No, I'm all right."

I continued reading. But when I glanced at him again, I saw beads of perspiration on his forehead. "Doc, are you sure you don't have any chest pain?" I asked. I was a director of the Vermont Heart Association and was aware of what his symptoms could mean.

Again, he said no, insisting he was all right.

Not liking how he looked, I called the Rescue Squad. Then I called Dr. Richard Davis, our friend who was an internal medicine specialist, to ask him to meet Doc at the hospital.

"What are you doing that for? I can wait until morning," Doc said.

"Doc, I think you are having a heart attack," I warned.

He got up, dressed, and sat in the chair waiting for the Rescue Squad. I phoned Roger, who was at a friend's, to let him know that Doc was going to the hospital. Then I drove to Bennington. There was fresh snow on the ground. On the way, the ambulance hit a deer but kept going.

When I arrived, Dr. Davis told me that the EKG showed Doc had suffered a severe coronary. After making sure Doc was okay and was in good hands, I accepted Dr. Davis's invitation to stay at his home for the night. The following morning at six-thirty, he told me that the hospital had phoned and that Doc wanted me to come as soon as possible.

I said I would go right up, but Dr. Davis advised that Doc was doing all right. He added we would both go up after breakfast.

When I arrived at the intensive care unit, Doc told me he had been watching the monitor and saw the line fall to a straight line. Then he lost consciousness. After feeling a thump on his chest, he came to. They had used the paddles on him to get his heart beating again.

It was a most frightening experience. Thank the Lord, he was in the hospital where the nurses knew what to do. Had he remained at home as he had suggested, he would not have survived. With all of this going through my mind, I was a wreck.

Doc, however, was his usual calm self. There were many important matters he wanted me to take care of at the office. He wanted me to pay the bills and be sure the insurance policies were paid before they expired. Doc also wanted me to get the Red Cross to bring Rick home. He was stationed in Europe in the Air Force at the time. I had been a director of the Bennington Red Cross so I knew whom to call, and they were able to get Rick home in two days. What a wonderful organization!

After a three-week hospital stay, Doc was released. He would not be able to go back to practicing medicine for some time. I was due back in Montpelier to serve in the Senate in early January so Doc went with me. We had a lovely room in the Montpelier Tavern where he could rest and recuperate. It was nice to have him with me and to be able to keep an eye on him. Modern medicine and the dedicated people in the medical profession had kept him alive. Now he was willing to do his part and take it easy. I was grateful.

My political activities became more involved on the national level when I was elected Republican National Committee Woman on July 3, 1973. The position had been held by Consuelo Bailey (Vermont's first female lieutenant governor in 1955) of Burlington for thirty-seven years. I considered it a great honor to be selected to follow in her shoes. My nomination was seconded by Richard A. Snelling, a state representative from Shelburne.

The Republican National Committee (RNC) consists of three people from each state: the state chairman of the Republican Party and one woman and one man. They meet twice a year, usually in Washington, and are charged with selecting the site for the National Convention, the plans for its program, and many miscellaneous tasks. There are several

Seated, Consuelo N. Bailey; standing l to r, Governor Deane C. Davis, Stewart Smith, Madeline, Ronald Reagan, and Roland Seward. Madeline replaced Consuelo as GOP National Committee Woman, serving 1973-1992.

standing committees that function within the RNC. I had the honor of serving on the Rules Committee for many years.

I found the meetings to be educational and interesting. We always had at least one member of Congress or the Senate speak to us on current affairs. And, when a Republican was president, we were invited to a White House reception and were addressed by the President himself.

George Bush was chairman of the RNC at the time I was elected to serve. He was an honest, straight forward chairman. He was also serving at a rather unusual time as Watergate was of great concern that year. Many people had questions of who did what, when and why, along with what was the President's role, if any.

By April 30, 1973, two of Nixon's top aides, Bob Haldeman and John Ehrlichman, had resigned. Things were in a general state of turmoil, but George told us that at one of his meetings with the President, Nixon had informed him that he was not involved in the Watergate affair. If I find that the President has not leveled with me, I will resign as your chairman, he added. Unfortunately, it was not long before we received his resignation. George Bush was a very honest man who could not serve knowing the President had not been straight forward with him. Vice Chairman Mary Louise Smith, of Iowa, became the chairman for the remainder of the term.

When we met in October 1973, we were invited to the White House. I fully expected we would be welcomed by President Nixon. Instead, Vice President Spiro T. Agnew met us. I thanked him for being there to greet us, but as I shook his hand, I noticed that he didn't seem very relaxed. (I had previously met him when he spoke at a fundraiser in Norwich, Vermont.)

A few days later, I learned the reason for his tension. President Nixon had asked him to resign on October 10 (for reasons that had to do with alleged income-tax evasion, not the Watergate affair). Two days later, President Nixon nominated U.S. House Minority Leader Gerald Ford to serve as vice president.

While I enjoyed serving on this committee for many years, this was certainly a distressing time for both the party and the committee — and a somewhat sad introduction to its many challenges for me.

Early in 1973, Vermont's longtime U.S. Senator George Aiken announced that he would not seek re-election in 1974. Richard Mallary (a former Vermont State Senator) had been serving in Congress as our lone Representative to the U.S. House. It seemed likely that Mallary would run for the Senate seat being vacated (he did) and that the Congressman's seat would be up for grabs. By early spring both James Jeffords, Vermont's Attorney General, and Lieutenant Governor John Burgess (also a Republican) had announced they would be candidates.

Many of my friends got in touch with me and convinced me that it was time for a woman to be Vermont's Representative in Washington. After some soul searching and consultation with my family, I decided to run. My family and a few friends were present when I made my announcement on May 16, 1974. Reporters were also present to bombard me with questions as to why I was running and for details like how much I was planning to spend.

The truth was I had a late start on this campaign, and I didn't have those answers yet. I had time to make up and lots to learn. Both Jim and Jack had run for statewide office at least twice. They knew the ropes. I was a novice who began to feel like she was on the ropes. Whereas they knew the locations of all the radio stations and town clerks' offices, had their own mailing lists, and even campaign staff, I was starting green and with very little in the way of expertise for such an important position. It would prove to be a very different and educational experience.

Running for the U.S. House

Running for Congress turned out to be an entirely different political ball game. First, it was a very expensive venture. I soon learned it was necessary to raise a far larger amount of money than I ever had to raise before. William Lassiter, a neighbor, offered to be my treasurer. This was a difficult task as people were not in the habit of giving to women candidates.

Doc also came to my rescue by volunteering to be my campaign manager, pledging to take time from his own busy schedule to help me.

The newspapers noted that I had a volunteer staff. This was true, but I got some mileage (and laughs) by the confession that I slept with my campaign manager.

I was already behind time wise, so our first order of business was to do brochures, print letterheads, draw up mailing lists, and establish a functioning committee. Then there were candidates' forums to attend, tough questions to be answered, and supporters to line up to attend the forums.

As a native of Orange County, I knew many people there. We had lived in Windsor County while in South Royalton, but I had not gotten acquainted with many voters there. I knew a few folks from when we lived in Brandon in Rutland County and a few from when we lived in Windham County (Whitingham). I was better known in Bennington County where I had been re-elected twice already.

Feeling I needed some professional advice, I consulted our friends and fellow Republicans. Noble Smith suggested that professional ads were necessary for radio and television. John Wu told me there was a fellow from Maryland named Robert Goodman who was an expert. Doc and I discussed the fact that he might be expensive, but I felt the need for good radio and TV ads. Every time I picked up the paper, I saw lists of supporters signed up for Jim. Even my good friend Connie Bailey

Madeline Harwood
for United States Congress.

Because people remember what she has done and believe in what she can do for America.

"She led the fight to give financial aid to widows of policemen killed in action . . . and that meant a lot to me."

"Without Madeline, the Vermont farmer would still be taking it on the chin in livestock property taxes. She's been a friend for a long time."

"I think the bill Mrs. Harwood sponsored against drug abuse is the most important thing that happened in the Vermont Senate all last year."

"When other Republicans turned their back on the party, Madeline stayed with us. I'll never forget that."

"Madeline was the Senator who introduced the bill to end discrimination against women applying for bank loans and credit cards."

Madeline's 1974 brochure.

had come out for him. She signed on as honorary co-chair of his campaign. After talking it over with Bill Lassiter, we decided to contact Goodman.

Mr. Goodman got in touch with a New York company that wrote a theme song of sorts for radio and TV spots. I thought it was a bit corny when he first presented it to me, but it did have a catchy tune. The song was sung by a Vic Damone type voice and repeated a refrain: "Someone to believe in, someone we can all join hands with . . . Madeline, Madeline Harwood." I made short statements to go with it and we did six versions in all. He advised using that refrain on my brochures and also took photos of me with different people for use on the brochures.

For the television ads, we also had film of me driving the car as I was discussing the issues. It aired on the Burlington station very effectively. The frugal, grassroots approach to my campaign seemed to go over well with Vermonters, and we also received exposure at the candidate forums.

As the deadline for filing our petition of voter support was approaching, Jack Burgess called on me at our home. It was a Sunday evening and Doc had been called to the office to attend to an auto-accident patient. He had called me to help him suture the patient. So Roger sent Jack to the office to find me. Seeing we were busy, however, he returned to our home to wait for me there.

Jack had his assistant with him. He also had a very important mission. After a short exchange of pleasantries, he wondered if Doc didn't need me at the office to help him.

I explained to him that Doc had decided to give up his practice and go to Washington to be with me if I were elected.

It was about midnight when Jack came to the purpose of his mission. He told me he had taken a poll that showed us drawing from each other. It was his conclusion that neither of us could win against Jim if we both stayed in the race. Observing that it looked like Doc could use me to help him, he asked if I would consider dropping out of the race.

This took us by surprise. I had never even considered dropping out. I was indebted to Mr. Goodman for quite a sum of money. We had many expenses for brochures, stationery, as well as for contracts for radio and TV time.

I told him, I didn't see how I could possibly drop out, noting that we were too indebted to many people.

We were all standing in the kitchen talking when Jack asked if there was anyone I could call for advice?

"Not at this hour of the night, Jack. I'm sure all my friends are asleep. The Lord is the only one I could ask at this hour. Besides, you know tomorrow is the day we file our petitions with the Secretary of State," I reminded him.

"Yes, I know it is. That's why I think we should make a decision. Would you consider calling Fred Hackett?" he asked.

I told him I would have to think about it, but I was going to go to Montpelier in the morning and file my petitions as planned.

Still, he persisted and asked if I didn't think I should call Fred before filing.

I told him I was not sure I would call Fred and repeated I felt I owed too much to get out that early.

Jack finally said, "Well, Madeline, if you don't get out of the race, I will. We can't win this way."

Doc also informed Jack that we didn't feel we could afford to get out of the race. With that, Jack and his assistant left our home. It was a about 12:30 a.m. and I needed to get some rest for the long drive to Montpelier.

I left early Monday, determined to get my petitions filed on time. As I entered the Secretary of State's Office, I noticed reporters were there to check on filings. I told them I had doubled the number of signatures required. For most candidates this would have been newsworthy. Not for me though — no mention was made of my efforts.

As I was leaving the office, one of the secretaries called to me, saying that Fred Hackett had called and wanted me to phone him before filing.

I told her it was too late, that I had already filed but assured her I would call him later.

Wondering what Jack was up to and feeling uncertain as to how to proceed, I called Doc. He advised me to call Fred anyway. At that point I was so distressed that I couldn't recall much of our conversation after I got off the phone with Fred. He basically told me he had wanted to talk with me before I filed and that he had had a call from Jack regarding our filing.

A few days later I had a call from a reporter asking me if there was anything to the rumor that I was going to withdraw from the race. I said I had no idea where that rumor came from and had no intentions of getting out. From that point on, I was determined to campaign as hard as I could. I felt a new urgency to reach as many people as possible and to prove something to my fellow politicians as well as to myself.

I began to realize that there were still some serious barriers to women in politics. This was 1973. Consuelo Bailey had made it all the way to lieutenant governor in 1955 but despite her years of experience and dedication, she had not run for governor because she felt a woman would not get elected. The party and people just weren't ready yet, she felt. But they would never be ready if we didn't get out there and show them we could do the job, I reasoned. Of course Doc didn't know the meaning of not trying — his can-do attitude just encouraged me as did his high expectations, God bless him.

Jack Burgess did stay in the race. Many times during the next weeks, we met at forums and at radio stations. He never once mentioned his offer to get out, and I never brought it up. I understood what had happened, and it just egged me on to win.

Sometimes things like adversity and challenge can energize you. When I look back at the hectic schedule I followed (at age sixty), I can see that must have been the case. The following is a sample of what my days were like.

Sunday, August 25: 2:30-6 p.m. Forum in Morrisville.
Monday, August 26: 8:45-10 a.m. Radio interview with call-in questions, Burlington; 11:30-3 p.m. campaign in downtown St. Albans; 4-7 p.m. campaign at Fair.
Tuesday, August 27: 6:40 a.m.-8:05 campaign at GE Plant, Vergennes; 9-11 campaign downtown Vergennes; 12:30-2 campaign in Bristol; 3-5 campaign in Middlebury; 6:30 potluck supper in Cornwall.
Wednesday, August 28: 8:45-10 a.m. Burlington Radio with live call-ins; 3 p.m. campaign with Orin Johnson in Winooski; rest of day at Fair.
Thursday, August 29: 6:40-8:05 a.m. IBM Plant (Essex) meeting workers; 11-1:30 p.m. Senior Citizen lunch; 2-3 ETV Taping; 4-5:30 Middlebury radio, taping advertisements.

I still did not have any paid staff. This was unheard of for an important office of this level. I also did all my own driving. As I told Doc, I wasn't going to risk the possible gossip attached to employing a male driver.

Campaign workers Dorothy Treat, Betty Goff, Al Webb, and Bernice Graham were pictured in this campaign poster for Madeline's 1974 run along with the following information:

"Over 55 Vermont kitchens located all over the state have become the official headquarters for Madeline B. Harwood, Republican for Congress.

"When good ideas and good people get together for Madeline, it just isn't necessary to hire a staff of managers and coordinators. From the beginning, Madeline has taken her campaign to the people herself . . . and the spirit that has followed has become a new chapter of Vermont history."

However, my dear campaign manager also wanted me at home each night. So there were many times when I drove great distances at the end of a long day. There were times when I was so tired that I would begin wondering if I had reached Rutland yet. Had I driven through Rutland? Did I slow down going through Rutland? I always seemed to reach home, sometimes in the wee hours of night. Many days I would be up at six the next morning to head out for the next engagement.

"I take the issues to the people," I announced. "That is the approach of local involvement that is needed."

I established HARWOOD-FOR-CONGRESS-KITCHENS throughout the state. These were my "kitchen cabinets" where I met with housewives in each county. The ladies would then distribute my brochures to their friends. The political reference to FDR's use of the term kitchen cabinets (which was used to refer to his meetings with close advisers) was deliberate. I enjoyed the play on words and took pride in meeting in those kitchens.

One morning I was invited to a coffee hour in Essex Junction at the home of a friend Barbara Fondrey. I made my opening remarks, then took questions. Someone wanted to know why she should vote for me instead of Jim Jeffords. He has had lots of experience as attorney general, she noted.

I thanked her for that question, and responded that I was not going to speak against Jim as he was a friend of mine. But I also told the group that I had legislative experience and that I had participated at the national level, trying to point out my own qualifications as I did so. I spoke of a need for a strong national defense and other goals I would work for if elected, ending with, "The decision of who you want to represent you is up to you."

After the meeting, my hostess told me the lady was Jim's sister-in-law Jane Mendicino.

Long before I entered the campaign and before Watergate had become an issue, I had made a speech at a Lincoln Day dinner, stating that I thought President Nixon would go down in history as "one of our great presidents for having opened the door to China."

The press took note. After Agnew resigned, things began to shape up in Washington against President Nixon. When he admitted in August that he was involved in Watergate, reporters went after me. If you were in Congress now, would you vote to impeach the President, I was asked.

I told them I would withhold any final decision until I had studied all the evidence thoroughly. I added I thought that our elected officials in Washington had that opportunity to study the evidence and were better qualified to make that decision.

I was also asked if I felt there would be a voter backlash against all Republicans in the fall elections

"I can't see why that would happen. More than 117,000 Vermonters supported the President in the 1972 election," I noted.

At every radio interview following Nixon's admission of involvement, the interviewer questioned me extensively about Watergate.

Reporters were always present at forums. Occasionally one would follow me for a while when I was campaigning in a town. They would listen to my answers, then try to quote me in their news stories.

I never read an article written about my opponents where they mentioned what the candidate was wearing. But they would often report what I was wearing. I decided to turn that to my advantage. I began wearing red, white and blue outfits. They immediately picked up on that. This made me recognizable when I went to an area. We found you because of your red, white, and blue dress, people would say.

One day I had an appointment to pick up a member of the media in Randolph at 8 a.m. to spend the day with me. We drove to Craftsbury where Eunice Kinsey met us for some campaigning in that area. We had lunch with Miss Mary Jean Simpson, former Dean of Women at UVM at her home. Her sister was also present and it was a most enjoyable occasion.

From there we drove to Newport, where a friend, Representative Arthur Mooney, took us through the business district and introduced me to many of his friends. We had dinner at his home, another enjoyable occasion.

Following the dinner, we attended a square dance program that lasted until late. It was 9 p.m. before I managed to beg off so I could head back to Manchester, 150 miles away. After leaving my media friend off in Randolph, I arrived home at 1:30 a.m.

The next day I was in Brattleboro, working Jack Burgess's town. We attended a forum that evening. After each candidate spoke, we were asked questions. Following that, one man asked me to go to his table.

"I like what you say. You know what you are talking about, but I can't vote for you," he said.

"Why, do you live in New Hampshire?" I asked.

"No, I can't vote for you because you are a woman. A woman's place is in the home."

So much for my efforts and years of hard work.

A very good friend, Barbara Cummings of Springfield, served as my campaign chairman for Windsor County. She really worked hard. She held a coffee hour for me, inviting many of her friends. She then enrolled them in my Kitchen Cabinet as workers for me. She also would try to arrange to have me invited to speak at Rotary meetings when I found that one of my opponents had done so. Equal time, Barbara would suggest.

We were told not to discuss politics at these meetings. This made it very difficult. At some meetings I would explain some bill that had passed. There were always questions that followed. When I was in Chester, one member asked me a very technical question on economics.

"I am sorry, sir, I am unable to answer your question. However, if you will give me your name and address, I will look into it and write you," I replied.

"No thank you, that won't be necessary," he responded.

Later, I was told that he had asked one of my opponents the same question. My opponent responded but gave the wrong answer, leaving a bad impression. I carried that town. It was another lesson learned. It really does pay to be honest and to admit that you don't know everything but are willing to learn and get back to them. People do want to be listened to and taken seriously.

When I spoke to the Bethel Rotary, I decided to show some marijuana plants and speak on the bill I had gotten passed, which made its use illegal in Vermont. I visited our police station to see if they had some plants I could use for show and tell.

They gave some to me along with a permit to have them in my possession in case I got picked up. Doc went with me that day and carried the permit in his pocket.

Early the next day, I had an urgent call from my sister-in-law in Massachusetts, telling me my brother John had had a heart attack and would I come right away. Of course, I said, and headed for Worcester. I soon realized I had the plant in the car and no permit, so I returned it to Manchester to avoid an arrest and then continued my trip.

With the voting date coming upon us, I began to feel like I was running out of time. I still had lots of material to distribute. I had been told that the Republican State Committee would allow each candidate access to the address plates with the names and addresses of Vermont Republicans. We could use them for mailing purposes, but for one mailing only.

I had already done mailings to special interest groups and now needed to use the plates. Jim Jeffords had used the plates for his mailings, but when I went to the office to do mine, I was told the machine was broken. They were sorry, but I would be unable to use it. This was indeed a great disappointment. I never did find out if Jack had used the plates.

The last week of the primary campaign, our son Rick was able to be with me. He was a great help with my scheduling and did all my driving. We covered the northeastern part of the state, attending fairs and other functions. It was a great relief to have a chauffeur and to have time to spend preparing for the next stop. It was important to appear "bright eyed and bushy tailed" if one wanted the public to listen — this was not always easy with a demanding schedule but having a driver definitely helped.

On Election Night, we drove to Montpelier where the media had reporting equipment set up in the hall behind the Tavern Motor Inn. Many people were there waiting for the returns. Suspense ran high. Returns started to come in at what seemed a very slow pace. Neither of my opponents was there.

As we stood watching the ever-changing score board, there were times when I felt very encouraged. But soon a flash would appear that put Jim many votes ahead.

Occasionally one of the press would come over to me and say it was beginning to look real good for me. Like a yo-yo the next half hour report would deflate me.

When the Springfield vote came in, showing I had carried that city, we were elated. Barbara had sure helped there. But by 11 p.m., it became apparent that I had lost to Jim. The final tally showed Jim Jeffords had 18,563 votes for 40 percent. I had received 16,345, for 35.2 percent, and Jack Burgess got 11,453 for 24.7 percent. Jack was right. We had taken from each other.

I had been told that Jim was at a large hall near Northfield and tried to phone him several times to congratulate him. Not being able to get through, I asked Doc to drive us there. The hall was jubilant with the celebration of victory. As I offered Jim my congratulations, he commented, that he never knew of the defeated candidate coming to his opponent.

I explained that the phone line had been constantly busy and then offered him my support adding I would ask my supporters to work for his election. They did and many times Jim remarked about my good sportsmanship. To this day, Liz Dailey Jeffords, his wife, will comment about that election, saying, "She almost beat him."

But almost is small consolation. I wouldn't be truthful if I didn't say that the defeat left me feeling depressed. I still owed $17,000 and had campaign materials left over that were of no use now. The debt was most depressing.

This was another lesson. Women at that time did not get the financial support that male candidates did. And yes, Watergate did have a great effect on the election. Jim Jeffords was the only Republican to win that fall at the statewide level. Richard Mallary lost his bid for the Senate to Democrat Patrick Leahy[1] and Democrat Thomas P. Salmon was re-elected governor.

[1] *When this book went to print in October 2000, Pat Leahy was still Vermont's senior U.S. Senator and Jim Jeffords was also a U.S. Senator, having served as Representative from 1975-1988 and in the Senate since 1989. Independent Bernie Sanders, a self-described Progressive, was Vermont's Representative in the U.S. House, having served since 1990 when he replaced Republican Peter Smith. Vermont still did not have a woman in Washington, although Democratic State Senator Jan Backus had run against Jeffords in 1994 (with a respectable 41 percent of the vote versus Jeffords' 50 percent), and Republican State Senator Susan Sweetser had run unsuccessfully against Sanders in 1996.*

Democrat Madeleine Kunin had broken another female barrier. After being elected lieutenant governor in 1978, she went on to become the first woman Governor of Vermont in 1985, after narrowly defeating Republican John Easton in the November 1984 elections. She served three terms, showing a woman could get the job done. Republican Barbara Snelling also was elected a lieutenant governor in 1992 and 1994, the third woman to hold that position in Vermont history.

Doc and Madeline (l) attend a GOP function. Stewart Smith, National Republican Committee Man and his wife Priscilla are on the right.

Two members of the President's Commission on Mental Retardation (far left) and Vermont Senator Robert Stafford, Madeline, Representative Jim Jeffords, and Senator Pat Leahy in Washington D.C. in the mid-1980s.

Chapter Thirteen

A Meaningful Journey
&
New Challenges

I did not run for state senator in 1974 as you could not run for two offices in one year (even though the primary was held earlier than the November elections). Having lost in the primary for the U.S. House, I took a rest from the state legislature for two years. But with politics still in my blood, I ran again for the senate in 1976 and returned to Montpelier for my fourth term, 1977-78.

This time, when asked what committees I would like to serve on, I chose Health and Welfare and the Government Operations Committee, which had a vacancy. Senator Niquette had been appointed chairman of Health and Welfare while I was away, so when asked if I would like to be chair again, I declined as he was most capable.

Government Operations turned out to be a very interesting committee under chairman Sandy Partridge. We dealt with election laws, local government problems, and redistricting. The U.S. Supreme Court Decision of 1964, based on *Reynolds v. Sims* case, said that all state legislatures had to be apportioned on the basis of a one-person one-vote rule so as to reflect density of population in certain areas. This meant that every so many years we had to redistrict to reflect current populations. Of course, redrawing districts was rife with political implications so this was a challenging task.

The Health and Welfare Committee continued to be inundated with bills, but again I enjoyed the work. With some medical knowledge and interest, I felt useful to the committee.

On September 4, 1977, Doc and I flew from New York to London for a vacation and sight-seeing trip. Our four children were grown and settled and this was to be an extended trip, the "vacation of a lifetime."

It did not start out well, though. There were delays in New York and problems clearing customs at Heathrow Airport at three in the morning. Then we couldn't find a taxi. As we stood out in the cold, I noticed several buses being loaded with tourists. Doc advised that they were for charter groups and wouldn't take us. He was right, but I insisted we had to get out of the cold and that it was worth trying. We boarded a bus with a group from Israel and, much to his surprise, we were allowed to ride to their hotel. There, we found a cab to take us to our hotel, the Royal Horseguards.

After several hours of much needed sleep, we asked for afternoon tea, only to be informed, "Madam, we do not serve tea." And so began our twenty-three day vacation. Like all vacations, it had its ups and downs as well as its memorable moments.

There was Patrick, our Irish bus driver and guide for a tour of England, Scotland, and Wales. He was a most entertaining host and a great story teller. On the first day as we were heading out for York, he announced he'd been in an accident several months earlier and had to appear in court the following day so we would be on our own touring York. Soon after explaining this, we came to a Y in the road with a stop sign. Pat started up too soon and struck the car in front of us. No harm was done, however, so we still had confidence in our driver.

As we left the bus at our hotel, one of the members said they were not sure what to wear on the tour.

"Oh, don't you worry, m' dear," Pat sang. "I'll give you the dress for the day at dinner tonight." We knew he was kidding.

Later, when we were all on board the bus to leave York, I noticed all the ladies had slacks on while I was still wearing a skirt. I went up to him and said, "I'm sorry, Pat, I didn't get your announcement for the dress of the day. It looks like I'm the only one here with no pants on."

"Oh, do tell," he said, laughing heartily.

I felt sure I had added another amusing story to his long added to my repertoire with his expression, "Oh, do tell." came a favorite in our family.

Of more historical note, our travels with Pat took us from th nificent Minster Cathedral in York to the Roman Wall in Cheste saw Scotland with its beautiful countryside, dotted with sheep and gra cattle, and Inverness Castle high on a hill. In Wales, Pat drove on ba roads to show us wild horses. We visited the ruins of Tintern Abbey, twelfth century monastery and an impressive walk back in time.

Our ten-day tour ended in London with a fond farewell to Patrick and our fellow travelers. Indeed, the journey had been a Canterbury Tale all of our own.

We added four more days, seeing the sights of London and took a train to Shakespeare country followed by a bus ride to Stonehenge, a most famous prehistoric site with huge rocks placed in a circle and wrapped in an air of mystery. We would liked to have stayed longer, but as Robert Frost once observed, we had "promises to keep."

Our friend Anne Mauger of Manchester had asked us to visit the Isle of Guernsey, the place of her birth. We flew there from London. Guernsey was a very old Channel Island that had been occupied by the Germans during World War II. We visited the cemetery where Anne's relatives were buried. A very quaint and small church stood at the entrance. We also located the home of Anne's family. It had been turned into an eatery. We ate lunch in what had once been their living room. It was an interesting experience to visit a place where we felt this special connection to the past.

From there we went by hydroplane to St. Malo where we had dinner and spent the night. We had arranged for a rental car to be delivered to us the next morning. The front desk phoned us when the car arrived. We went down with some of our luggage to pick up the car and pay our bill. The concierge, a large unfriendly lady would not accept our traveler's checks. She insisted that we go up the street to the bank and bring back cash.

As I started to take some luggage to the car, she looked up and ordered me to leave it where it was until we had paid the bill. I explained

ır room, thinking it would serve as our
again instructed us to leave it and get
as ordered. When we returned, we
ur luggage into the hall. So much

...ere the magnificent sight of the ancient
...ck of granite greeted us. At high tide the area
Doc never liked the idea of commercializing such
, and was not interested in visiting the abbey due to the
...ocated in the doorways. I had a great interest in the church,
...ver, so I did walk past the shops and inspected all I could of the
...obey without paying the fee for a tour.

Next we drove to the lovely city of Granville in France. We had a reservation in a delightful hotel where we received a warm welcome. Doc had spent Christmas 1944 in Granville, and he wanted to show me the church where he had attended the Christmas Eve service. The small church was still there just as he remembered it. It was a memorable and meaningful visit, and we enjoyed our time there.

From Granville we drove on to St. Lo, where we visited a museum with World War II items on display. I still remember the mock-up of a paratrooper who had been dropped in the night before the invasion and got hung up on a steeple. Luckily, he was cut down and lived to tell about it. There were also letters on display about the events, recalling what the men had experienced with the D-Day invasion. It was a very moving exhibit, reminding us of the cause and price of freedom.

Then it was on to Utah Beach where Doc had landed on D-Day. I took Doc's picture by the monument, which had been erected in memory of the outfit he served with. Of course, it brought back a flood of memories for both of us.

Then, just when we thought our experience could not possibly get any more emotional, we visited the large cemetery where United States servicemen killed in action are buried. While there, we saw a rainbow which extended over the entire width of the cemetery. It seemed like a blessing from God.

Reliving our connection to freedom this way was really the highlight of our trip. It made us both more mindful and appreciative of the role the Allies had played in protecting the world from Nazi Germany. It was not easy to see what we saw, but it did hold a deeper meaning for us. We were both proud that Doc had done his patriotic duty and had helped to save countless lives. We were thankful once again that miraculously he had escaped injury himself and come home in one piece.

It certainly had been a scary time for me, but now, over thirty years later, I could rejoice in our small roles and in our country's involvement in preserving freedom from tyranny for so many. The experience was one of pride and thankfulness.

It also reinforced my own deep feeling that had gotten me into politics in the first place — that we can and should work through the system to achieve a better way of life for all people. It made me appreciative of the sacrifices our service men and women make and especially the danger they face. It also made me mindful of the serving professions in general — doctors, nurses, teachers, elected officials, and others who serve the public in various ways. I could look at legislative work in a different, more appreciative light now.

Elated by this experience and the opportunity to put perspective on our lives, we left our rental car in Caen and took the train to Paris where we were to spend a few days before flying home. Over the weekend we ran low on money and found there was no bank open where we could get a cash advance on our credit card. We did some sight-seeing, walking around the city and taking a bus to see the Arc d'Triomph where we found a pleasant cafe and ate our last dinner before running out of money. For the remainder of our time there, we subsisted on French bread and Coca Cola.

On September 27, we flew out of Charles de Gaulle Airport for an uneventful trip home. All together, it was a very educational and meaningful journey. We came home relaxed and invigorated. (Some years later, we had the occasion to board and visit the *Missouri* when the battleship was stationed in New York. To see where the final surrender of Japan had been signed was another significant occasion for us.)

I ran for my fifth term in the Senate in 1978 and my sixth in 1980. Although I always enjoyed the work of campaigning and learned something new and educational during my visits with people, I had another most unusual and unforgettable experience while campaigning in Bennington. There, I visited stores and homes as I had done in previous elections. As I went into one store, the Oasis, I had to walk by several teenagers who were sitting on the steps smoking. I instantly recognized the odor of marijuana.

I entered the store, noticing an interesting display of different style pipes and other paraphernalia such as spoons and measuring instruments. At that moment, a gentleman appeared from behind a curtain. I introduced myself as Madeline Harwood, a candidate for the Vermont Senate.

As I offered one of my fliers, he refused it, saying there was no solicitation allowed in the store and told me I could leave.

I just wanted you to have one of my fliers, I responded.

You are not welcome here, came the reply.

Disturbed that we had laws banning the possession or use of marijuana, yet still had places that would promote its illegal use by selling such paraphernalia, I looked into the possibility of introducing a bill that would ban the sale or purchase of drug paraphernalia when the new session started. Upon checking with the Legislative Council, I learned that there was a model bill that had passed in several states and that, most importantly, it had also withstood the test of the courts.

I introduced the bill and it was sent to the Health and Welfare Committee, of which I was chairman again. I thought this was going to be an easy process, but, much to my surprise, I soon found there were many groups in opposition, including some of my own committee members!

Several weeks of testimony followed. This included some members who wanted to see marijuana legalized for medicinal use so as to ease the reaction to chemotherapy. While the argument was made that smoking cannabis would reduce chemo-induced nausea, we were able to show evidence of other anti-nausea alternatives. Eventually, after much discussion and debate, we were able to get the Drug Paraphernalia bill passed in the Senate.

Even so, when it reached the House Health and Welfare Committee, it met with even stronger opposition. That committee had spent the entire session working on a bill that would place a cap on hospital expenditures. In time, the "Maxi-Cap" bill came before my committee. When I asked Gretchen Morse, who was chairman of the House Health and Welfare Committee about the progress of the Drug Paraphernalia bill, she replied that they might get to it later. That was not encouraging news as the session was nearing the end.

A few weeks later, it appeared my bill wasn't going to be considered. One day Gretchen approached me regarding her Maxi-Cap bill, and I told her we "might get to it later."

But that is an important bill; we have worked on it all session, she protested.

So is the drug paraphernalia bill, I countered, adding we also had worked long and hard on it.

In fact, our committee did work on her bill, and we came up with a proposed solution to the hospital cost problem. It was to establish a Hospital Data Council that would meet with hospital personnel and review their income and expenditures and make suggestions and recommendations as to where they might make cuts or do things differently to effect cost savings. This process would then allow the two parties to come to an agreement on hospital budgets.

However, we held up final action on it until she had "voted out" the drug bill. Then we addressed her bill; as a result of our recommendations for a different solution, a Committee of Conference (composed of three members from our respective committees) was set in motion to settle the differences in the House and Senate versions. The result was to establish the Hospital Data Council in 1983; it was in effect until 1996 when it transitioned into the Public Oversight Commission (POC) due to various other changes in administrative bodies.[1]

---

[1] *The establishment of the HDC (Title 18, Section 1952) was a good example of how changes in our statutes occur. From 1983 to 1992 the five-person board made decisions but with the Reform Act of 1992 creating a Health Care Authority (HCA), the membership changed some and it became an advisory board that presented findings to the HCA (Title 18 Section 9452). When the HCA disappeared in 1996 and became a division in the Department of Banking, Insurance, Securities, and Health Care Administration, the POC was established (Section 9407 of Title 18) with a different breadth of duties and changed board membership.*

Over the years, there have been many many revisions to Vermont's various statutes, indicating just how complex and involved law-making really is. The layers upon layers of revisions and amendments, have caused legislators to work hard to understand them all in order to proceed with new bills and laws.

My drug bill also became law (Title 18, VSA Sections 4475 -4478) in 1983 and is still in effect (with a few amendments added in 1999). In an article which appeared in the October 20, 1991 issue of the *Vermont Sunday Magazine*, Tzaims Luksus of Bennington, who happened to be the owner of the store I had visited, stated: "It was a new darkness (in reference to the investigation of sales at the Oasis and the subsequent closing of the store). People like Madeline Harwood felt it was their role to discipline the people of this state."

The bills we need to pass are not always the most popular ones. I had never before used my influence with the chair of another committee to get a bill passed. But I was learning that there are times when such actions are necessary.

This was a type of politics that some are more adept at than others, i.e., the wielding of power. I was more comfortable with the concept of public service and doing what I felt was good for the people of our state by doing my homework and proceeding according to established procedures. I was not of the "power politics" persuasion. I tried to do things on a reasonable basis even when the system seemed to weigh down at times. But when push came to shove, I was offended that someone thought their bill was important and mine was not. That one instance of being tough stands out in my memory, although I can't say that I really enjoyed giving "tit for tat."

Of course, I made the acquaintance of some who enjoyed wielding power as well as being public servants. But as I also eventually learned, there was a new brand of politicians who got into politics because they really enjoyed power and where it would take them. I saw this more on a national level than in Vermont. Interestingly, I also saw some people enter our Legislature for that very reason and then eventually become great public servants. Government service is like that — full of surprises, educational, and sometimes downright nitty gritty. I may have been an old-fashioned conservative and a lady, but I could play that game when I had to.

The issue of drugs was one of those situations. It had always been an important issue that concerned me greatly as a nurse, mother, community member, and legislator. This was a decade before the highly visible "war on drugs" so it wasn't as well known an issue in Vermont at that time. But my medical training and my experience on those national committees as well as the state medical auxiliary made me aware of the dangers that illicit drug use presents to society.

The bills I supported did not make me popular with some, but I am proud to have done what I felt was in the best interest of the health and welfare of all Vermonters, especially our youth. Young people are vulnerable to peer pressure and the use of drugs offered an easy way out of their problems. I thought it was important that teenagers learn how to handle their problems without resorting to feel-good drugs. After all, how could they become responsible adults if they didn't learn to manage their issues when they had the support of their families and others who cared about them.

As adults, they certainly would be on their own and would require their own inner resources to confront life's problems. If they didn't develop those resources when young, they would not be well equipped to deal with the everyday frustrations of life. If they began to use drugs early on, I felt certain that there was a serious danger that they would continue to do so.

There was, and still is, no doubt in my mind that drugs are addictive and can lead to further trouble. The brave parent who testified about his loss helped to convince me (and others) of that. I felt, and still feel, that strong marijuana, alcohol, and other drug legislation is the only way to prevent more tragedies. If the ban on drug paraphernalia made some unhappy, that was okay by me, and I chuckled to read the article about my "disciplining" the people of this state. (I felt similarly about alcohol use by eighteen-year old teenagers, which put me in direct opposition to fellow Republican Governor Richard Snelling, but I will get to that story a bit later.)

I often was referred to in the newspapers as "one of the most conservative senators in Vermont," which I was. However, my stand on making drug use, pushing, and sales (including sales of drug paraphernalia) illegal and a criminal offense (with possibilities of fines and imprisonment) was rooted in a preventive mode, not a purely reactive one — as it seemed to people like the store owner who had a vested interest in selling pipes and such.

By penalizing and punishing the pushers or anyone who sold illicit drugs or equipment, we were really aiming for prevention of addiction and more problems. I think that history has borne out that prevention is really a progressive concept; and to my way of thinking, making it hard to get away with introducing people to drugs just made common sense. One of the reasons we had included a possibility of jail time as a penalty for selling was to allow the authorities time to check out the backgrounds of persons and to see if they were major pushers. Harsher penalties for pushers was part of a preventive strategy, also. Jail time and a stiff fine could be strong deterrents to those who just wanted to make a "fast buck" on the drug trade.

Of course, educating young people was also a prevention strategy that became accepted practice in the late 1980s and the 1990s. Such education was not limited to the dangers of illicit drug use and the penalties, however. Part of education was to teach facts like the tremendous number of chemicals in substances like marijuana (over 400 chemicals in addition to the main ingredient THC, the mood-altering chemical in cannabis) and what was known about how such chemicals might affect the human body and mind. It was the harmful effects, from memory problems to psychological dependence, that concerned us.

When our committee dealt with complex and emotionally-charged issues like making marijuana use or the sale of drug paraphernalia a criminal offense, we really had to became experts on the issue, or at least as informed as possible. The process of hearing testimony from both the public and professionals helped in this regard. (And that included the opposition as well.) This was generally hard work that entailed a great deal of homework, too, but I found our legislators very dedicated to the job.

This, I think, held true for all kinds of issues that came before the various committees in the Senate. While one senator could not possibly become totally informed on each issue, the system of committees and reporting bills really did work to help us all become informed enough to vote intelligently on bills that might become our laws (or amendments to existing laws). Although I did not always agree on every outcome of a vote, I do think that the system generally works admirably well in Vermont.

The early 1980s were exciting times on the national front of politics, too. The national campaign of 1980 was an unusual one for us in that it split Doc's and my usual agreement on Republican candidates. George Bush was in Vermont on a campaign swing early in the year. Ronald Reagan was also an announced candidate. As a National Committee Woman, it didn't seem advisable to take sides at such an early date. Moreover, Doc, who had been a longtime supporter of Ronald Reagan, agreed to be his finance chairman in the state of Vermont.

When George Bush later returned to Vermont, his workers and campaign manager Jim Baker asked me to announce my support for Mr. Bush. After due consideration, I decided he was the one I wanted to see elected president. Stewart Smith of Rutland, who was Vermont Republican National Committee Man, also decided to support Bush, so we became co-chairs of the Bush campaign in Vermont.

The duties were very time consuming. Candidate Bush made several trips to Vermont, usually in conjunction with visits to other New England states. Stewart and I were responsible for meeting him at airports and escorting him to the assigned appointments. Barbara Bush visited Vermont on another occasion so we were responsible for taking her around as well.

One day Stewart and I met Mr. Bush at the Burlington Airport and prepared to drive him to Montpelier for a meeting. Stewart was a Buick dealer and had a new car to transport the candidate. He asked me to do the chauffeuring so he and George could sit in the back seat and visit. I was also in on the conversation, but Stewart felt he could concentrate better if he wasn't driving!

Returning to Burlington, I rode on the bus with George, and Stewart drove his new car home. Spirits were high, and we were all so full of optimism that it made campaigning fun.

The fact that Doc was Finance Chair for Reagan, however, caused quite a stir. Doc and I were comfortable with our positions, but the media and others found it newsworthy and in at least one case a cause for not trusting me! If a call came for Doc from the Reagan Headquarters and he was not in, they would not leave a message with me!

The Reagan Committee was very strong in Vermont. When the State Convention was held in May to elect the National Committee Man and

Woman for the ensuing four years, they replaced Stewart. I was allowed to continue — I assumed because of Doc. Neither Stewart nor I was elected as a delegate or an alternate, however. The "winner takes all" rule prevailed. Vermont Republicans were supporting Reagan in this election, which meant Bush supporters were out.

The National Republican Convention was held in Detroit that year from July 14 to 17. I attended as a Committee Woman and Doc went with me as was his custom. We stayed with the Vermont delegates, who as usual, were housed a distance away. This time we stayed in Windsor, Canada, and were taken by bus each day to the convention site.

Congressman John Rhodes of Arizona served as chairman of the Convention. The usual speeches were delivered by leaders of the party, including my friend from Texas, Ann Armstrong, who was the first woman to serve as Ambassador to Great Britain.

It was a foregone conclusion that Ronald Reagan would be the nominee for President, but the question of who would be his running mate added some excitement to the proceedings.

Stewart Smith, who was filling his Committee Man term, and I received an invitation to meet with George and Barbara Bush in their hotel suite the afternoon prior to the Reagan announcement. He wanted to thank us for all we had done for him. "Without your devotion, we wouldn't be here today," George told us.

It isn't over yet, is it, I asked him in a hopeful tone.

He confided that it was doubtful from what he was hearing that he would get the nod for vice president.

I asked if there was anything we could do to help at that late hour, not wanting to give up.

He said he was afraid not and that he and Barbara planned to go to Maine for a short rest when it was over.

We thanked him for calling us to his hotel and left on this rather sad, personal note.

That night the Vermont delegation was seated in the front row at the convention. We believed we would have to wait until the next night to learn who the candidate for VP was and that we would have to endure many speeches. But as the night wore on, rumors began circulate about the choice for VP and a certain excitement began to be felt. Being in the front row gave us better access to the media as they walked by. At one point, a reporter told us the nominee was considering President Ford. Later, we heard it would be Howard Baker.

At about eleven thirty, Governor Snelling, who was one of our delegates, felt sure it would be Ford. He was tired and went to his room, feeling his wish was about to be fulfilled. In the meantime, Stewart, feeling very disappointed, decided to go to the parking lot and wait in the bus for the ride back to the hotel.

We were all taken by surprise when Ronald Reagan suddenly appeared at the podium. When he was introduced, the entire delegation broke into cheers. Once the group quieted, he said:

> Delegates to this convention, ladies and gentlemen, and those of you who are viewing, I know that I am breaking with precedent to come here tonight, and I assure you at this late hour, I am not going to give you my acceptance address tonight. I will wait for the scheduled time.
>
> But in watching the television at the hotel and seeing the rumors that were going around and the gossip that was taking place here, I felt that it was necessary to break the tradition, just as probably in this campaign we are going to break with tradition a lot of times.

He then told of his discussions with President Ford and Betty, and with party leaders and his decision to "advance the schedule a little bit."

> And I talked with a man we all know and a man who was a candidate, a man who has great experience in government — and a man who told me he can enthusiastically support the platform across the board. I have asked, and I am recommending to this convention, that tomorrow when the session reconvenes that George Bush be nominated as Vice President of the United States.
>
> I have only one more thing to say. It is past the witching hour. It is late. God bless you. Good night, and we will see you tomorrow night. Thank you very much.

The great suspense was over. The convention erupted in cheers.

And what a glorious moment for the Harwoods! Doc and I got the best of two worlds. He got Ronald Reagan and I got George Bush. Peace in the Harwood house at last!

Doc and I both worked for my re-election and the Reagan-Bush team. With the fall 1980 elections over, the Republican National Committee once again had a friend in the White House. That meant we would be invited to a reception followed by an appearance from the President and Mrs. Reagan. We looked forward to these occasions as we had enjoyed such past occasions and the mingling of the President and First Lady with members of the committee. President Reagan did not let us down. He gave an inspiring talk and we very much enjoyed our reward for working for the party.

In 1982, I received a great personal honor from President Reagan when he appointed me to serve on the President's Committee on Mental Retardation. I had been a member of the board for the Mount Laurel School for the Mentally Retarded in Manchester for many years so I was familiar with some of the issues facing the committee.

Doc and Madeline with the "two dummies" as Madeline irreverently calls the two cardboard cutouts of their favorite presidents. With the Reagan-Bush team, there was peace in the Harwood House.

There were twenty-one members on the committee — lawyers, doctors, a governor's wife, college professors, and many people with varying interests in mental retardation. We met four times a year for two or three days each time. It was a hard working group of professionals trying to make life better for some of our less fortunate citizens.

We had staff support for our subcommittees who worked long hours in an effort to establish some policy positions on different mental-health needs. I was assigned to the subcommittee on prevention, which was chaired by Dr. Lee Christoferson, a North Dakota neurosurgeon. I found the work very stimulating and rewarding.

After much serious study, we produced a prototype booklet to be distributed to doctors' offices, clinics, and planned parenthood groups. This was an attempt to reach women, warning them against drinking and smoking during pregnancy. (Today, the dangers to the fetus are well known, including low birth weight and fetal alcohol syndrome among others; but back then, this was new ground.) The entire committee felt the publication was excellent. But first it had to be approved by certain administrative agencies, deputies, and others in a chain of command before it could be published for circulation.

It was discouraging to learn that it was rejected as were some of our other efforts. To have worked so hard and for so long with such obviously dedicated and talented people and to have such excellent projects meet such a fate was a terrible and deflating blow.

Nevertheless, we continued to work on various issues. We attended the Special Skiing Olympics in Salt Lake City and saw how mentally retarded youngsters of all ages could enjoy the various competitions on snow and the good it did for their spirits and confidence. Such experiences helped us to gain further insight as to what programs could work.

In fact, we gathered one year in San Francisco where we visited some excellent health-care institutions that had good programs. We considered the issue of de-institutionalization and studied the alternatives. But the committee was divided in its opinion regarding de-institutionalization of all mentally retarded people so we didn't come to a consensus during my term. Such major issues took time before progress could be made.

We had also tried to alert the public to the connection between lead poisoning and mental retardation, but it appeared that we failed in that, too, as it went nowhere at that time. As a result of some of these failures, after serving for six years on the committee, I felt that these committees entailed a great expense to the taxpayer (for travel, room and board, a full-time staff, and each member's $100 a day stipend while meeting) yet accomplished very little in concrete programs or policy.

The committee assignment was most interesting, but in the end, it was a huge disappointment not to see anything enacted due to the bureaucratic procedures that negated our work. Today, the validity of the prevention initiatives we suggested are all accepted practice as is de-institutionalization. But, it took many years for our suggestions to become public policy. Another lesson learned — sometimes the wheels turn so slowly as to seem worthless even to a political veteran.

The 1982 Senate election was more difficult for me. I had an opponent Harvey Carter, who was a lawyer and had served in the Vermont House as a Republican before he had switched parties. I had not felt his campaign was too much of a challenge until the election results showed that I had won by only thirty-five votes. It is probable that my work on the drug paraphernalia bill, which had been highly publicized, had cost me some votes.

Naturally, Harvey called for a recount to be held. That made it necessary for me to hire a lawyer to represent me at the December 2 recount. There was great suspense until the final tally showed that I had picked up an additional twelve votes. I was about to start my thirteenth year in the Vermont Senate in January 1983.

In 1983, I was elected to serve on the Site Committee for the 1984 Republican National Convention. We selected Dallas and met there in June to visit the various facilities. Doc went with me. As I was leaving for a meeting one day, he said he was going to see if he could attend a local Rotary meeting. That seemed like a good idea as he always seemed bored when I attended meetings.

When I returned, however, I found he had not gone because he had felt a discomfort in his chest. Concerned, I suggested calling the desk and asking if there was a house physician who could take a look at him. Instead, he told me to take him to the Parkland Memorial Hospital.

When I asked why there, he replied, if it was good enough for President Kennedy, it was good enough for him.

I couldn't believe my conservative husband's thinking, but there was no talking him out of it. He was, after all, a patriot first and a Republican second. We hailed a taxi and upon arriving at 4 p.m., Doc was ushered into the Emergency Room. I was sent to the waiting room.

After an hour, I tried to get taken to Doc but was told I could not see him. As I sat waiting (no reading material was available), many patients were admitted. One girl with shackles on her ankles came in screaming. The police brought in a man who had been badly beaten. It was a real horror story watching all the emergencies arriving. Finally, at 7 p.m., I was allowed to see Doc in a side room. The doctor attending him was waiting for reports on tests they had taken.

By 11 p.m. the doctor had decided to admit him. He called a taxi to take me to the hotel and offered to go to the waiting room with me, telling me he didn't want me waiting there alone. As we reached the ER area, the police were bringing in a man on a stretcher. He was bleeding badly. "Are you all right," the solicitous doctor inquired.

"Oh yes," I answered, "I saw much worse while waiting earlier."

After another wait, we learned that the taxi driver had arrived and then left without me because he didn't dare come in to get me for fear his cab might be damaged in such a rough area. The doctor then took me back to my hotel.

Doc was discharged ten days later. (My meetings had ended and arrangements were made for me to stay in a private home until Doc could travel.) The doctors didn't find anything seriously wrong with Doc, but they did make sure oxygen was on the plane for his return to Vermont. Fortunately, it was not needed and he made a good recovery.

Doc finally retired on December 7, 1983. He was just a month shy of his seventieth birthday and had put in forty-five years of service as a family doctor, including thirty-eight years in Manchester, four in the army, and one each in the towns of South Royalton, Brandon, and Whitingham. He certainly had earned a rest from his labors on behalf of others, but he was not one to take retirement as a time of being "put out to pasture." I thought I might retire also and we would go to Florida for the winters, but as I soon learned, Doc had other ideas.

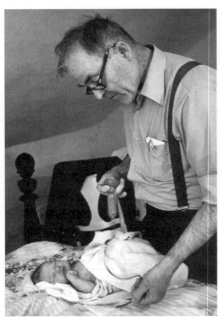

Doc clearing mucous from a baby's throat on his last home delivery. (Roth)

Being sworn into the House, 1985

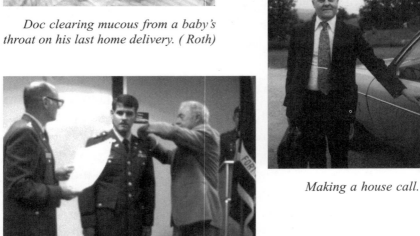

Making a house call.

Left, Doc placing Major insignia on son Rick.

Chapter Fourteen

Two Harwoods in the House

While Doc was still actively practicing medicine, he was always interested in politics and my activities and was very supportive of my efforts. He usually accompanied me on various trips and enjoyed the national conventions as much as I did, although he could be bored at times when I was at meetings. He himself had served several terms as an alternate delegate to the Republican National Conventions and was elected a delegate to the 1984 convention. Sometimes, though, I went on trips alone, such as when they were for events for women only or when he couldn't get away. Once he retired, however, he was eager to join me on any trip he could. I am sure that my experiences and enthusiasm also encouraged his further participation.

In January 1984, Republican women from the northeast region of the country were invited to attend a White House briefing to be held February 3, 1984. It was most informative with Vice President Bush and several cabinet secretaries, including Secretary of Health and Human Services Margaret Heckler, speaking to us and then taking questions.

Following this program, we went to the White House for a luncheon with President and Mrs. Reagan. Each legislator was given a small envelope and instructed to pass it to the hostess at the door. My envelope held a card indicating I was to go to table nine (by the Lincoln Portrait). My seat was at the right of President Reagan. What an honor! (Nancy was seated at another table, as were Vice President and Mrs. Bush, thus dividing the honors.)

We had place cards, beautifully inscribed with the presidential seal. I asked the President if he would sign his card for me, and he said he would be honored to.

We all watched attentively as he was served first. When he lifted his fork to start eating, we followed suit. The menu included: Watercress Soup, Cheese Twists, Paupiettes of Sole in Curry, Rice with Mushrooms, Macedoine of Vegetables, Lemon Mousse, Strawberry Grand Marnier, and Grand Cru Chenin Blanc 1981. Each course was followed by finger bowls. Once again, we watched the President as he approached the finger bowl.

"Do you know what that leaf floating in your bowl is," he asked me.

I told him I thought it looked like a leaf from a Martha Washington Geranium.

"Squeeze it. It has a nice aroma," he replied.

I gently reached in and tried to do as he suggested with one hand.

"Oh, get in there with both hands," he said with gusto.

I told him I didn't want to damage it as I thought I might take it home and slip it. He laughed and my leaf floated on unharmed.

There was lively conversation during lunch. The President spoke of his concerns regarding the invasion of Granada. He told us the hardest thing he ever had to do was to inform a parent of the loss of a son in war. Tears filled his eyes as he spoke of one such incident.

Following dinner, we were all invited to have our pictures taken with the President and Mrs. Reagan. Having had lunch with him, I thanked him and said, "Mr. President, I wish you would give me your formula for looking so young. I'm nowhere near your age, and I'm looking worn out."

He put his arm around Nancy and said, "Nancy wraps me up every night." President Reagan always seemed to have a charming answer.

That was one of the many more pleasant highlights of my years serving on various Republican committees. The 1984 convention in Dallas was another one. As a National Committee Woman I had been on the site committee but had less responsibilities for the actual convention. Instead, I enjoyed watching Doc do all the work as he was a delegate again and had been elected to serve on the Platform Committee.

The year 1984 was not to be all fun for me, however. Harvey Carter, who was originally from Bennington, had moved his law practice to Manchester and had become better known in the Northshire. He ran again for the Senate, and this time I lost to him. Maybe fourteen years in the Senate was enough, I thought.

Perhaps I took this defeat somewhat philosophically because Doc had decided to run for the House and had won. We went to Montpelier to spend the winter of 1985, this time with Doc doing the honors. His father had served a term in the house in 1931, representing the town of Rupert. I think Doc felt a certain pride in having a male Harwood carry on this tradition. Of course, he was also interested in the position as he had been participating in party politics for many years now.

During the summer of 1985, we took another memorable vacation trip. This time we went by Amtrak to the West Coast. We stopped in Albuquerque, New Mexico to visit our good friends Chaplain Rowland Adams and his wife Dora. Next we visited Joyce and George Wenger in Santa Barbara. They gave us a grand tour of the area, and we enjoyed catching up and sharing memories of the times we had spent together, including a good laugh over my gun-slinging roommate.

Our next stop was Washington State to visit Rick and Jan. Rick, who was now an army nurse practitioner, had time off and took us to many interesting sites, including Victoria, British Columbia, to see the Butchart Gardens. It was the most beautiful spot I had ever visited! What a glorious and fun trip to see family and friends and so much of our magnificent country. And what a delight to be on a real vacation.

Doc served in the House again for the 1986 session, and we returned to Montpelier for the winter (we still traveled back to Manchester on most weekends). Although he enjoyed it, he decided not to run again. So the summer of 1986 found us celebrating our fiftieth wedding anniversary without any concerns for duties other than enjoying ourselves.

Our entire family gathered on July 4, 1986, for the renewal of our wedding vows. My sister Charlotte and Doc's brother Clarence stood up with us once again. The ceremony took place in the little chapel of the Manchester Congregational Church, where we had been worshipping with our family since 1945. Reverend Paul Douglas, the minister who had performed the ceremony fifty years earlier, participated in the service along with our Pastor, Reverend Jerry Hevey.

The chapel was full with our children and their children and many friends and relatives, including my sister Evelyn and brother John. (My two other brothers had died a few years prior as had Doc's brother Raymond.) A reception followed in the church parlor with many friends present. Then a dinner party followed at the Masonic Lodge. It was a truly wonderful day and a more elaborate occasion than the day we were married!

That summer, we bought a used nineteen-foot travel trailer and large secondhand Ford station wagon to pull it. We planned to go to Florida for the winter and thought it would make sense to take our things with us and camp on the way. The entire operation turned out to be far more complicated than we had anticipated, however,

We left home the day before Christmas 1986 and drove by way of Pennsylvania. There we got caught in sleet and went into a skid that frightened both of us. We skirted the Capitol in heavy rain between 5

Clarence, Doc, Madeline, and Charlotte at 50th Wedding Anniversary.

and 6 p.m., which meant horrendous traffic, and finally reached our son Cliff's home in North Carolina at midnight.

After our overnight stay with his family, we continued on our journey, staying at campsites on the way. Many times we found ourselves in situations that required backing up the trailer. It was not a simple task! Finally, we reached our destination, a camp area near Disneyland in Davenport, Florida. What relief to be settled at last in the sunshine state.

Not too long after our arrival, however, I awoke one morning with a bad cold. Doc had gotten up and taken the dog for her walk. When he returned, he tried to tell me something, but I could not understand a word he was saying. At first I thought it was something wrong with me, but then I realized he was having a stroke.

I took him to the hospital where he stayed for four days and his speech cleared up, $5,000 later. He was allowed to return to the park on January 28. Fortunately, the rest of our two months there were enjoyable and relaxing.

We drove home by way of Texas so we could visit Jan and Rick, who had been reassigned to Fort Hood. That was a long hard trip. Too many things to remember in hitching the trailer for hauling.

The next year I was packing to go to Florida when Doc announced, "I don't want to die in Florida."

"Is that a message, Doc?" I queried.

We didn't go to Florida, and the next spring we sold the trailer.

In July 1988, I was asked to recruit a candidate for Representative from the Northshire area to run against the incumbent Democrat Robert Stannard. That proved difficult as no one would agree to run. I was finally persuaded to run for the office myself.

After I announced on July 26 that I would be a candidate for the House, the following letter appeared in the *Vermont News Guide*, a Manchester newspaper.

I was surprised to hear of Madeline Harwood's announcement of her candidacy for the Vermont House covering the Manchester-Dorset area.

After her defeat in her Senate race in 1984 at the hands of two Democrats, Jane Gardner and Harvey Carter, the *Manchester Journal* reported:

"Mrs. Harwood said she doubted she would run again for public office. 'I'm getting too old,' she said."

While I oppose age discrimination at any level, I think that Mrs. Harwood owes an explanation of her statements of 1984.

The job of a legislator requires a high level of energy to endure the rough and tumble of a legislative session, not to mention the weekly travel to and from Montpelier. It is essential that our elected representative vigorously and energetically represents our interests in Montpelier. We must also elect our legislators on the basis of their qualifications and abilities, instead of either how long they have lived in the area or their relative personal popularity in the community.

Very truly yours,
Bradley Myerson

Mr. Myerson was the chairman of the Democratic Party in Manchester. On August 3, in response to his letter, the following appeared in the letters to the editor of the *Manchester Journal*.

I would like to introduce Bradley Myerson to Madeline Harwood, for apparently he does not know her.

As a former legislator and member of several boards for ten years, I have known Madeline for many years and can vouch for her ability and integrity. She will be loyal to her constituents and not turn on them following election for political gain of committee appointments.

Former Senator Harwood knows well the route to Montpelier for she has traveled it for 14 years while representing Bennington County. She knows well the legislative process for she served on two Senate committees each session and was chairman of Health and Welfare for several terms; therefore she knows the job requirements.

Reports from Montpelier of Supreme Court members, the Education Department, and the inability of the legislature to come to grips with important problems, show there is certainly a great need for good Vermont mature thinking, hard work, and sound judgment. Madeline Harwood would contribute all of that.

Eugene A. Bond
Dorset

This letter was followed by several others in support of my candidacy. Excerpts from two follow:

. . . my first thought was how fortunate we are to have a person of her character, experience, knowledge, and most particularly, her boundless energy who is willing to run for office. I can't think of many around here who can match her in many of these qualities . . .
                    Paul Buzzell, Manchester

When you elect her to the Vermont Legislature this fall, you will know that you have done your share to promote good government in our state, as well as in your home town . . .
                    Lawrence Harrington

I also wrote a reply of my own, stating:

My campaign committee is grateful to the Democratic Town Chairman for his letter regarding my candidacy to the Vermont House. Also, I greatly appreciate my friends for their letters of support. The other writer's letter was worth a thousand dollars [Myerson] toward my campaign.

My energy level is such that I extend a challenge to the Democrat Chairman to play 27 holes of golf at the Manchester Country Club, pulling our own carts . . .   I may have to swing the club more but would look forward to the game.

On September 14, I defeated Robert Stannard, receiving the most votes of all four candidates in the primary. The General Election results were also gratifying. I returned to Montpelier where I served two busy sessions in the Vermont House (1989 and 1990).

For years I had been saying that members of the Senate worked twice as hard as those in the House. Nothing that I saw in the House changed my mind. House members served on only one committee compared with a senator's two.

With more members on those committees, however, (our state Constitution calls for 150 representatives), there were more opinions to be considered, and it was even more difficult to come to a consensus and it often took longer. Used to the greater workload of a senator, with one committee meeting in the morning and another in the afternoon, I felt that less was accomplished. I found that rather amusing in view of the fact that I had been questioned for my energy level. I was also gratified that I easily had the energy to carry on. I was, after all, seventy-four years of age.

For my first term in the House, I served on the Municipal Corporation and Elections Committee. It dealt with issues affecting towns: charter changes, dumps and their locations, problems concerning town government, and of course election results and challenges. We were the watch dog over elections as well as changes concerning local and state elections.

My return to Montpelier in January 1989 was marred by a late month call from Rick's wife Jan who phoned to tell us he was in the army hospital. They thought he had acute appendicitis and would operate in the morning.

Following the surgery, Rick called us to say his problem turned out to be a growth on the large colon, but he would know more in a few days. He called again to tell us that the growth was malignant and that there was involvement of the lymph nodes, but they thought they had gotten all of it. The oncologist would be seeing him, and he would keep us informed.

Needless to say, our hearts sank as we realized the danger he was in. Rick was so optimistic each time he called; trying to reassure us — and I thought himself — that he would be all right once they gave him chemotherapy.

But Rick was the in-charge nurse in the Hypertension and Diabetics Department in the hospital. He knew the circumstances regarding his illness. In spite of his condition, he continued working for over a year. Finally, he was given a medical discharge and retired as a Major.

We went to Texas to visit Rick and his family in mid-December 1989. While we were there, the doctors discovered a brain tumor for which Rick received radiation. Rick and Jan insisted that we stay over and spend Christmas with them.

This was to be Rick's last Christmas. He left us on April 9, 1990, at the age of forty. It was a devastating time for the Harwood family. The loss of any family member is difficult — over the years we had experienced the deaths of our parents and siblings and the sadness that follows

Doc, Madeline, Rick, Janice and Seth.

— but the loss of a child is just too painful for words. Our faith in God and support of friends sustained us during a period of unbelievable grief.

Deciding that keeping busy would be good for us, I campaigned one more time the following fall. I was re-elected to the House in the November 1990 elections. This time the Speaker of the House appointed me to the Committee on Highways and Transportation. We dealt with problems concerning highways, bridges, seat belts, auto and boat registrations, bike safety, bicycle paths, and other related issues. It proved to be yet another educational experience.

While serving in the House in the session of 1992, I had to take a week off the first of March to have surgery. I had torn the muscles of my left shoulder when removing old shrubbery at our home in Manchester. I wore a sling for several weeks after but was able to return to my duties at the Statehouse.

Doc and I were staying at the Days Inn in Montpelier directly across the street from the Statehouse at this time. Our room was on the fourth floor. At 7 a.m. on March 11, Doc looked out the window and wondered aloud as to where the water on the side street by the post office was coming from. There was no water to be seen on the Main Street so I suggested that maybe a water main had broken somewhere. But while eating breakfast in the dining room on the first floor, one of the legislators told us that there was an ice jam in the river and that the water was coming up.

Sure enough, we went back to our room, only to see the water rise in front of the Inn. We thought we were safe where we were and were watching people leave their flooded cars to walk knee-deep through the water, when someone pounded on our door. It was an employee ordering us to evacuate as the wall of the Inn didn't appear to be safe.

I grabbed my pocketbook, threw my cape over my shoulder, and Doc picked up our poodle Suzie. He was about to put his rubbers on, but the anxious employee told him there was no time. We were to hurry and follow him as the electrical power was off and he had a flashlight to show us the way down the stairs. Once we reached the lobby, we were escorted to higher ground along with several others.

Officers and rescue personnel were busy trying to keep people moving across the bridge to the other side of the river. We were told to proceed to the Grand Union parking lot where we would be picked up and taken to shelter at the Vermont College.

While we were getting these orders to move, Doc spied our car getting flooded in the Inn's parking lot. He said he was going to get the AAA garage to get it out and quickly disappeared with Suzie. I had no choice but to follow the crowd to the lot.

It began to rain hard, but no buses showed up to take people to the shelter so some started walking up the hill toward the college. I decided to wait for Doc as I was worried about him. He finally appeared, telling me it was too late for the car. By the time he reached the AAA garage, they, too, were flooded.

One of the legislators drove by and gave us a ride to the college. By then it was full of excited school children from Bennington who had come to Montpelier to visit the legislature. No seats were available for us.

Senator Carlson of Arlington came to the shelter and got us and two other legislators and took us to her apartment nearby. We spent the day watching accounts of the flood on television. We saw boat rescues in the streets and photos of the ruined cars at the Inn lot. We spent the night with our considerate hostess, and the next day Doc was allowed to return to our room to get his heart medicine.

Many businesses suffered great damage. The ice jam at the railroad bridge, which had caused this mess, was finally removed by a wrecker's crane dropping a 26-foot I-beam, like a pile driver, to break up the ice.

Fortunately, the water did not reach the Statehouse. Legislators who could reach the building carried on. Others arrived the following day. It was business as usual despite the need for emergency disaster assistance. Ironically, I had once worked on such measures (on the Civil Defense Committee), never dreaming they would be necessary while we were serving in the capitol. Another lesson learned about the work legislators do.

Doc's health had always been a concern to me. He had suffered a major heart attack (in 1972) and two strokes. With Governor Snelling's sudden death in 1991, I was more aware of how fragile life can be. I decided not to run again for the House after my term was up in 1992. I felt the time had come to give up the stress and strain of politics and journeying to Montpelier each winter for enjoying our remaining years together in Manchester.

I had served for fourteen years in the Senate and four in the House. I was happy to have worked for my constituents and our state, but now I felt it was time to concentrate on Doc and family once again. People often asked me if I missed being in the legislature, and I would answer that "I missed the people but not the political process," which was strenuous work. At age seventy-eight I was finally ready to retire.

During my tenure in Montpelier, it was my privilege to work with several Vermont governors. Deane C. Davis was one of the older governors to serve. We got to know him when he was campaigning in 1968 with his delightful wife Marjorie and we had lunch together. He was governor from 1969-1972 and did much for environmental causes in Vermont (including initiating Green-Up Day) and was instrumental in garnering support for Act 250, the state's pioneering environmental land-use law. To return Vermont to a sound fiscal basis, he realized the state needed to generate more revenue and so he argued for and won the Vermont sales tax, which was three percent at that time and helped to pay for the mounting costs of welfare. He also reorganized state government into a cabinet system. These initiatives gave the legislature plenty of work during his term in office.

Governor Philip Hoff, the first Democrat to be elected governor since the Civil War, served as a member of my Health and Welfare Committee when he became a senator after having served as governor (1964-1968). He was a most valuable member of the committee. I also had the honor of serving in the Senate when Thomas Salmon, another Democrat, was governor (1973-76). He continued the environmental work begun by Davis and also accomplished a property-tax relief program. He led the way to making the property tax more progressive by using state revenue-sharing money and land-gains tax funds to refund local taxpayers part of their property tax assessment according to an income-level scale. He also became a fiscal conservative during the mid-1970s recession, adopting a more prudent spending policy which I supported.

Democrat Madeleine Kunin, served as lieutenant governor from 1979-83. She was the second woman to hold that position in Vermont [Republican Consuelo Bailey was first in 1955] and thus presided over the Senate during those years. She was elected governor, Vermont's first female governor, following Governor Richard Snelling's decision not to run in 1984 and served three terms, 1985 through 1990.

Although she did much to further the cause of women in politics and appointed many women to high positions in state government, I did not approve of all her programs which I felt led to a fiscal deficit. However, I did get a kick out of the fact that when she presided over the Senate, which she did most capably, there were two Madelines/Madeleines in the Senate who were both married to doctors, were both left handed, and each had four children (three boys and a girl). The difference was the spelling of our first names and our politics: she was a liberal Democrat and I a conservative Republican. Because we respected each other, however, we worked well together.

Richard Snelling, a Republican, was the governor I admired most. He had served on the Vermont State Committee with me for several years. I always admired his ability to express himself. He also served with distinction as a member of the Vermont House representing Chittenden County. When Ralph Foote ran for governor, Dick ran for lieutenant governor. They both spent the night in our home while campaigning in Manchester. Dick brought his sleeping bag, prepared to sleep on the floor if necessary!

Dancing with Richard Snelling during an Octoberfest event.

When Dick ran for governor in 1976, I worked on his campaign and for his re-election in 1978, 1980 and 1982. I was very happy to see him return to an unprecedented fifth term as our governor in 1991. In fact, I was assigned the same House seat he had once occupied when serving in the House.

I felt his "don't spend it if you haven't got it" policy was very necessary after the excessive spending of the Kunin years. Vermont was in an economic recession at that time (as was the rest of the East). True to his style, Dick plunged into getting the state back on an even keel — fiscal restraint and considered expenditures were the order of the day. When it came to hard decisions, Dick was ready with a logical outline, carefully explaining what was needed. As a true conservative, I heartily approved of his measures.

My admiration and appreciation for his hard work and leadership did not stem from always agreeing with him, however. When I was chairman of the Senate Health and Welfare Committee, he had often called me into his office to discuss his health-care concerns. Once, he wanted me to listen to some officials from a national health group in an effort to solicit my support for the Maxi-Cap bill. But at that time, I did not feel it was necessary to dictate to hospitals what their expenditures should be. I was also a member of the State of Vermont Health Policy Council. Our mission was to help control health-care costs, not to set them. So my committee came up with the aforementioned Hospital Data Council which, although it was not exactly what the governor wished, was signed into law by him anyway. He was a fair man I thought.

Another time, the teenage drinking age came up.[1] He felt strongly that it should be legal for a teenager to be able to possess alcohol or beer and drink at age eighteen if he or she so wished. Dick knew I opposed him on that. There are often times when eighteen-year-olds are still in high school. I felt approval of their drinking would make it too inviting for older students to furnish beer to the younger ones. I also felt we should not make college drinking so inviting.

"Madeline, do you mean to tell me that an eighteen-year-old can get married today, conceive a child tonight, sign a contract to buy a car or house tomorrow and not be allowed to drink at his or her wedding?" he asked me.

"Gosh, Dick, I would hope he would be sober when doing all of the things you have outlined," I answered.

Tim Haywood, Dick's deputy, burst into laughter but Dick just stood there looking very serious. He took his causes to heart, as did I. But I also could not resist an opportunity to make a point.

When serving as governor, Dick held open house in his office each morning from eight to nine-thirty. This was a great opportunity to have

---

[1]*Vermont went to an age 18 age of majority law in 1971. It survived challenges to raise the legal right to drink part of it to 21 until 1985. That year, due to changes in federal policy, the state of Vermont returned to the 21 drinking age in order to maintain its federal funding of highway programs, while retaining the age 18 age of majority for voting and legal contracts.*

a formal or informal chat with him. I am sure he enjoyed the all-business conversations best. But many times we would hear his laughter as we entered through the door.

While he could be very serious, Dick also enjoyed a good time and a joke. While Barbara did not seem to like the noisy atmosphere of the National Conventions, Dick did, marching and dancing around the hall during the joyous celebrations. I once had a delightful time dancing with him when he attended an October Fest while campaigning in Bennington.

When Dick was campaigning and marching in parades, his wife Barbara could always be found marching at his side, waving and smiling. Everyone loved Barbara. She had a great interest in the Vermont State House and was instrumental in restoring it to its original style. I had also served with her during my last term as a trustee on the Champlain College Board. She had served as chairman of the Vermont School Boards Association and was most knowledgeable about educational needs.

Having this close and friendly relationship with the Snellings, it meant a great deal to us when he attended a parade in Newbury. My sister Evelyn Clark had contacted many descendants of General Jacob Bayley to march in that parade. Governor Snelling was invited to lead the parade, which was held in August 1991.

As we gathered at 6 p.m. to march, it began raining. By the time we reached the reviewing stand, the heavens had opened wide. Everyone got soaked. After it was over, I went looking for Dick to thank him for attending, but by the time I reached the parking area he was gone.

Two days later on August 13, I received a shocking phone call from our daughter Cathy. She told me she had heard on the news that Governor Snelling had been found dead by his pool. At that point I reached a state of disbelief. It couldn't be so; he had been so active, so full of life. It was a loss Doc and I felt both personally and for our state.

Governor Snelling was eulogized as a leader who did a superior job as he took on the great difficulties of the recession (*Rutland Herald*) and as a great governor "who continued to take risks, to follow his heart, to protect and serve the Vermont he loved" (*Burlington Free Press*). In an outpouring of love and respect, over 2,000 Vermonters traveled to Montpelier to attend his service. He had served just 220 days of his term but was widely regarded for having "successfully rallied Vermonters to his vision of responsible government, helping to renew faith in state government as Vermont entered its third century."[2]

Just a few days after his death, Vermont celebrated its statehood Bicentennial. Governor Howard Dean[3] asked for a moment of silence to honor Dick Snelling, and Barbara Snelling[4] spoke briefly. Sister Marie Candon, the Commissioner of Health and Welfare at that time, said she knew everything was in good order in heaven with Dick there. It was just what we needed to hear — an observation that was so appropriate that it brought relief and release in the good laugh we all enjoyed.

On Columbus Day weekend, 1992, I had a phone call from the local post office, telling me to come quickly; something had happened to Doc.

In a state of panic, I drove through heavy traffic, arriving just as they were putting him into the ambulance. He was perspiring profusely and was very pale, although he had recovered consciousness. He was taken to the doctor's office and then to the hospital in Bennington where he remained for several days before being transferred to Burlington Medical Center for evaluation. He was later released with a monitor to check his heartbeat.

Six months later, following a shower, he felt dizzy and sat on the toilet seat to dry himself. A short while later, I found him passed out. His face was flushed and I was unable to detect a pulse or get any response by shaking him.

Fearing he had died, I phoned the Rescue Squad and a physician. While waiting I pulled him to the floor, striking his head on the heater unit. Thinking I had fractured his skull, I started giving him CPR, opening the airway by tilting his head, then compressing his chest several

---

[2] *William Doyle,* The Vermont Political Tradition, *page 231.*

[3] *Lieutenant Governor Howard Dean became governor in August 1991 and was still serving in the year 2000.*

[4] *Barbara was elected lieutenant governor for two terms, serving 1993-1996. She withdrew from the race for governor after suffering a stroke in 1996 but was elected state senator from Chittenden County later that year.*

times. As I went to force air into his lungs, he took a breath, looked up, and asked what I was doing!

At about that moment, Police Chief Wessner and an officer arrived and administered oxygen until the Rescue Squad got there.

Once he was revived, they suggested getting him on the stretcher and to the hospital. At that point, Doc really came to and said, "Help me up and to my chair in the living room; we have to talk this over."

He was helped to the chair and I threw a blanket over him. "I'm all right," he insisted as they administered oxygen.

Dr. Michl, who had also arrived, examined him. He advised Doc to let the Rescue Squad take him to the hospital for a checkup and observation. But Doc said that there was no need of that, that I could drive him there. He had no idea of the state I was in.

He went by ambulance, and I drove down a little later — after I had stopped shaking and felt it was safe to drive. Relieved that he was alive and okay, I told him I had had ten years taken off my life.

Doc returned home, three days later, revived and ready to go. He must have nine lives, I thought to myself, all the while saying many grateful prayers that he had been watched over once again. In time, I got over my scare. My concern about Doc also served to distract me from missing the November 1992 elections. In fact, it made me more certain that I had made the right choice to focus on us. I also stepped down from the Vermont National Committee Woman position, choosing not to run again. [Madeline ranked eighth in seniority on the National Committee at this time.]

It was good to be in our own house, just the two of us now. No Statehouse to return to. Just a golf course for me and some occasional Republican Party events for both of us and, of course, family to see from time to time. We really could enjoy life, even if it was less full now without constant political activity.

But that is as it should be, I thought. We had lost much, first with our son Rick and then our friend Dick Snelling. Now it was time to savor our life together and enjoy ourselves and the years we had left. Of course, Doc never retired from having an opinion. He continued to write letters to the editor, enjoying the opportunity to express himself in this way.

Doc, son Clifford, grandson Clifford, and great-grandson Clifford Harwood.

Debbie and Cathy

Cliff and Helen

Granddaughter Edith Ward

Seth, Jan, Rick

Emily, David, Abby, Heidi and Roger

Chapter Fifteen

A Reflection

When first married in 1936, I needed to keep quiet about my marital status and my first pregnancy. There were "barriers" to women doing certain things in those days just because we were women. In the 1930s, 1940s, and 1950s, it was still very much a man's world.

For me, however, that all began to change with the war and the three years Clifford was away. Living on my own with fear and worry was not easy, but I knew others were experiencing the same thing. That was some help and consolation and kept me from feeling sorry for myself. Being totally responsible for the well-being of two children as well as for myself taught me to be resourceful and self-reliant and most importantly to make my own decisions. It was during wartime that I learned to manage on my own, as did many other American women.

The Women's Lib movement of the 1960s and 1970s is most often credited for the change in women's roles and rights, but I really think it started much earlier. It may have been a subtle transition with my generation, but it was significant because it provided a foundation for much of the progress made during the latter half of the twentieth century. Because men and women of my generation experienced other roles during the war — men went from being workers to soldiers and women from homemakers to workers — there was more openness to new roles afterward. Of course not everyone of my generation was receptive to change. But some were, and I often wonder if it wasn't their experiences during the war that helped both men and women to see more possibilities for themselves afterward and to explore new roles, whether in the workplace, the home, or in government.

During our first years in Manchester after the war, I was learning some important lessons about tolerance. Doc could put up with much more than I could. Things may have bothered him, but he took a pragmatic approach, wishing to choose his battles wisely. For him, that meant you didn't start off in a new town by making enemies, even if it meant letting someone get away with taking your rug and candlesticks. If we went out to eat and the food or service was bad, he would never complain. He didn't wish to "rock the boat."

I was more willing and ready to state my mind. Doc had been right that there were some people who would take advantage of you. Not everyone, but certainly some. I bristled at the injustice of it, whether it was kids fooling with my shoelaces in church or movers taking one piece of furniture at a time so as to charge us more. Gradually, my way of handling such episodes was to speak out or to put my foot down — to demand my money back for an inferior product or to dare to tell Clifford that I didn't want that house under any conditions.

It may seem a little thing today, but back then speaking to your husband like that was a radical thing to do. However, I had learned to have a little more self-expression, something I think I got from making my own decisions when he was away those three years.

Looking back now, I can see that although it bothered me at times, I realized that Doc's more carefree and casual approach to life had its merits. Our children never got murdered in New York City. They never suffered a terrible injury, although they had their share of bumps and bruises. By Doc being so willing to let them attempt things, they were learning to be their own persons. Some of that was true for me, too. His expectations of all of us, himself included, were very high.

His willingness to let the children learn by trial and error occurred at a time when "self-empowerment" was not yet in vogue. So, being a mother, I saw it as a source of constant worry and did not always appreciate such experiential lessons. I think it was partly habit on his part that Doc permitted the children to make their own way, to do things as he had done without the fetters of a mother's apron strings. But he also would say things that told me he was weighing the situation to determine what would be in their best interest.

Doc observed the situation as a doctor was trained to do and then made his decision based on his own experience, learning, and intuition. When it came to swimming out into the lake, he figured it would be better for Cliff's self esteem to try to reach his goal. For Doc, to attempt something was worth the risk. Allowing Rick to make a cross-country motorcycle trip was another such decision. Obviously, I was more concerned about Cliff's possibly drowning or Rick's getting lost or hurt, or worse, killed.

Occasionally, Doc's expectations backfired. His insistence that anything was possible, that a new driver could handle a dirt road proved more eventful than even he had contemplated. He learned what most parents learn at some point — that it is sometimes impossible not to overreact to things our kids do. Grabbing the wheel may have wrecked another car, but it also taught Doc to understand something of what I was going through, and why I was more apt to worry or be more protective.

For me personally, Doc's high expectations proved life changing. The attitude that anything was possible offset my own inclination to be fearful. In our earlier years, I was not yet a truly "liberated" woman who considered herself an equal to him or to men in general. I took care of the children, our home, and my husband as was expected of a woman at that time. I answered Doc's every call at the office and did the accounts.

I was proud to use my abilities and skills, but I also labored under an impossible ideal — in my case that both the family and the patient could come first. And that I could perfectly follow my mother's injunction, "Whatever you do, do with your might; for things done in halves are never done right."

I was good at juggling diverse responsibilities, and I really enjoyed being a nurse and helping Doc and his patients. But the demands that two full-time jobs placed upon me had created a difficult situation. As we had more children, I began to resent being called in to the office for someone else's needs when my own baby was nursing and needed me. My instincts were telling me that my family should come first, not the patients. This tension caused such bad headaches that I was convinced I had a brain tumor.

In retrospect, I can see that this illness allowed me to stop and take stock of the situation. It gave me an opportunity to learn that I didn't have to do everything one-hundred percent. I had learned that much could be accomplished with hard work, but now I woke up to the fact that sometimes family had to come first. Part-time nursing, learning to play golf, and spending more time with my growing family proved to be a good antidote to my former hard working, perfectionist ways. I enjoyed our children's years of growing up and attending their many sports events, concerts, and other activities. I was proud of each of them.

My experience taught me that true liberation meant being able to make my own choices. It wasn't just high expectations that mattered, it was what one did with them.

I was also beginning to feel a stirring for public life. My feelings about war and my volunteer work with the Republican Party during the 1950s and 1960s made me realize that there were many issues about which I cared deeply. The 1964 National Convention was an exciting initiation for me, and by 1968 I was ready to seek elective office. I was ready to put my convictions into practice. It was another turning point in my life — and the start of another very satisfying career.

I first chose nursing because my mother's experience had indicated that it was an occupation that could make a difference. Being a legislator wasn't an option presented to women when I graduated from high school in 1932. Thanks to changing times and Doc's support, however, becoming a state senator was a possibility for me in 1968. I now saw a similar potential for making a difference in politics and welcomed the opportunity to campaign in hopes of getting to Montpelier.

At age fifty-five, becoming a freshman state senator was a humbling, yet challenging experience. But the realization that serving in the legislature could be productive and beneficial — that we did in fact labor for the public good — was truly inspiring. Once I saw that, I was hooked.

On Golf and Politics

When I was in the hospital for migraines in 1954 and the doctor advised me to take up tennis or golf, I warned my first teacher that I was left handed. Unmoved and unconcerned, he told me that I should be able to play right handed since I had "such a strong left arm from doing everything left handed." Thinking a golf pro would surely know what he was talking about, I started lessons playing with the right-handed club he loaned me. This proved so awkward, however, that when I was in New York with Doc, I went to a pawn shop and bought a used set of left-handed clubs.

At my next lesson, I showed the pro that I could actually swing through and hit the ball with a left-handed club. At that point, he decided I didn't need any more lessons but insisted I buy the right-handed set of odd-numbered clubs from which he had taken the seven iron for my lessons. Being ignorant of the ways of golf, I paid him. Without too much success, I spent the rest of the summer trying to play with my left-handed clubs. (It appeared the pro had no desire to teach left-handed people.)

The following year I joined the Equinox Country Club and again struggled on my own. My second year there, the golf pro told me I should take lessons. He also told me I should be able to play better if I played right-handed. I took several lessons. Part way through the summer, I found I was not enjoying the game. I told Doc I was going to go back to left-handed playing, but he told me I shouldn't do that as it might hurt the pro's feelings. So I continued to struggle along, wondering all the while if my feelings counted for anything.

The next year I took lessons from John Lombardy, the pro at the Ekwanok Country Club. He saw my difficulty and asked why I was trying to play right handed when in fact I was left handed. What a relief when he said I didn't have to play right handed! My game improved as did my enjoyment. I have played with clubs for lefties ever since, and I even won a few tournaments when I became the best of the worst of them!

My "progress" was uneven as I didn't have much time for lessons and practice. Once I hit the ball over a nearby barn and it landed in a farmer's dump truck (an unplayable lie). So much for the head tucked and concentration. Another time I arrived late from a meeting and since I had left my shoes in Doc's car, I joined my group at the second tee in my socks. Shoeless, I drove the ball the longest and straightest I ever had on that hole.

I never became a great golfer but I did get down to a handicap of 28. I also found it relaxing to be on the course where I could forget my cares as I worked on "mastering the game." By allowing me to lose myself in the concentration it demands, golf served its purpose for recreation. It also gave me the opportunity to have fun and to laugh at myself and socialize with friends. And to bemoan the high cost of country-club memberships forty-six years later!

As with my introduction to golf, there were struggles in my life and a learning process that didn't always go smoothly. But I persevered and survived. Eventually I even made progress. That went for my life in politics, too.

Politics can be viewed as a game. Or it can be viewed as public service. Or public service with games played. I think each person will have his or her own unique view on this. I see public service as trying to solve life's problems by looking at them as interesting challenges. The challenge is to resolve the issues in a way that will benefit all people, or if that is not possible at least the majority.

That is the way the legislature operates most of the time. Senators and representatives react to some problem and create a bill to address it; then they try to convince their peers to pass a statute (law) that will make government and/or life work better. In presenting a bill and arguing for or against it, legislators are ultimately working not only for their own constituents but for everyone in their state.

When I was out on the golf course, I didn't interrupt the game the time Clifford came running out to tell me I had a call from the White House and needed to come home right away. Much to everyone's surprise, I said I would finish the game first. I knew it was probably just a minor thing like needing my social security number (for screening me for some upcoming event there), and I let the matter wait — first things first.

We need to have our priorities straight. I think that is what I tried to do in life in general and in the legislature as well. I focused on the task at hand and gave it my best shot. Nurse, wife, mother, volunteer, golfer, and legislator — it was all interesting, challenging, and rewarding work.

Madeline, 1997

A Great Loss But Much to Celebrate

Regardless of the weather, it was Doc's habit to go out for the newspaper very early in the morning. As soon as he heard the truck drive up (about 4 a.m.), he would get up and walk down to the end of the driveway to get the paper that had been delivered to our box. In his later years, at my request, he would wake me when he got up. I wanted to be sure he got back okay and didn't fall in the snow or have a stroke. I could go back to sleep, knowing he was all right. Usually, after reading the paper in his chair in the living room, he would come back to bed.

Two doctors, Dr. Guerrero and Dr. Frost, were very attentive to Doc's medical needs. He had poor circulation in his legs and sometimes suffered so much pain that he could not walk. When he had trouble breathing, he would get up and read in his chair for hours. He still enjoyed attending Rotary and church, reading, and writing letters to the editor. He also still insisted on driving to the post office at 6 to 6:30 a.m. most mornings to mail something.

On February 24, 1995, when there was heavy wet snow on the ground and when he was gone too long, I called the police to ask if they would check on him. I learned that Doc had been in an accident and had been taken to the hospital in Bennington by our rescue squad. He had been unable to stop at an intersection and had hit another vehicle broadside. He had severe head injuries and was sent to Fletcher Allen in Burlington, where he had several surgeries for brain swelling. After his hospital stay, he went to a rehabilitation center. Then he came home for awhile, and I took care of him. But it didn't work out — his injuries were such that he had to go back to the hospital in Burlington. I sat by his bedside daily, staying at our son Roger's home nights. Roger checked on him daily, and our other children visited Doc frequently.

The day before he died, Doc seemed fine and was able to enjoy sitting up and talking with us, including Cliff who had come up from North Carolina. But during the night he took a turn for the worse and was placed on life support. He died on May 25, 1995, at age eighty-one.

Doc was the human being I most loved. Even though he qualified as an old-fashioned male when I married him, he always treated me as someone who could do anything. Doc taught me to drive at a time when few women of my generation learned to drive In fact, some never did. The man did the driving just as he earned the paycheck, ruled the roost, and told his wife what clothes to buy. Knowing how to drive made me more independent and confident. It came in handy during the war and when running for office. I got a lot of mileage out of changing my own flat tire during a campaign, too!

Doc and I were fortunate to find each other and to have each other's support and respect. We shared a love for family, community, and politics. His support of my role in public service made him my partner just as my work as a nurse made me his partner. I think being partners and supportive of one another was a key ingredient in our long and happy marriage. It was highly unusual for a man to be so supportive of a woman taking on such a nontraditional role as a run for office in those times. But that went with Doc's belief that I could do anything!

Doc not only encouraged me with words and moral support, he also put his "pocketbook" into my political efforts. When I lost to Jim Jeffords in 1974, we were in debt, but rather than turn to a party fundraiser to pay it off as people usually do, Doc insisted that we would do it ourselves. I took on a nursing job, working nights at the Odd Fellows Home in Ludlow to help. Even after that defeat and debt, he encouraged me to run for my old senate seat again.

The stereotypical "old-fashioned" man expected his wife to be at home for him, to take care of his children and his needs, and to support him in his job. Doc went beyond that — he also wanted me to be happy and to do what I enjoyed doing. He was not threatened by my emergence into my own person, nor did he mind my being in the political limelight. He always encouraged my involvement and that was a wonderful gift.

Only much later did I realize that he was also proud of me. It was in 1995, while he was in the hospital and a nurse was attending to his needs, that I overheard him telling her all about me. My first reaction was to tell him not to brag, but I held my tongue and let this final gift to me sink in.

I used to feel sorry for Mother Harwood because she didn't feel free to buy a hat or a dress without Father Harwood's approval. In our lifetime, Doc and I made the transition to being partners and a relationship based on mutual respect. You might say we were both liberated. Having seen life both ways, I can appreciate the change and progress we made.

Doc always saw the bright side of life, dismissing problems easily. As the selectmen said in a tribute to him, "No day was too long, no hour too late, or no weather so bad that Doc failed to answer a call for distress."

He never refused to make a house call, sometimes traveling over forty miles round-trip. Pay was never a consideration for Doc. He was always

Doc, Christmas 1994.

ready to help his fellow man or woman. When a patient would call him at 2 a.m. saying she needed sleeping pills, he would leave his warm bed and drive to the office to put out the medicine for this inconsiderate person who never paid her bill. Many were the times he would answer a call when he was ill himself.

I recall one home delivery many miles from our home. The father was so grateful for Doc's services that he offered to pay as soon as the baby was delivered (a charge of $35). Doc responded with, "Let's wait and see how many times I need to come."

When he returned to make his follow-up call, Doc was greeted by the husband who said, "Sorry Doc, you lost out. I had to use your money to make a payment on a tractor I needed." He never did pay the bill.

This did not bother Doc. He had fulfilled his obligation as a physician. Living up to the Hippocratic Oath was what was important to him. He had many "RFDs" (Rural Free Deliveries)! Upon retirement, he did not send out bills although there were thousands of dollars owed to him and we were by no means well off. He found joy in helping people and that was all the reward he needed. He was indeed a good human being.

A Full House

Our four children were another important part of our lives for which Doc and I were always thankful. We enjoyed our visits with them as we got older and getting to know our eight grandchildren and seven great-grandchildren. Doc and I loved each other, our family, the medical profession, and politics. That is a full house for which we both felt truly blessed.

After graduating from Champlain College, Rick went into the Air Force for four years and then to UVM for nurse's training to become an RN. He joined the army as a medical assistant and traveled to different stations before he and his wife Janice ended up in Texas with their son Seth. Rick had served in the military for seventeen years when he died in 1990. Janice and Seth still live in Texas; I see them once a year when they come up in the summer.

Roger graduated from UVM and then went to the University of Rhode Island where he studied pharmacy. He became a pharmacist at Mary Fletcher (now Fletcher Allen) in 1980 and is still there. He and his wife Heidi live in Burlington and have three children.

After the Navy, Cliff settled in North Carolina where he worked for Firestone Tire until retiring in 2000. He and his wife Helen have two boys and a girl and now have seven grandchildren. Cliff is still a Free Will Baptist minister.

Cathy graduated from Bates, worked for a while, married and settled in Burlington. Her daughter Debbie, graduated from UVM in 1992. Cathy now lives closest to me in Bennington.

Some of our family home for Thanksgiving

Manchester

Manchester was a delightful but smaller and quieter town when we first arrived in 1945. It had one dentist, three doctors, one lawyer, several churches, and two grocery stores. Those who needed food and were not able to go shopping could always call in an order which would be delivered to their homes. There were three post offices that served Manchester's 2,139 residents; one in Manchester Village, one at the Depot, and one at the Center. Manchester also had one bank, the Factory Point. Many times a dollar changed hands so often that it became worn before reaching the bank.

The Quality Restaurant and Hill's Restaurant took care of tourists and local citizens. One police officer, Munson Nelson, looked after the safety of the public. The road to Bromley Mountain was a dirt road. One could get stuck in the snow in winter and grounded in the mud come spring. Most of the large houses on "the Street" in Manchester Village were closed for the winter months as was the Equinox Hotel.

Tourists now find Manchester a shopping mecca that boasts many outlet and specialty stores, from newer names like Calvin Klein, J. Crew, and the Gap to the older establishments like Orvis Outfitters and the Orvis Fly Fishing School. There are restaurants to satisfy anyone's taste or pocketbook and a variety of food stores from gourmet to supermarket chain. A host of motels and inns offer luxurious accommodations. One does not have to search far to find a real estate office to answer the need for housing.

We have some additional religious denominations and greater diversity in our population now. We also have assisted-living facilities, housing for the elderly, low-income housing, a trailer park, and a new affordable housing project.

Our larger population of 3,737 is well served by a large police force (nine or ten officers), many lawyers, several doctors, and a well-trained Rescue Squad. When Doc started practicing, the local hearse served as an ambulance (with the undertaker the driver) to take people to the hospital in an emergency. Doc would ride with the patient when needed for something like an intravenous that had to be kept elevated. Today there are EMTs who attend to such emergencies and a specially equipped ambulance that can keep people alive with oxygen, defibrillator, and modern medicines.

There is an expanded Southern Vermont Arts Center with a large new addition; a new Civic Center which serves as home to the Vermont Symphony in summer and becomes an indoor skating rink in winter; an active historical society; and one of the best bookstores in the state at the Northshire. Hildene, Robert Todd Lincoln's restored summer home, is an historic mansion that draws over 50,000 visitors a year, and the Equinox has been beautifully renovated and operates year round now. Enhancing our cultural and recreational opportunities are nearby theaters at Dorset, Weston, and Williamstown along with winter playgrounds at Bromley, Magic, and Stratton.

Many have welcomed progress in Manchester, noting the town has historically embraced entrepreneurial opportunities. They would note that the town's population has grown slowly at about 30 additional residents annually for the last 55 years. Others vocally deplore the town's commercial success.

Success and growth have come with a price. One must be flexible to adjust to the many changes that have occurred. With the hustle and bustle of lively retail and tourist trades, there is traffic to be tolerated, crowded times at the supermarkets, and a steadily rising cost of living that includes higher taxes and housing costs. The Quality Restaurant and Ben Franklin Variety Store are gone (and greatly missed) as is the small-town feeling that came with knowing all your neighbors. The many small farms that once dotted the countryside are mostly gone (just two operating now), and Manchester has become more dependent upon tourism and shopping dollars from out of town as well as the second-home industry for its economic livelihood. There is a busy lumber supply/home center and a few small manufacturing concerns as well.

When the new Manchester Country Club opened in 1970, residents who wanted to join could buy a $100 share plus pay annual dues of about $250 to play. Since that time, a new deluxe clubhouse has been built and improvements to the course have been made in an effort to keep up with other clubs. The result is that the initiation fee has risen to $6,000, yearly dues to $955 (single) and there is now a $150 restaurant minimum and a similar $50 pro-shop assessment. (Guests of a member pay a $65 greens fee.)

The original intent of affordable golf membership has been lost as this is beyond the means of many. Just as leisurely walking for exercise has given way to riding in motorized carts to save time, so too, the ideal of making the game accessible to all has gone by the boards. Like so many other sports, the price has gone up as improvements have been made. For each change and advance, we often lose something in the name of "progress." That, too, is part of life today. That doesn't make change bad, but it does make it challenging to get it right.

Such changes have occurred throughout Vermont. Some — better education, health care, and other services — have come at a great price in the form of higher taxes. We are one of the highest per-capita taxed states, but that is also largely due to being one of the least populated states with under 600,000 people. Today, Vermonters struggle with issues related to rising taxes, better employment opportunities, preserving the environment and maintaining rural beauty. For all these challenges, however, Vermont is still a beautiful state. Although not immune to such problems and issues, Manchester is still a wonderful place to call home.

Life's Lessons

One of the most positive changes I have witnessed in my lifetime is that not too many men cannot vote for a woman now. We have gone beyond the kitchen! But as I learned, the kitchen also remains an important place. It is where we can nourish and nurture ourselves, our families, and each other. When we meet our neighbors or constituents around a table with a meal or a cup of coffee, we find our common concerns do more to unite us than our differences do to divide us. My "kitchen cabinets" also provided me with a lesson in how important it is for women to support women and the difference that makes.

I was surprised and amazed when my good friend Connie Bailey told me that she was supporting Jim Jeffords because I was a woman. She implied that the job of U.S. Representative was more than a woman

ortunately, women have proved themselves and that they
llenging positions. The role of women in government in
hanged for the better. More women are involved at all
levels   both as elected and appointed state officials. That means
better representation of Vermont's growing population. There is still
room for more improvement, however; as of this writing Vermonters
had yet to elect a female to represent the state in the U.S. Senate or
House.

When I entered the Vermont Senate in the 1969-1970 Biennium,
there were eighteen women in the House and three in the Senate. When
I left the House at the end of my 1991-92 term, those figures had risen
to forty-eight and seven respectively. In 1997-98, the numbers were
forty-six and twelve. To me that is progress. I don't think that view
makes me a liberal or a feminist, but it does make me proud that women
are interested in and seeking government positions where they can make
a difference.

Today that's possible for women and many others who once weren't
even in the game. That is real progress, not some here-today and gone-
tomorrow fad.

As I begin my eighty-seventh year, I am grateful for the goodness of
life and the potential for all human beings to grow, learn, and give something back. That is one of life's greatest blessings, and it helps to give
meaning to our time here. It is also a source of fulfillment and content-
ment. It made Doc and me happy that we could serve and help others
through medicine and politics.

I see life as a journey to be undertaken with love and laughter, responsibility and reflection. Its outcome is affected by who we are and
how we approach the journey. Realizing that we do have choices and
that we can listen to our hearts and act with compassion is an important
step. Giving it our best shot at any age is another, while seeking to make
a difference in some way is perhaps the most significant part of our
progress. It is what connects us to our fellow man in a lasting and meaningful way.

I say this with a keen appreciation for life's tough times, with empa-
thy for those who experience fear, pain, and loss. When our family home

burned down when I was away at nursing school, like so many victims I was in shock and felt lost and asked "Why Me?" When our son died, I asked, "Why?"

Now I see that such tragedies serve to teach us important lessons. I learned to appreciate things more when I realized they could all go up in smoke so quickly and at anytime. With the loss of our son, I came to see that difficulties and sorrows are a part of our shared human experience. I came to have greater understanding of what others go through and the importance of one's faith and the support of friends. I also came to know that calling on the Lord now and then provides a source of strength and realized the importance of a higher being for all people.

Some of us have more than our share of bad luck, accidents, illness or other misfortunes, yet despite those trials and tribulations, we learn to appreciate what we have and to move on. From misfortunes, problems, and sorrows, we learn the lessons of optimism and hope, of possibilities and opportunities. Of continually striving — of accepting that for every step we take forward, we often take a half-step backward but can, and must, help each other to keep going.

Nursing taught me to marvel at the birth process and the miracle of a perfect newborn. Life taught me to see the possibilities for that child and to accept the responsibilities that come with making sure that each tiny new being has a good chance at success.

Politics and good government do have an important role to play in this respect, as do the many helping professions and we ordinary human beings. I believe it is possible for all people to make a difference and that with vision, hard work, and a dose of compassion, we can work for better lives for everyone.

At my age, I do not miss the long grueling hours of government service (or the bullying of power politics at the federal level these days), but I do miss the many wonderful people I worked with in the legislature and on various committees. I continue to be thankful for my many experiences and the people who were part of them, especially the people who still greet me and tell me they remember when I was a legislator or when Doc made house calls. That is still fun, too, as has been sharing my memories and what I have learned.

Greeting George Bush.

The Harwood and Johnson twins (Doc delivered them), 1970. (Philip R. Jordan)

Another "Doc baby" Mary F. Mylott, 1970. (Aldo Merusi)

Gov. Deane Davis speaks at July 7,1970 festivities.

Hobnobbing with Carol and John Wu, 1974.

Last RNC, 1992, "I never did anything crazy like this hat before."

Postscript

The Community Remembers

by Karen Lorentz

During their long and productive lives, Madeline and Doc were often honored for their service to their community and state. Madeline mentioned some of these special occasions in passing — in her modesty, she was not one to dwell on them. In asking her about them, however, it became clear that such honors were a source of quiet pride and joy for both of them. A few of these special moments are included here to indicate the esteem and affection that so many felt for Doc and Madeline.

They are followed by stories told by others and shared here in the hope that you will enjoy knowing Madeline and Doc from another perspective. The contributors, whose names follow their stories, are representative of the many people who appreciated the Harwoods as good friends to their fellow man.

Esteemed Good Vermonters

Doc was still actively practicing medicine when the townspeople of Manchester chose to honor him for his first twenty-five years of service as a doctor. The selectmen designated the "Week of July 7, 1970, as Dr. Clifford B. Harwood Week" and the day "July 7 as Dr. Clifford B.

Harwood Day." Vermont Governor Deane C. Davis also issued a state proclamation designating "July 7 as Dr. Clifford B. Harwood Day."

On that day, the community turned out in force, and the Governor as well as town, school, and church officials, representatives of the 1300 babies he had delivered, and Madeline and Clarence recognized Doc for his services to state, town, fellow citizens, and family. John W. West, who served as the master of ceremonies, jokingly declared a moratorium on births that afternoon so that Dr. Harwood could be feted and not called out to a delivery! Madeline was honored on that day, too.

The 1970 Annual Report of Manchester was dedicated to Doc, praising him for his devotion to the children and the schools of the community as "evidenced by his service as School Director and as attending Doctor at athletic events, school clinics, and for school physical examinations." His and Madeline's many years of serving in various positions in the Republican Party on local, county, state, and national levels were also noted. But it was the statement by the selectmen that said it all: "No day was too long, no hour too late, or no weather so bad that Doc failed to answer a call of distress."

Thirteen years later, after he retired on December 7, 1983, the community threw a retirement party for Doc in early January. Feted in the press as well, Doc joked that he switched out of agriculture his first year at UVM because getting up at 4 a.m. "didn't appeal" to him. Beneath the drollery was the story of a passionate love affair with medicine, people, and politics. "Now," Doc told the press, "I can devote myself to my hobby — fundraising for the Republican Party."

Doc had been the top fundraiser in the county for many years. In fact, local committee members decided to initiate a plaque with the annual top fundraiser's name on it in recognition of Doc's efforts. He received the honor of being the first recipient.

Among numerous earlier awards, the Manchester School Board had recognized Doc for twelve years of service, and the Vermont State Medical Society bestowed honors and a medal upon him for his many years of service and for serving as its president. A new building that now houses the Manchester Health Services was named the Dr. Clifford B. Harwood facility when it was dedicated in 1996. This building is located across the street from the office where Doc practiced medicine for 38 years, a fitting reminder of a doctor who carried a black bag and made house calls and left his mark on the community with his caring and dedication.

Madeline was similarly honored on many occasions for her work with the Republican party and various other organizations, including the Woman of the Year bestowed in 1971 by the Bennington County Business and Professional Women's Association. She was frequently an honored guest and/or speaker, and she developed a repertoire of topics from the history of medicine to the need for good citizenship. Two very special awards, given in 1990 and 1991, recognize her for her life's work.

The Vermont Republican Woman of the Year award was given to Madeline at the June 2, 1990, Annual Meeting of the Vermont Federation of Republican Women. In addition to commending her for all her work as a volunteer on various boards and in Republican politics and state government, Madeline was hailed as:

> earning the recognition and respect in many more enduring ways than even these. She reaches out to teach and help newcomers. She encourages others who strive to improve the Green Mountain State and its government. A woman with credentials like Madeline's doesn't have to march in parades in the rain, come to meetings after long days in the State House to help others reach their goals, or give advice on organizing her community to one more political candidate. But she does all this and more, and that's why we are honoring her today. THANK YOU, MADELINE!!

Messages on this special day included congratulatory notes from George Bush, Peter Smith, Robert Stafford, John Easton, Jr, Sara Gear, Susan Auld, Susan Sweetser, Jeffrey Amestroy, Richard Snelling, Barbara Snelling, Mary Wing, and Jim Jeffords among other notable Republicans and friends. Their greetings praised Madeline for being a source of inspiration, a tireless worker, and a good role model, as well as for having a vision of a philosophical basis for the Republican Party.

The expressions of appreciation often echoed Jim Jeffords observation that, "Although the award suggests a year, those of us who have been in politics for years know that this could well be an award for decades of outstanding service."

Or as Mary Wing wrote, "As far as I'm concerned, you are the Republican Woman of EVERY year — this is a long overdue honor!!"

Pointing to the essence of good public service, Barbara Snelling included these words in her congratulations:

> You have been an inspiration for all Republican women — a real leader who has always been very knowledgeable on the issues and a strong worker for the party and for candidates. You have always been there for the good of the state and our nation.

Many women thanked Madeline for serving as a role model and friend as this message from Susan W. Sweetser so heartfeltly noted:

> Words are not adequate. Thank you so much for everything, especially for serving as a role model to me and many many other women. Your commitment to the Republican Party is second to none. Thank you for showing me the Republican way, for being my mentor, my teacher, my friend. Your example has been a warm, shining beacon in what has sometimes been a dark night. I so look forward to working with you for many years to come. Thank you.

On November 13, 1991, Madeline was awarded the first Richard A. Snelling Achievement Award. It was given for outstanding service in memory of Governor Snelling. It was the recognition that "meant the most" to her because Madeline so admired her friend and fellow politician and what he stood for. It was a fitting tribute to her own career and lifetime of public service.

There were many times when Madeline or Doc or both were guests of honor for some event that also served as a fundraiser. Most often this occurred within Republican Party circles, but one special tribute was a benefit for The March of Dimes. The well-attended dinner was held at the Equinox and featured a good-natured "Roast" of the Harwoods. The MC, Madeline's sister Charlotte, and Doc's brother Clarence did

He continued in the vein of the evening's numerous tributes to the Harwoods, noting: "These are real people, with real sincerity. Throughout their entire lives, they really cared. They are unique . . . people who help because they care. What impresses me most . . . is the diversity of interest." He went on to describe Madeline's interest in education and serving on two college boards as a trustee, adding, "I admire her sense of focus and leadership." He also read messages from President Reagan, Governor Madeleine Kunin, Vermont Representative James Jeffords, and Vermont Republican Committee Chairman Patrick Garahan.

As on so many similar occasions, the sentiments expressed that night shared a common thread of thanking the Harwoods for selfless dedication and hard work on behalf of the various groups and causes to which they devoted their considerable attention and talents.

Roasting and Toasting

The following stories were told or written by various people — personal friends, former patients, fellow politicians, co-workers, and neighbors. We start with John Wu and Joyce Wenger who both served in Republican circles with Madeline but, who along with their spouses, became lifelong friends with both Madeline and Doc.

Communists and Cows,
Integrity, Independence, and Loyalty

I met Madeline and Doc through my work on the Windsor County Republican Committee and got to know them better when we worked on the state committee.

I am a Chinese American. I came to this country from what is now Communist China. My father had a saying that "the only way you ever wanted to deal with a Communist was if *they* were looking down the barrel of a gun and *your* hand was on the trigger." The Communists would let a son or daughter leave mainland China but not the whole family. My parents were not allowed to leave, but I was. I understand why Doc was against Communism because of what my family lived through. Our mistrust of Communists and our knowledge of the threat of Communism gave Doc and me a common bond. We understood each other and got along as a result.

Doc was very sincerely worried about the Communist threat, and history has proved him right. I think that having seen the atrocities he saw in World War II made him fear Communism. People today don't know what his generation saw and the real fear they lived with. The Soviet Union has since collapsed, and I am so glad Doc lived to see the Berlin Wall come down. My father wished to live to see Communism overthrown, but he was not so fortunate.

One time my wife Carol and I were visiting at their house. A truck pulled up and Madeline said two men were unloading wood; did Doc order any wood? Well, he hadn't so Madeline sent him outside to tell them they must have the wrong house. It turned out that Doc had helped the man's wife in a medical emergency years before, and the man hadn't been able to pay. He was so grateful that he never forgot Doc's kindness; now he was repaying him with wood.

You know Doc never charged people who could not pay — even when he was first starting out and needed the money himself. He was generous, and he didn't complain. He was happy to help people. People appreciated that, too.

One time Madeline was campaigning and was running late to get somewhere. A reporter was traveling with her. When Madeline saw a farmer's fence was open and the cows were getting out, she insisted on stopping and shooing the cows back in. The reporter was surprised by her actions and protested it would make them even later and might hurt Madeline. But Madeline told him that the farmer probably didn't know the gate had been left open. That was the way she was — thoughtful and helpful to others. That is the way they both were.

I was the executive director of the Republican State Committee when Madeline was in the three-way race with Jeffords and Burgess. You know her campaign was a volunteer effort. I told them that they needed an organization. Jeffords and Burgess had statewide-election experience and a professional campaign organization. But she and Doc said they didn't have that kind of money, but they had faith they could do it on a grassroots level.

I told them that they had to at least have professional radio and television ads. I knew John Goodman who had helped defeat the Rockefeller nephew for governor in West Virginia. I said he would probably do Madeline's media publicity at a reasonable cost just to get national campaign exposure.

So that is how she got the theme song *Someone to Believe In*. She thought it was a little hokey, but she let it be played. It had a catchy tune and was very effective. (After she lost by a small margin, she used the theme *Someone to Believe In* on her next campaign for state senator.)

Madeline just had volunteer help. She kept her schedules on the side of their refrigerator with magnets. She did all her own driving. That was really incredible for a statewide campaign.

I would say, "But you have to do such and such." Doc would say they would do it themselves — it was amazing. "We have faith we can do it," he would tell me. I know it sounds incredible, but they really did.

When the campaign laws changed and you could no longer give corporate money directly to a candidate, someone in the party wanted me to do something, but I said no because it would be illegal under the new rules. Some powerful people got mad at me, but Doc and Madeline stood by me. They were very loyal and that meant a great deal to me. Years later, the party was fined $800 and I was vindicated, but all those years in between they believed in me and that helped me when others didn't.

Do you know about what a wonderful fundraiser Doc was? He was amazing. If there was a $100-a-plate function and people could not afford that, Doc would ask for what they could afford. Then when several people had put in enough to cover a ticket, he would give one of them the ticket so they could attend the dinner. He was thoughtful like that.

When he was asking for money, he would explain to people why they should give. He would say that we need the money to support the Republican candidate so that such and such would happen. He treated people with the same respect for a small contribution as for a large one. I think that helped to make him so successful.

He never bullied or pressured anyone to give money, but he was the top fundraiser for many years. That was because he knew so many people — just think of all those babies he delivered and meeting them later as young adults! Even the town chairman [of the Manchester Republican Committee] Andy Shaw used to say the first person he met in this world was Doc. So many knew him because he took care of them. Think how much people loved him because he cared for them. So he didn't have to do a hard sell. He just asked people to give something to help the effort and to be part of the system

My favorite story is the Reagan and Bush campaigns. It made national news stories that Doc supported Reagan and Madeline, Bush. Everyone liked the ending when Bush got vice president so Madeline and Doc could both be happy.

The National Committee Woman position is a very prestigious position. It is an elective position that goes to a person who has been very active and loyal to the party and is held in high esteem. Madeline earned this honor and served for a long time — almost twenty years [1973-1992].

Madeline was like Doc. She was nice to work with; she was not pushy or a bully. But when she took a stand on something, she could dig her heels in. She did not let people push her around. Like the time she did not bow out in the three-way Congressional race. She could be tough in that sense — she was not a bully but she was not a wimp either.

You know Bennington, the town, is a Democratic stronghold. But they supported Madeline. *The people didn't just like Madeline, they loved her.*

Another thing Doc and Madeline did for Bennington County. They would help young people, teenagers and college kids, get interested in politics. They would speak to them to interest them and then see that they got to attend fundraisers and other events. They always made sure that Bennington County had its share of pages for the state and National Committee. Southern Vermont was well represented and Chittenden and Rutland Counties did not dominate these positions when Madeline was around. She would say, "Now it is Southern Vermont's turn" and dig in her heels until they got their fair share.

One time I was supposed to be doing some thing at the White House, but there was some glitch. Doc asked me how it was going, and I told him of the problem. He said, "Oh, I can help you."

I said, "Doc this is the White House; I don't think it's the same as how things work in Vermont." I really didn't think he could help.

The next day, Doc called me and told me it was all taken care of. I couldn't believe it. He thought nothing of it; it was just his way of helping people any time he could. They were very close friends with the Reagan and Bush families.

Doc and Madeline were like the Chinese. We are not openly demonstrative people. We do not show our feelings like Americans. Madeline and Doc did not boast about themselves or each other. They were modest like the Chinese are. I understand this. Their way was to do the work and not talk about it.

But Doc was very proud of Madeline — you could tell. And everyone respected them for their dedication and loyalty to the Republican Party and their work for the state.

John Wu

Mr. and Mrs. Republican

I was very into Republican Politics in California and was an officer in a group with 40,000 members. For the San Francisco Convention, we Southern California supporters of Goldwater had not been given tickets to the convention.

I met Madeline and told her about our problem. She spoke to Governor Keyser, and through him we were able to get some tickets from the Vermont people who were not using them. She would help you like that.

We were visiting Doc and Madeline and they took us to the Weston Country Store and introduced us to Vrest Orton. "What are we going to do about Madeline?" he asked me. He wanted me to try to change her mind and get her to support Reagan the year she supported Bush. Of course, I wouldn't do that. I knew that she had her reasons, just as I had mine.

Another time we were visiting them and attended a big Republican dinner at the Vermont Military College in Norwich. Doc had beat the bushes to sell tickets to this event. There were over 800 people there even though it was a stormy October night. There was a private reception and then after the dinner and before the program (U. N. Representative Jean Kirkpatrick was the speaker), Doc and Madeline walked down the center aisle and there was such an ovation — they were Mr. and Mrs. Republican.

When we stayed at their house, sometimes we would bring our family. Their kids would play with ours even though ours were younger. They were so nice to them. We could hear Clifford go out on calls many times during the night. One time he was up all night, but he still took us to see Fort Ticonderoga the next day. On the way, he stopped to see a patient.

Another time a friend whose husband was a very successful California doctor visited them with me. She was amazed to hear Doc go out during the night on calls. She couldn't believe it. This was long after doctors had stopped making housecalls!

After one particularly busy visit — going off to events, sightseeing and everything — we needed to get up and go to church with them on Sunday. This caused my husband to comment that visiting the Harwoods was more like work than a vacation because we did so much! Doc and Madeline were always energetic and hard working like that.

Joyce Wenger

Our Friends

We moved to Manchester Center on July 4, 1971. My husband Marshall had acquired *The Guide*, now known as *The Vermont News Guide*.

Our youngest son Christopher was six and suffered from asthma. I wanted to be sure there was medical help in town. I learned that there were two doctors, Dr. Harrigan, who was not taking any new patients, and Dr. Harwood. We contacted Dr. Harwood. He was wonderful. He went anywhere, anytime, and would treat people at home if they could not come to his office. He took great care of us.

He was also a fierce Republican. My husband is a Republican also, so we became friends and met his wife Madeline. There was instant rapport. We visited each other often. They took us to Republican happenings. When Madeline was a Representative they took us to the inauguration of Governor Snelling. I sat with Madeline in the House in Montpelier. It was great. We also drove with them to the inauguration of President Bush and spent three glorious days in Washington, doing lots of special things thanks to Madeline who was close to Bush.

Traveling with the Harwoods was not boring. They never stopped telling stories or remembering events. Among the most interesting were their remembrances of World War II when Doc was in Europe. We found out that after the war ended, Dr. Harwood and I were practically standing next to each other watching the victorious troops march down the Champs Elyses on July 14, 1945 (Bastille Day). After we discovered this "coincidence," Doc, as we called him, always mentioned the episode when introducing me to someone.

Now it is the year 2000. My husband and I are retired and celebrating our fiftieth anniversary, happy to have six healthy children and many grandchildren. But we still miss Doc, who passed away some years ago. He is fondly remembered by everyone. Bravely, Madeline goes on alone.

Hugette Peck

A "Patient" Remembers

I have three children; two were delivered by Dr. Harwood. Cathy Ann Lake was born in 1968 at the Bennington Hospital. Toby Charles Lake was born in Dr. Harwood's office on December 22, 1969. My mother and I caught the flu a few days after Toby was born. We were both flat on our back and trying to take turns taking care of the baby and Cathy who was just a year old. Dr.

Harwood came to check on us and the baby almost every day. Dr. Harwood was a life saver. He was the greatest. We all loved him.

Also, if it wasn't for Dr. Harwood, I would have lost the tip of a finger. My mother says that I got it shut in a door when I was about a year old. It was just hanging, but Dr. Harwood fixed it. The finger is slanted on the tip, but I still have it.

Ann Towsley

Caring & Compassion

It was the summer of 1961 or 62, and I was driving to Arlington with my family. Dr. Harwood's car was off to the side of the road. He had run out of gas, so I took him to Arlington to get some.

On Christmas Eve my three children were sick. He had church to go to and family but he came anyway. Two had to have shots. I asked him how much for the call. He said, "$4 — one good turn deserves another."

I couldn't believe that was all he was charging for a house call and two shots, but he never forgot a good deed. He was grateful.

He wasn't in the medical profession for the money. He was in it for the oath that doctors take. He cared for the people he treated.

I had five children in five years. We would go up in the evening and the boys sat on his lap. They thought he was their best buddy.

Gen Bell, his office nurse, was a rare individual. He wrote an article about her that was in the paper. He was so thoughtful.

I thought Madeline was the perfect Doctor's wife. She had compassion. I called her about my diabetic father and told her the problem. She said you need a doctor and to call Dr. Harrigan because Doc was out.

Doc was very well informed on everything. He had a lot of books and he read up on everything. He was a good citizen.

Before our Bicentennial in 1976 I suggested that we should display our flags on January 1 and it was in the newspaper. I drove around that day to see them. Doc Harwood's wasn't displayed, but he had seen me drive by. He called to tell me why it wasn't out (he had been away on a call and hadn't had a chance to display it). He was so patriotic that he took the time to explain that to me.

Our family and the whole town was blessed by the presence of both of them.

There is a saying, "I lived. I loved. I laughed." That was so true of both Doc and Madeline.

Alberta Harrington

A Couch for Doc
A Baby for the Children

We moved to Manchester in 1959 when we had four small children. Each day I took a walk with them down the street to get our mail. Dr. Harwood always went by and waved to us. The children looked forward to seeing this nice man go by and wave. When my son got in school, he came home with colds, chicken pox — all the childhood health problems. I remember he treated all four of them for $3 for an office call. They got to know him and trusted him, not only as a doctor but as a friend.

One year we moved to Sunderland. Our sixth child was born there on March 16, 1967. There was a winter storm so Dr. Harwood came early and stayed all night. The children got up to go to school and they saw him sleeping on our couch in the living room. They thought that was so funny, and they laughed and laughed. Then they came home from school to find a new baby girl in the house. They thought the doctor left a baby for them and they loved her, Robin Lee, so much.

They all loved him. Robin Lee and the others always remember Dr. Harwood. We will never forget his kindnesses and what a good doctor he was to us.

The Colvin Family,
Nella, Wally, Gladys, Priscilla, Foster Jr., Jim, Robin Lee

Thoughtfulness

Attendance at weekly divine worship was as important to Dr. Harwood as breathing. With his true tenor voice, he was a valued member of the choir, often slipping in late to his accustomed seat after having made a house call.

I think of a summer Sunday when the choir was on vacation. He had a house call to make, but he took time to come first to church. He sat near me in a rear pew for twenty minutes of the service. Then he rose to leave, handing me a clipping from the newspaper. It was a piece about one of his elderly patients. "Please see that she gets this when church is over," he whispered. "I thought she'd like an extra copy." And off he went.

Madeline has led an interesting life and a good one. She went from being a nurse who made $10 a month during training to sitting at the right hand of the president. She and Doc had strong beliefs and they worked hard for them. Her story is a piece of real Americana.

Phebe Ann Lewis

On the Golf Course

Madeline loves to play golf. She took her game seriously enough to improve but not too seriously that she didn't have fun and enjoy the game. She always liked to walk instead of using a motorized cart to get around.

Madeline has a great sense of humor, that dry Yankee wit and Vermont understatement. She likes to joke around. We have a good time together, and I enjoy her company. She is quite an accomplished person but most of all, she is a good friend and a wonderful person. It's pretty amazing at her age to be writing a book, but if anyone can do it, Madeline can.

Mary Lou Burditt

The Competition Remembers

I remember hearing Jim humming that catchy tune that was Madeline's campaign song in 1974. Once I heard him singing it in the shower, and I asked him whom he was going to vote for.

You know she almost beat him in that race. It was very close.

Liz Daley Jeffords

Powerful Decision Making

When Snelling was Governor and Madeline was a senator, there was a big issue about decoupling the state's income tax from the federal tax. As a CPA, I got a call to contact Madeline because she was undecided. She could be the vote to kill the bill to decouple.

We took her through the process and showed her a stack of books four feet high that represented the federal IRS income tax codes. We made a case that it was easier and simpler to use the "piggyback" (25 percent of the federal-income-tax due) formula for the state income-tax. We explained that it would be more work to decouple and to create another system for Vermont, but that it could be done. The trouble is we thought it would cost Vermont taxpayers more in the end. She listened to us and asked us to explain exactly how everything worked.

I think she was the swing vote. She went against her party and did what she thought was right for Vermonters. I was impressed by her willingness to tackle such a difficult and complex issue and to vote independent of a party line.

Dick Engel

Another Doctor Remembers

When I met Cliff Harwood, it was 1948. I had spent a year at Walter Reed as an intern and after military service had taken a fifth year as a surgical resident at Beaumont General. But I decided I wanted to get practical experience so I resigned my commission.

I was up in Vermont on vacation and knew of the Harwoods from medical school so I stopped in to see Cliff. He was desperate for someone to help. Dr. Campbell was in his 80s then but still active and another doctor was leaving so there was only Dr. Bashaw in Dorset and the two of them in Manchester. They were very busy. I went to work for Cliff for awhile and then had my own practice. I thought I might stay for three to five years but I stayed for fifty. I'm retired now, but occasionally I see a former patient pro bono or give aviation physicals.

Back in 1948 life was simpler. There were 35 working farms surrounding Manchester. There were fewer regulations. We didn't have medicines to treat things like hypertension. With no medicines to lower blood pressure, we saw a lot of weakened hearts and cardiac asthma. When there was fluid in the lungs, you were more or less in a holding action. Today, we have more potent diuretics. Your practice back then was more dedication and common sense. There were definite limitations on what you could do. You had to anticipate the patient's needs and know your own medical limitations.

Then sulfa drugs came along and then penicillin and later, tetracycline. It was the first broad spectrum antibiotic.

One day Cliff called to tell me that the family he had taken care of in the only brick house in the village at that time had discharged him. He said I should feel free to go there if I got a call. Cliff had prescribed tetracycline for the woman who had shingles. She had sent her chauffeur to the pharmacy for sixteen capsules and when she found out the bill was $16 she was upset with Cliff. Back then a house call was $3, an office call was $2 and we charged 50 cents a mile beyond the town limits. People were surprised by the cost of the new medicines!

We had mechanical scales (for weighing people) that were based on levers. One patient told Cliff there was something wrong with his scale, so Cliff called the Department of Weights and Measures. They checked his scales and put state seals of approval on them. Then Cliff sent the man over to check my scales, too. He was thoughtful like that and was an unusually generous person.

Cliff always thought of how he could be helpful to others. He put his patients' welfare ahead of his own. One woman caught a ride with a milk truck so she came in at 6:30 a.m. for routine visits and he would accommodate her. He kept office hours at night, too. People would come in without appointments, and I would see his office full at nights. His light would still be on when I was on my way home from a movie.

He worked long hours and would go almost anywhere, anytime. He was easy going and put up with a lot. He always put his patients first and he never complained.

Dr. Frank Harrigan, Jr.

A "Doc Baby" Remembers

I am one of hundreds of Dr. Harwood babies, having been delivered "by Doc" in 1957.

I had an interest in politics from a very young age. When I reached adulthood, I was invited to join the Rotary Club of Manchester. Doc was a longtime member. I also became active in the local Republican Committee — Doc and Madeline were the mainstays of that group.

A few years ago I was asked to say a few words at a fundraising dinner of the Bennington County Republican Committee. Madeline was the guest of honor in recognition of her long service to the party. When thanking her for her leadership, dedication, and service to the party, I included some of the following remarks:

"There is no woman and hardly a man in Vermont who would not support her candidacy!"

So wrote a *Manchester Journal* columnist Bernice Graham in 1974, endorsing the woman we are honoring tonight. We honor Madeline Harwood for her outstanding service to the Republican Party and our State of Vermont.

Old timers around here might say Madeline was "from away." She was born and grew up in Newbury . . .

Her service to our party is legendary. Madeline was a delegate to the Republican National Convention in 1964, 1968, 1972, and 1976. She served on the Republican State Committee for years and was Vermont's Republican National Committee Woman from 1973-1992.

She was a Presidential Elector in 1976 and 1984, casting electoral votes for Ford and Dole and then Reagan and Bush.

There is a funny story in the 1980 election with Doc backing Reagan and Madeline supporting Bush. Locally, I think Bush prevailed, but Doc got the last laugh when Reagan won the nomination. It is widely assumed that Reagan chose Bush as his VP in order to bring peace to the Harwood household.

Madeline's seven terms in the Senate were interrupted when she sought the Republican Nomination for Vermont's seat in the U.S. Congress. It was 1974, the year the nation was fixated on the infamous Watergate scandal. Jim Jeffords of Rutland, John Burgess of Brattleboro, and Madeline all announced for the Republican Primary. We really had a lot of Republicans around back then — all south of Route 4, too!

Having not run in a statewide campaign before, Madeline had her work cut out for her. She took to the task like a fish to water. She even had commercials on the "Cronkite News" and "Hee-Haw."

By the time primary day arrived, Madeline was breathing down Jim Jeffords' neck and had left Jack Burgess in the dust. She finished second by 2200 votes — 5 percent behind Jeffords . . . Madeline returned to the Vermont Senate after the 1976 election and "retired" in 1984. Or so she may have thought.

When Doc Harwood stepped down from his term in the House, we found out that his former seatmate Robert Stannard who had been re-elected to represent the Northshire as a Republican was turned into a Democrat by none other than Ralph Wright. Needless to say this did not sit well with a lot of voters in Manchester. The county chair asked Madeline to find a good candidate to take back the seat that was rightfully Republican. As you know, not finding anyone, Madeline did it herself and carried the day decisively in 1988.

Her opponent came back in 1990 for another spanking. One of my favorite memories of this campaign was when her opponent's supporter suggested to the local paper that she might be too old and not have the energy. She handled this with characteristic grace and humor, challenging him to 18 holes of golf. Of course, she won . . . .

I recall that Doc enjoyed recounting his exploits as an automobile driver and how he had a hard time keeping his car on all four wheels. I think he tipped his car over on three or four separate occasions.

When he died, I was asked to be a bearer at his funeral. As I recall, there were five Republicans and one Democrat as bearers.

Elaine Nowrath wrote a wonderful tribute that appeared in the *Manchester Journal* . . . it would be nice to include it in the book. [It arrived three days earlier with Elaine's "happy to have it included" and follows.]

Andrew Shaw

The Quintessential Vermonter
Remembering Clifford B. Harwood, M.D.

My mother was not one to enjoy ill health. As a matter of fact, the total of her visits to Dr. Harwood's office could probably have been counted on the fingers of one hand, thumb excluded. Her association with him was as a friend rather than on a professional basis. They shared a lifelong faithful and active affiliation with the Congregational Church and the Republican Party, and the young doctor had quickly earned my mother's respect, admiration, and affection.

But it was in his physician's role that he was summoned by my mother one evening some 25 years ago, when she was stricken with a painful attack of severe indigestion. When none of my home remedies or consoling words succeeded in allaying her anxiety, the call went out for Dr. Harwood.

It was late in the evening and there was some delay since, as I recall, he was at a dinner meeting. In due time he arrived on the scene, cheerfully and with no evidence of regret at having his evening interrupted.

The immediate change in my mother's condition was only slightly less than miraculous. Whatever medication he administered, it was readily apparent that his reassuring presence was the real healing agent. Dr. Harwood was there (she would not have dreamed of calling him "Doc" or "Clifford"), and now everything would be all right.

It was like that for many of his patients. His was not the conventional bedside manner, but he succeeded in instilling in his patients complete confidence in his ability to take care of them.

Clifford Harwood was the quintessential Vermonter — a country boy to the core. He was born in a small town where his forefathers had lived before him, and he left only when he went to the university to earn his medical degree.

After serving his country honorably in World War II, he came home to Vermont to establish a thriving medical practice and to fulfill, as well, the kind of civic duty that he believed implicitly was the obligation of every American — not only in his own community, but also at the state and federal level. He was a steadfast patriot and when he espoused a cause in which he believed, he did it with an uncommon fervor and persistence.

Nonetheless, in spite of a long life of involvement with people and places far removed in every way from Rupert, he remained in his heart a country boy. He would not have chosen other than a return to his home town and it is as it should be. The circle is completed for Clifford B. Harwood, M.D., and it is as it should be. The people of his adopted community here in Manchester are united in a common thought: "Rest in peace, Doc."

Elaine G. Nawrath

A 1995 Tribute by the Bennington County Committee

WHEREAS, Dr. Harwood has been a dedicated and tireless worker for the Republican Party since his return from military life in 1945 and the most effective finance chairman and fundraiser this County has ever had, and

WHEREAS, he has commanded the highest respect and deepest affection possible from all who have been active in Republican affairs throughout the State of Vermont, and

WHEREAS, Madeline Harwood has, throughout all of those years, been a stalwart helpmate to Doc, and herself a dedicated leader among Republicans;

NOW THEREFORE, Be it resolved by the Bennington County Republican Committee in meeting assembled:

1) That we engage in a minute of silence in grateful remembrance of all that Doc has done for the party and for the County of Bennington as a community, and

2) That a sincere vote of thanks be extended to Madeline Harwood, both for her share in Doc's career and for the valiant work she has done on her own for the party.

Rep. Judy Livingston on behalf of the
Bennington County Republican Committee

Another Quintessential "Good Vermonter"

Just as Doctor Clifford B. Harwood was a quintessential country doctor, Madeline was a quintessential Vermont woman. She was independent, industrious, and resourceful. Her frugality was reflected in her conservative views while her sense of honor and right and wrong were reflected in both her politics and her behavior.

Never one to shy away from a challenge, Madeline became a role model and mentor for others as she made the transition from the traditional role of mother, wife, and nurse to her husband's partner, party stalwart, and pioneering politician.

Madeline never considered herself a pioneer, but the fact was that through her work in state government and for the Republican Party, she was one of the first females to lead the way. She showed what women could accomplish.

The very accomplished attorney, Lieutenant Governor, and National Committee Woman Consuelo Bailey thought the time had not yet come for women to be elected to the highest offices, but Madeline forged ahead in an attempt to show Vermonters differently. Although she lost to Jim Jeffords for U.S. Representative in 1974, she helped pave the way for a younger generation of women like

Doc and Madeline

Madeleine Kunin, who would successfully win the state's top office when elected Governor in 1984.

Although she did not overtly support feminist causes such as the passage of the ERA, Madeline did in fact support women through her actions and the example she set for others. Her politics were deliberate and well thought out — her understanding of issues was admirable, her insights astute. Her approach of slow and steady wins the race and showing people what a woman could achieve has led to lasting and significant change and better roles for women in state government. She takes pride in the progress made and the greater options open to women today. With her own penchant for humor and having the last word, Madeline still likes to point out that, "We did it without having to change the Constitution."

Raised on Vermont farms, Madeline and Clifford Harwood were humble, hard working people who did their jobs uncommonly well. Whether serving family or patients in their house or their constituents and fellow Vermonters in Vermont's Statehouse, or hobnobing with presidents in the White House, Clifford and Madeline demonstrated the dedication and commitment to service that made them special. Manchester and the people of Bennington County were indeed lucky to claim them as residents, neighbors, and legislators — and so was Vermont.

Karen Lorentz

A Prayer

by
Catherine Harwood Shepard

Dear God,

I cannot tell you all the grief I have known.
I cannot believe the beauty I have seen.

At one time in space I had at church,
I heard a black friend sing
"Nobody Knows . . ."
It was a work of art we all shared.

But in the valley and the shadows,
it is more than dust —
it is beyond awe;
and beneath are the
busy ants and bees,
carrying out their place
in the constellation.

You have a place for us,
and it echoes from the hills and mountains
to the depths of the ocean floor,
forever — and ever more.

Scenes from a Political Life

Visiting farmer Stan Zecher, 1974.

Madeline, showing photographer Aldo Merusi she could change her own tire.

Talking with Barbara Kehoe, head of the Home Health Agency, 1974.

While attending the Republican Women's Conference in Washington in 1968, the Vermont women were guests of their Congressional Delegation for lunch in the Capitol. L to R: Senator Prouty, Mrs. Stafford, Senator Aiken, Mrs. Aiken, Consuelo Bailey, Mrs. Carlton Monaghan, Mrs. Richard Sykes, Mrs. Raymond Goss, Congressman Stafford, Mrs. Prouty, Madeline, and Mrs. S.T. Hudson.

Madeline, Francis Salmon, VP National Federation of Republican Women, and Consuelo Bailey at meeting of Vermont Federation of Republican Women.

A few of our favorite friends.

Madeline, Ronald Reagan, Mrs. Richard Sykes of Brattleboro, 1966.

With Bob Dole, VP candidate, 1976.

To Clifford and Madeline
Harwood
with best wishes

with love—
and Barbara Bush

At the White House, 1987.

At the Vermont Statehouse with Doc doing the honors, 1985. (Associated Press)

Madeline showing the "Republican Hat" she made with her many souvenir buttons. Photo, August 2000. (Karen Lorentz)

Photo Credits

Appreciation is extended to photographers whose photographs appear within this book.

Where photographers are known, their credits are given in parenthesis following the picture caption. The photographs with the various presidents are Official White House Photos, courtesy of the White House.

The photograph on the front cover was taken by the late Aldo Merusi for the *Rutland Herald* on "Doc Harwood Day," which was also Madeline's birthday, July 7, 1970.

The photo on the back cover is a White House photo taken on July 16, 1987.

Bibliography

Bailey, Consuelo Northrup. *Leaves Before the Wind*. Burlington, Vermont, Consuelo N. Bailey Publisher, 1976.

Doyle, William. *The Vermont Political Tradition: And Those Who Helped Make It*. Montpelier, Vermont, William Doyle Publisher, 1999.

Kunin, Madeleine. *Living a Political Life*. New York, Alfred Knopf, 1994.

Meeks, Harold A. *Time and Change in Vermont*. Chester, Connecticut, Globe Pequot Press, 1986.

Morrisey, Charles T. *Vermont: A History*. Nashville: American Association for State and Local History and New York: W.W. Norton, 1981.

Smallwood, Frank. *Free and Independent*. Brattleboro, Vermont. Stephen Green Press, 1976.

Vermont Statutes Annotated. Charlottesville, Virginia, LEXIS Law Publishing, 1999.

Wells, Frederic P. *The History of Newbury*. St. Johnsbury, Vermont, Caldeonia Company, 1902.

Chronology

1726   General Jacob Bayley born.

1753   Jacob's son Joshua Bayley born.

1775   Revolutionary War begins, Jacob Bayley becomes a General.

1761   Bridget Harwood settles in Bennington, Vermont.

1762   General Bayley settles in Newbury, Vermont.

1763   NH Gov. Wentworth granted charter of Newbury to Bayley, others.

1773   New York granted charter for Newbury to Bayley and others.

1776   Jacob Bayley begins road to Canada, now Bayley-Hazen Road.

1777   Republic of Vermont framed a constitution much like that of Pennsylvania's but added prohibition of slavery and establishment of universal manhood suffrage. Bayley involved in first government.

1785   Joshua Bayley settles in Newbury Village (VT).

1789   Joshua's son Jacob Bayley born

1791   Vermont became the nation's 14th state, joining the original 13.

1826   Jacob's son George W. Bayley born and lived at Jefferson Hill.

1849   Building of railroads in VT.

1861   Civil War; Vermont sent 34,238 volunteers, 5,224 were killed.

1872   George A. Bailey born, resides at Jefferson Hill.

1893   Ford built his first auto.

1900   Average U.S. Life Expectancy is 49 years (plus 7 for women).

1901   Marconi sent transatlantic wireless message.

1903   Henry Ford started Ford Motor Company.
First crossing of the American Continent by car took 65 days.
Wilbur and Orville Wright flew homemade plane for 59 seconds.

1908   George A. Bailey marries Maude Smith.
Ford introduced the Model T.

1914   Twins Clifford and Clarence Harwood born on January 3.
Madeline Bailey born on July 7. World War I began.

1920s   Era of "flappers" and carefree self-indulgence of 1920s;
changing role of women as they cut hair and wear short dresses.

1921   First U.S. radio programs.

1927   Great Flood in November, Vermont's worst disaster to date.
The Jazz Singer with Al Jolson first talking motion picture.
Lindbergh first to fly solo nonstop across Atlantic.

1929   Great Depression began.

1930   Clifford Harwood graduated high school, entered UVM.
New Deal I & II Programs began (WPA, CCC, etcetera).

1932   Madeline Bailey graduated from Newbury High School.

1933   Madeline begins nurse's training at Mary Fletcher Hospital.

1934   Madeline meets Clifford at Mary Fletcher where both work.

1936   Madeline marries Clifford on July 4.

1938   Move to S. Royalton to set up practice.
Clifford Jr. born in Burlington.

1939   Move to Brandon; daughter Catherine Ann born in Burlington.
World War II begins.

1940   Move to Whitingham where Clifford establishes a successful practice.
U.S. population 132 million; life expectancy 64 years; 30 million
homes have radios.

1941   Clifford reports for military duty. Family moves to Fort Devens, MA.

1942   Captain Harwood goes overseas.
Madeline on own with two children, moves to VT.

1945   WW II ends on May 8. Captain Harwood returns in July.
Harwoods move to Manchester, start a new medical practice.
Women make up more than 1/3 of nation's labor force; first atomic
bomb test; U.S. drops atomic bomb on Hiroshima.

1949   Richard "Rick" Harwood born in Burlington.

1950   Korean War.

1952   Roger Harwood born in Burlington.

1955   Consuelo Northrup Bailey first woman elected Lt. Governor of VT.
Madeline and Clifford ("Doc") active in Republican Party.

1964   Madeline serves as delegate & Doc as an alternate to Republican
National Convention (RNC), CA.
Madeline serves on Drafting Committee at RNC, introduces the
Harwood Amendment, which passes.

1965	Vietnam War began.
1968	Madeline and Doc attend Republican National Convention in Florida. Madeline runs for Vermont Senate and wins in November elections.
1969	Madeline sworn in to first term as a state senator on January 3.
1970	Dr. Clifford B. Harwood Week proclaimed by Manchester Selectmen. Dr. Clifford B. Harwood Day proclaimed by Gov. Deane Davis and town selectmen and held July 7 in Manchester.
1972	Madeline serves as Delegate to National Republican Convention.
1973	Madeline elected Vermont Republican National Committee Woman.
1974	Madeline runs for U.S. House; loses in close primary to Jim Jeffords.
1976	Madeline runs again for Bennington County state senator and wins; serves as delegate to RNC and as a presidential elector.
1978	Madeline wins reelection for state senator.
1980	Madeline reelected state senator. Doc and Madeline attend RNC in Detroit. Doc serves as a Presidential Elector.
1982	Madeline wins reelection for state senator in a close race; appointed by President Reagan to President's Committee on Mental Retardation.
1983	Doc retires after 45 years as a general practitioner and 1300 deliveries.
1984	Doc elected Representative to VT House; also delegate to RNC and serves on Platform Committee. Madeline loses senate seat as Democrats sweep elections and take majority in senate. Madeleine Kunin (D) first woman to be elected Governor of VT.
1988	Madeline runs for VT House seat, wins.
1990	Son Richard dies. Madeline runs again for VT House, serves last term. Madeline is honored as Woman of the Year by the VT Federation of Republican Women.
1991	Madeline receives first Richard A. Snelling Achievement Award.
1992	Madeline retires from Vermont House after serving 18 years as a legislator; also steps down from post as National Committee Woman.
1995	Doc dies May 25. Remembered as dedicated, caring physician.
2000	Madeline moves into an apartment in Manchester Center, finishes her memoir, and looks forward to its publication.

About the Co-Author

Karen D. Lorentz grew up in West Hartford, Connecticut and graduated from the University of Connecticut in 1968. She taught English at Scotch Plains-Fanwood High School in New Jersey before moving with her husband John to a remote mountaintop in Shrewsbury, Vermont, in 1978.

There, they learned to heat with wood, plow four-foot snowdrifts, and survive long cold winters as John developed a law practice in nearby Killington and taught college courses, and Karen ran a bed and breakfast (Lorenwood) in their home and raised their three sons.

Karen Lorentz enjoys writing about Vermonters, mountains, and skiing.

Karen turned to freelance writing in 1979 and has written more than 2,500 articles for various publications, including a column "Country Roads" for seven years. She has written for the *Rutland Business Journal* since its debut in 1984 as well as for the *Valley* and *Champlain Business Journals* among others.

Her interest in writing books began with copy editing the history of the town of Shrewsbury. She has since edited and produced an anthology of works by Vermont writers, *Vermont Voices*, and has written four books, including one on drug-abuse prevention, two ski-area histories (Killington and Okemo), and one biography of a quintessential Vermont family, entitled *Good Vermonters, The Pierces of North Shrewsbury.*

Finding Vermont conducive to the small press business, Karen formed Mountain Publishing, Inc. in 1990. Currently, she is working on a history of Vermont skiing and ski areas.

Besides being a volunteer with the Boy Scouts (and the proud parent of three Eagle Scouts), Karen serves as president of the Southern Vermont Branch of the National League of American Pen Women and treasurer of the League of Vermont Writers. She is a member of several ski-writer and ski-history organizations and enjoys learning about Vermont and New Hampshire mountain history. She welcomes feedback from readers and hopes you enjoy this story of the lives of Doc and Madeline Harwood.

Order Form

To order books by mail, fill out legibly and mail with payment to:
Madeline Harwood, Manchester Center, VT 05255

Name_____

Street Address _____

Town, State, Zip_____

Phone (   )_____

Two Harwoods in the House, A Vermont Memoir

One copy @$22 East of Mississippi (includes Shipping)$_____

"   @$24 West of Mississippi "   _____

#_____Multiple copies to same address @ $20   _____

#_____Multiple copies to one address West of
the Mississippi River @ $22   _____

Vermont residents, please add $1 sales tax per book   _____

Total enclosed $_____

Check here if you wish to have book autographed by Madeline   _____

Give name(s) if you would like book inscribed to a person or persons:

_____

Address books are to be sent to if not to the person ordering
above (use backside for any additional).

Name_____

Street Address _____

Town, State, Zip_____

Two Harwoods in the House, A Vermont Memoir is also
available in Vermont bookstores and gift shops at $19.95.

This page may be photocopied or removed.
Please make checks payable to Madeline Harwood.

Order Form

To order books by mail, fill out legibly and mail with payment to:
Madeline Harwood, Manchester Center, VT 05255

Name_____

Street Address _____

Town, State, Zip_____

Phone (   )_____

Two Harwoods in the House, A Vermont Memoir

One copy @$22 East of Mississippi (includes Shipping)$_____

"   @$24 <u>West of Mississippi</u> "   _____

#_____Multiple copies to same address @ $20   _____

#_____Multiple copies to one address West of
the Mississippi River @ $22   _____

Vermont residents, please add $1 sales tax per book   _____

Total enclosed $_____

Check here if you wish to have book autographed by Madeline _____

Give name(s) if you would like book inscribed to a person or persons:

_____

Address books are to be sent to if not to the person ordering
above (use backside for any additional).

Name _____

Street Address _____

Town, State, Zip_____

Two Harwoods in the House, A Vermont Memoir is also
available in Vermont bookstores and gift shops at $19.95.

This page may be photocopied or removed.
Please make checks payable to Madeline Harwood.

Order Form

To order other books about special Vermont people and places, fill out legibly and mail with check (payable to Mountain Publishing, Inc.) to:

Mountain Publishing, 1300 CCC Road, Shrewsbury, VT 05738.

Name_____

Street Address_____

Town, State, Zip _____

Phone   (   ) _____

Good Vermonters: The Pierces of North Shrewsbury *by Karen Lorentz*
The acclaimed story about real Vermonters who made a difference in their community & state. Softcover, 256 pages, 190 b/w photos, $19.95.
Number of copies ___ @$22 (includes shipping) $_____
        "   ___ @$24 West of Mississippi $_____

Killington, A Story of Mountains and Men *by Karen D. Lorentz*
A beautiful, illustrated history of the Killington Ski Resort; now a valuable collector's item. In limited supply.
Hardcover, 320 pages, 8.5 by 11 coffee-table book, over 200 color & b/w photographs @$39.95 + $5 UPS=$44.95
        Number ordered_____Total enclosed $_____

Okemo, All Come Home *by Karen D. Lorentz*
A colorful history of the Okemo Ski Resort and its people.
Hardcover, 288 pages, 8.5 by 11 coffee-table book, over 200 color & b/w photographs @$39.95 + $5 UPS=$44.95
        Number ordered_____Total enclosed $_____

Vermont Voices, III An Anthology by League of Vermont Writers
Real Vermontiana. Softcover, 248 pages, @ $17 #___ $_____

                Total order for #_____ books $_____

Please Autograph _____ Inscribe book to: _____

If you have any questions or do not receive your order within 10 days of mailing, call 802-492-3576. Satisfaction guaranteed.